MONTY HA
Great
Es

Also available from BBC Books:
Monty Halls' Great Escape: Beachcomber Cottage

MONTY HALLS'
Great Irish Escape

ADVENTURES ON THE WILD ATLANTIC COAST

Monty Halls

BOOKS

This book is published to accompany the television series entitled *Monty Halls' Great Irish Escape*, produced by Tigress Productions and first broadcast on BBC Two in 2011. Executive producer: Dick Colhurst. Series producer: Martin Pailthorpe.

3 5 7 9 10 8 6 4 2

Published in 2011 by BBC Books, an imprint of Ebury Publishing.
A Random House Group Company.

BBC Books and Ebury Publishing would like to thank Monty Halls, James Hemming, Martin Pailthorpe and Tamsyn Smith for the images used in this book.

The Random House Group Limited Reg. No. 954009.
Addresses for companies within the Random House Group can be found at www.randomhouse.co.uk

A CIP catalogue record for this book is available from the British Library.

ISBN 978 1 846 07705 0

Mixed Sources
Product group from well-managed forests and other controlled sources
www.fsc.org Cert no. TT-COC-2139
© 1996 Forest Stewardship Council
FSC

The Random House Group Limited supports The Forest Stewardship Council (FSC), the leading international forest certification organisation. All our titles that are printed on Greenpeace approved FSC certified paper carry the FSC logo. Our paper procurement policy can be found at www.rbooks.co.uk/environment

Commissioning editor: Albert DePetrillo
In-house editor: Caroline McArthur
Project editor: Steve Tribe
Production: Phil Spencer

Printed and bound in Great Britain by CPI Mackays, Chatham, ME5 8TD

To buy books by your favourite authors and register for offers,
visit www.rbooks.co.uk

Contents

To Tam
I was all at sea,
and you rescued me.

Introduction

Connemara has, of course, inspired so many writers through the ages. Reading various books on the region before I arrived, I was struck by the recurring themes of the power of the landscape, by the legends that lurked in every dark hollow and by the vast promise of an Atlantic horizon. It seemed to move visitors to such heights that I could hardly wait to pack a bag and get out there, hoping that it would unleash some literary giant within.

The snag with this otherwise splendid plan is that the superlatives are entirely true. It's the most majestic, wild, beautiful place and, instead of it creating a geyser of creativity in me, I found myself thoroughly intimidated, cowed by the grandeur of the scenery and my inability to translate it to the page in front of me. In the end I settled for simply recording the day-to-day ramblings of a man and his dog, telling the tale of their attempts to explore the land and sea around them, and record their wonder at the passage of giant animals in the sea at their very doorstep.

Once I'd reached that shameful pact with myself – acknowledging that translating the poetry of the Connemara landscape was going to be very tricky indeed – I began to thoroughly enjoy the writing process. I would rush to the cottage at the end of a day's work and tap away merrily on the keyboard, creating in effect a diary of someone living out their dreams. Every day held something new, great adventures to be played out against the extraordinary backdrop of this ragged edge of Europe.

The six months in the tiny cottage on Inishnee Island really was the most happy, fulfilling period of my life. It was a privilege to cruise the shores of Connemara seeking out dolphins, whales and sharks. To do so under the patient tutelage of Simon Berrow from the Irish Whale and Dolphin Group enhanced the experience beyond measure. Add to the mix the people of Roundstone – hospitable, wise, and entirely engaged with the landscape around them – and every day really did become an absolute treat.

The inhabitants of Connemara have always been known as being proud, resourceful and strong. They live in a land of staggering beauty, sometimes cruel and unforgiving, but always at the heart of the elements. There could not be a better place, or a finer group of people, amongst which to learn my trade as a marine biologist and a boat handler.

There are certain places that creep up on you, that seep through your skin in a kind of seductive osmosis. The picturesque drama of the region is beyond question, but it is the hidden side of Connemara that won me over utterly. The mystery and the legends, the darkness behind the ravishing façade, the wild hint of a truly ruthless land that remains beneath the immaculately manicured surface. To track a pod of gigantic Atlantic bottlenose dolphins beneath glowering cliffs, to watch a storm gather its immense dark shoulders at sea and then hurl itself at the land, to observe salmon trace a timeless route up peat-stained rivers – these are the moments that become seared on your psyche and demand you return again and again.

Eventually, we all have to turn for home, but for me the memory of this time in this place will always remain. In the words of one of my best friends from my time in Ireland: 'You can leave Connemara, but Connemara will never leave you.'

It is a relatively short stroll for us to the edge of our continent, where we can stand with our heels on the land and our toes dipped in the sea. It is a journey I have no hesitation in recommending – at your back will be mountains, bogs and lochs, whilst ahead of you will lie a deep ocean, mankind's last frontier. If there is even a whisper of a pioneering soul within you, then this is as good a place as any to nurture it.

1

A Man (and a Dog) on a Mission

The ramp rattled mightily beneath me as I drove the Land Rover onto the ferry, my eyes fixed on the somewhat surly crewman standing on the vehicle deck ahead. His spiralling right hand gestured me forward impatiently, drawing me ever closer to the car in front. I peered over the top of the steering wheel, brow furrowed in concentration and tongue projecting from the corner of my mouth as the gap between my bumper and the one ahead narrowed. Thankfully for all concerned he abruptly held up one oily palm to tell me to stop, and I obliged with a stamp on the brakes that brought me to a shuddering halt, the boat on the trailer behind me clanking and rocking in protest. The start of any journey is always intimidating, but when it is initiated by a gum-chewing, tattooed man in a Day-Glo jacket, it is doubly so. He glanced at me contemptuously as he walked past, and I smiled ingratiatingly whilst making an extraordinarily rude gesture at him under the dashboard.

With a sigh I switched off the engine. The air was filled with the sounds of cars arriving on the vehicle deck accompanied by the echoing chatter of excited tourists, whilst beneath it all was the rumble of the ferry itself. The cacophony was amplified by the metallic void of the space around me, a resonant backing track to announce the start of my journey.

As I climbed out of the Land Rover, it dawned on me how little I actually knew about Ireland. Although I had visited the country once or twice, mainly to undertake diving projects for various magazines, I had never spent any extended time there, flitting in and out via a series of rather nice hotels.* But I had never really explored Irish culture, tending to have a clichéd Englishman's view of Oirland: the flashing feet and plyboard hairdo of Michael Flatley; Guinness, fiddles and fighting. I was therefore as keen as mustard as I climbed the stairs from the vehicle deck, entirely ready to embrace a rich and glorious culture that has spawned more artists, writers and musicians per capita than anywhere else on Earth.

My enthusiasm was somewhat tempered by the fact that I was knackered. The reason had its face pressed up against my vehicle's side window behind me, colossal body stretched full length on the back seat of my Land Rover. My

---

* The boutique hotel is now something of a monoculture globally – one I am entirely happy to embrace I hasten to add, having decided some time ago that I will spend my dotage muttering darkly through an impressive set of whiskers in a bar called the Fug at a tiny hotel in Sidmouth. I intend to be known locally as 'the Colonel' and be bilious and flatulent – frequently simultaneously.

dog Reuben was not allowed out of the car for this crossing, four hours when potentially all he had to occupy himself was the plush interior of a spanking new vehicle. He had some previous convictions in this department, and I had resolved that I would wear him out during the course of the day leading up to the ferry trip. I had run five miles along a beach with him, thrown numerous sticks during frequent stops at service stations on the M4, run around the car park with him in the ferry port, and made a bed for him on the back seat that resembled an ermine-lined chaise longue. What this didn't take into account was that, whereas I am a 43-year-old man of questionable aerobic fitness, he is a 3-year-old Alsatian with a small brain and massive lungs. I left him bouncing up and down on the back seat like a demented toddler, my final despairing glance backwards noting that he had stilled momentarily to eye the seatbelts whilst licking his lips. I was convinced he would soon be swallowing one of my headrests like some egg-eating snake, before turning his attention to the upholstery – a hairy hand grenade about to explode on my stitched leather and shiny dashboard.

Arriving on the passenger deck, I was greeted with a scene of some bedlam, as the traditional bun-fight for the comfortable seats onboard was already taking place. I was elbowed aside by a sprinting pensioner, charging towards a vacant table with elbows out and a grimly fixed expression. From somewhere in the region of my left knee came a dark muttering, and glancing down I saw a toddler in the process of storming out of a mini-cinema that was showing cartoons. He looked, and now I come to think of it sounded, uncannily like Van Morrison. An Elvis impersonator moved past at some speed in a wheelchair, glancing at me through silver-rimmed sunglasses before dropping one heavy eyelid in a Graceland wink.

As an introduction to Ireland it left a little to be desired, and I retired to a quiet spot with a coffee. Glancing out of the porthole I felt the first stirrings of homesickness. Since leaving the tiny bothy at Applecross three years before, my life had seemed to consist almost entirely of a series of nomadic ventures that had spanned cultures and continents and I was becoming weary of the road. A pause in this incessant wandering had been working for several months as a voluntary nature ranger in the Outer Hebrides – a place of staggering beauty and hidden natural wonders. Guided by a series of gentle and knowledgeable local people, I had learned much about life in a genuine wilderness, about the day-to-day rigours of living on a rugged series of islands moored at the tempestuous border of a wild ocean. When my time there had come to an end, I had sought the sun, leading diving trips to Sudan, the Maldives and South Africa. Although this had presented me with a glorious sequence of flickering reefs and cruising predators, I had nonetheless begun to feel a powerful urge to settle in one place, to drop anchor and lift my head to survey the scene around me. My life had been a series of departure lounges and arrival halls, punctuated with brief periods at my home in Bristol before hastily packing another bag and awaiting the call to board. Such a lifestyle had inevitably had an impact on any type of stability I had managed to forge in the brief moments of calm. Antje, my long-suffering girlfriend of several years, had finally departed to take up her dream job working with her beloved penguins in Cape Town, and our relationship inevitably withered on the vine.

It is said that all of our lives are a journey of sorts, and I had suddenly found myself as a middle-aged man at something of a crossroads. There were all manner of great adventures in my rear-view mirrors, but I seemed to be staring out towards the horizon with an entirely new set of priorities. It didn't help that I had met a wonderful girl a few months previously, and was still (as a friend had described it) in the 'heart-skippingly-hand-holdingly-nauseating' phase. When the opportunity had come up to undertake a long-term post on the west coast of Ireland, a job that finally offered six months in a single location, I had seized it enthusiastically.

I watched the reception on my phone slowly weaken from five bars to one, with Pembroke Dock receding into the sea behind me. Despite my enthusiasm for the task ahead, I was keenly aware that I was leaving an old life behind and setting out on a great challenge, steaming west to a coastline that marked not only the edge of Europe but also the beginning of the great wilderness that is the Atlantic Ocean.

My journey was inspired by one man and one organisation. Simon Berrow is a bespectacled Englishman who runs the Irish Whale and Dolphin Group. From a vague notion hatched in the early 1990s, the IWDG has blossomed into a respected body dedicated to the study of dolphin and whale populations around Ireland, as well as to the education of holidaymakers and residents alike.

I had met Simon on one of my previous fleeting trips to Ireland, and it was immediately apparent why the IWDG had gone from strength to strength. He was, quite simply, the most enthusiastic man I had encountered in my entire life. Simon's stories – of which there were a great many – were delivered at enormous speed, with the odd miniscule pause to push his glasses back up his nose after they had been dislodged by one of his wilder gesticulations. I had met characters like Simon previously in my travels – driven, focused, energetic and mildly eccentric. All of these qualities are required to run a conservation organisation, as the concept of conserving and studying an animal will inevitably get up someone's nose at some point. It seems to me that the modern world is somewhat wary of an individual driven by anything other than personal gain, a perpetual problem for anyone who simply wants to conserve, study or celebrate a particular animal species. Simon had visited the town of Kilrush in 1991, perched on the northern edge of the mighty Shannon Estuary, and had noted the healthy populations of bottlenose dolphins in the murky, violently tidal waters. He had resolved then that something should be done to study and protect these animals as industry continued to spread like a virus along the banks, and so he plunged into the fray.

'It was a bit of a battle initially,' he told me, hand running through sandy-coloured hair that stuck up in a variety of directions, 'but then I started to make some headway. The people of Kilrush have supported me, and I feel we've really turned a corner now. Have a scone.'

Happily, any conversation with Simon at the neat building that is the headquarters of the IWDG is always accompanied by scones slathered in strawberry jam. There are many reasons for liking and admiring Simon Berrow, but this has to be one of the main ones.

'Is there any work you feel remains to be done?' I asked,

spraying small bits of scone for added effect.

'God, yes,' said Simon, voice increasing in speed and volume. 'I need more people like yourself, fully equipped and self-supporting, to conduct studies for me in the more remote regions of Ireland. I also want to push on with studies into the basking shark populations along this coast, and the work with the dolphins is perpetually ongoing. Lots to do, lots to do. Another scone?'

It is virtually impossible to walk away from a conversation with Simon without feeling energised. In fact it's virtually impossible to walk away from a conversation with Simon at all. We talked for several hours, with him eulogising about his adopted home, and speaking at length about the work that remained to be done. It was the simplest of decisions for me to offer my services and, after a great deal of planning and innumerable scones, we agreed that I should base myself in Connemara for six months. The aim would be to assess whale and dolphin populations in the region, act as a local representative for the IWDG, and set up a network of local people to continue the work after I had departed. Simon was also keen to initiate a tagging programme for what he suspected would be a very healthy basking shark population off Connemara.

'This really is exciting,' he said, eyes gleaming. 'I think I've figured out a way of tagging them that is far more efficient than any previous techniques. It essentially involves creeping up on them and poking them with a pointy broomstick. That's something you should certainly have a crack at – great fun.'

The basking shark is one of the true giants of the ocean, the second largest fish in the sea, a slate-grey monster that has seized mankind's imagination for centuries. The idea of sneaking up on one and ramming a tag into the base of a dorsal fin the size of a small sail seemed an elaborate form of suicide, akin to wandering up to a grazing bull elephant and knotting a ribbon on its tail. Or kicking a lion in the nuts.

'Ah nonsense,' Simon beamed when I mentioned this to him, 'besides I'm not that worried personally, as it's you that'll be doing your own tags in Connemara anyway. If it doesn't work out there are plenty more volunteers. Can we have your boat though?' He laughed, shook me vigorously by the hand, and scuttled off to attend to his beloved dolphins and his burgeoning empire.

Now, several months later, that self-same boat was bouncing and rattling on the trailer behind me, the sun setting and the roads narrowing as I travelled into the very heart of Ireland. I had docked in the south-eastern port of Rosslare, and over the next two days made my way to Roundstone, a tiny village perched at the western edge of the near-mythical province of Connemara, jutting into the Atlantic on Ireland's western coast. By now it was dark, and I had already tried – unsuccessfully – to book myself into various hotels for the night, being thwarted by the fact that I had a dog with me who still had the remnants of vehicle upholstery around his muzzle, and that every car park seemed to have a height limit enforced by a sturdy girder overhead. I trundled and rattled along, eventually finding a tiny bed and breakfast that was happy to take a yawning Englishman, a grumpy dog and a massive boat.

'Now there's a man who could use a cup of tea and some cake,' said Marianne, the owner of the B&B, as she met me in the immaculate entrance hall. Glancing in the mirror, I could see she had a point – I had the mildly deranged look of someone who had been staring fixedly at a narrowing road ahead, occasionally glancing behind to see that the boat was still with me, whilst studiously avoiding the reproachful 'you're a bad dad and this definitely counts as abuse' look from Reuben in the rear-view mirror.

And here was another face of Ireland. I was ushered into a large kitchen to find the family had waited up for me since my somewhat shrill call an hour previously. They smiled, shook my hand, ushered me to a seat. A piping hot cup of tea was placed before me along with a wedge of cake the size of a chunky doorstop, and we settled down for a good natter.

In Ireland, they love to chat. I hate to generalise, but it's true what everyone says – this is a nation that loves, above all other things, a good chinwag. Irish people engage, they smile, they enquire, they probe, they opine, they sympathise, they listen, they interrupt, they laugh, and you walk away feeling a little bit better about life. It's deeply civilised and utterly wonderful. I speak as a tightly wrapped Englishman – an ex-military, boarding-school boy at that – who can obviously only show emotion during the Queen's speech or when a favoured gun dog dies.

'Ah, so,' said Joe, Marianne's father, as he politely pushed the plate holding my cake a little closer to me, 'and what is it you're doing in Ireland?'

The whole family hushed, peering at me with gimlet eyes.

'I'm spending six months here studying dolphins, whales and sharks in Connemara.'

This was met with a cacophony of approval.

'Ah god,' said Marianne, 'I've a passion for whales. Always have had.'

'And these whales,' said Joe, holding up a hand to temporarily hush the group, 'would they eat the sharks at all?'

Tea, cake, a warm family kitchen, and a chat – it turns out that these are the thieves of time, and it was midnight before I stumbled to my room doing cakey burps and swishing with tea, suffused with a warm glow as my first day in Ireland drew to a close.

The next morning I was up bright and early to recommence my journey. Like Russian dolls, each larger road gradually gave way to a smaller one, until I was eyeing the rear-view mirrors with genuine alarm at the lack of space either side of the RIB, dry-stone walls passing in a blur like a buzz saw that would lacerate and tear the rubber on the slightest contact. RIB stands for Rigid Inflatable Boat – and it was the 'inflatable' bit that was occupying my attention at that precise moment, anticipating as I was some sort of explosive hiss and a fractional, jet-propelled increase in the speed of the Land Rover. I have actually wedged the RIB in a country road in Wales before, stuck like a massive orange bung containing a rising dam of irate holiday motorists. It was eventually freed under the instruction of a terrifying horsey woman who brayed commands accompanied by furious hand gestures. The boat bears the scars to this day. So do I.

But I was easily distracted from the imminent danger to my beloved boat as I neared my destination: Connemara, in the western part of County Galway, is a strong contender for the most beautiful place in this beautiful land.

Europe is a craggy and wild continent. At its western point sits Ireland, its storm-lashed coast staring straight down the barrel of the Atlantic. Over aeons of time the coming together of green breakers and spiralling low-pressure systems has sculpted a coastline convoluted and twisted into endless bays, coves, cliffs and inlets. If the continent may be described as Fortress Europe, then the west coast of Ireland represents the castle walls.

Jutting deeper into the wilderness of the Atlantic than virtually any other point on the coastline is Connemara. Even the name itself speaks of its intense link with the ocean, being a loose translation of the Conmaicne Mara, a medieval people long eradicated by other more martial tribes, but spoken of in folklore as the 'Community of the Sea'. Bordered by Lough Corrib to the east, Killary Fjord to the north and Galway Bay to the south, it is one of the most evocative and romantic places in Ireland.

At its heart lies a vast bog, from which rise the two mountain ranges of the Maumturks and the Twelve Pins. Their native Irish names do more justice to their grey peaks – Na Sléibhte Mhám Toirc and Na Beanna Beola. Intrigued by the stark beauty of the hills around me, I stopped at a gift shop and read the information board, which duly told me that the land of Connemara consisted of quartzite, gneiss, schist and green marble. I had absolutely no idea what any of those terms meant, but they sounded splendid, perfectly suited to the serried ranks of ridges that rise like a dragon's back from the bog beneath, falling away in boulder-strewn slopes that run into ochre loughs. The word 'gneiss' is certainly one I would have come up with if I had been given a blank piece of paper, plenty of time, and an eighteen-year-old bottle of Bushmills to aid my thought process.

Although it is tempting to eulogise about the manicured lawns and white cottages set against a backdrop of mountains, forests and shimmering loughs, there is a darker side to Connemara. As with so many beautiful places around the world, the fact that it has not been heavily colonised by man and tamed by agriculture tells a story. The land beneath my rumbling wheels has always been notoriously difficult to farm, and many of the roads, jetties and pretty harbours I passed were famine projects, initiated to provide work for the local population due to the miserly returns from the land for their efforts. Indeed, up until the early part of the nineteenth century, Connemara had very few roads, and had become a refuge for the lawless and the pursued. It was a natural haven, isolated by mountains, loughs and the sea, a place where it was easy to get lost and forget dark deeds. Smuggling and the making of *poitín* – a ludicrously potent liquor so powerful it would have you not only dancing like your dad, but also possibly making a clumsy pass at him a few moments later – were rife. As I drove through the pretty little town of Oughterard, I was crossing a border, a final outpost where only three generations previously bandit country began. With the mountains presenting a network of valleys and crags, dark loughs where many a rowing boat had carried shady figures with muffled oars, and a coastline frequented by pirates and smugglers, Connemara was a wilderness for a reason.

All of this changed with the construction of new roads in the 1820s and 1830s. These created routes into the very heart of Connemara, stripping the mountains of much of their menace, and opening the region up to speculators, travellers and the more adventurous brand of nineteenth-century tourist. Settlement was the inevitable next stage, although the brutal farming conditions of the barren interior – harsh rock and flooded bog – meant that the vast majority of farming took place on the coast, where there was ready access to the seaweed that was used to fertilise the crops. The inhospitable nature of the interior of Connemara meant that the region was never colonised on a mass scale, and as such the influence of the outside world remained relatively diluted. The mountains, loughs, villages and extraordinary beauty of the craggy coastline remain a bastion for genuine Irish culture to this day. Connemara has its own identity, unquestionably grand, beautiful, inspiring, but ultimately cruel and ruthless. It's the Tony Blair of landscapes.

Such a landscape has also forged a particularly robust, fiercely proud brand of local. Legend has it that in the eighth century the Vikings, who were wreaking havoc along the coastlines of Northern Europe at the time, saw the potential for rich pickings amongst the villages and fiefdoms of the Connemara coast. The first Viking raid resulted not in the locals running shrieking for the hills, as was the normal routine when the square sails appeared on the horizon. Oh no, this was Connemara after all. There was the eighth-century equivalent of a pint being put down on a bar, sleeves were rolled up, and the mother of all punch-ups ensued. Although triumphant, the raiders found that precisely the same ferocity greeted them only a few miles up the coast, as the land was divided into small clans and kingdoms. Having been involved in a monumental brawl in one area, to successfully conquer any decent area of land they then had to repeat that same brawl endlessly every few miles, each time with a fresh new group of opponents. I imagine as they sat in their longboat eyeing yet another beach with a group of long-haired, bellowing Irishmen doing complicated warm-up exercises, they took a moment to reflect on the wisdom of attempting to conquer this wild land. Glancing round their own boat to see lots of empty seats, several crew members with the horns of their helmets the wrong way up, and Ethelred the Invincible hiding in the loo and refusing to come out, they had a quick team talk and decided to sail elsewhere and find some monks to slaughter. This was a kingdom that the Viking Foreign Office website would suggest you avoid as the locals were too violent. Even today, the men of Connemara are said to be slightly taller and broader than those elsewhere in Ireland.

Staggeringly, there was actually an occasional tourist who ventured into Connemara before it was widely colonised. In 1689 a gentleman called John Dunton decided to take the seventeenth-century equivalent of a mini-break there, and noted: 'They were a parcel of lusty fellows with long hair, straight and well made, only clumsy with their legs, their ankles thicker in proportion to their legs than the English.' He was even more impressed when he met the women, who 'commonly on a Saturday night, or the night before they make their appearance at mass or any public meeting do wash their hair in a lee made with stale urine and ashes.' He was welcomed into a home and – a tad ungratefully, I thought – noted that the butter he was presented with by the lady of the house tasted odd because 'the heat which this labour put the good wife in must unavoidably have made some of the essence of arms pits trickle down her arm into the churn.' Something that would, admittedly, make your butter taste somewhat gamey, but there's no need to go on about it. Bloody tourists.

It was early evening when I finally arrived in the village closest to the cottage that was to be my home for six months. The tiny harbour held a number of brightly painted fishing boats, the rustle and murmur of the wind and the waves a suitably soporific accompaniment to my arrival. On first impressions Roundstone looked neat, compact and picturesque. It felt precisely like the opening scene of a film, and I had an unnerving feeling that I would turn off the main street to find that the houses were all made of a single sheet of colourful plywood and propped up by scaffolding, after which the opening credits would begin to roll.

Given the history of Roundstone, this somewhat ephemeral feeling was perhaps not such a strange sensation. Before 1822 and the appointment of an extraordinary Scotsman called Alexander Nimmo as the Chief Engineer of the Western District, this had indeed been nothing more than a rough quay and rugged cove. He decided to build a harbour here – one of thirteen built as famine-relief projects along the coastline – and, as is the way with these things, the community grew up swiftly around it. It appeared that Nimmo's ambitions for the place were not that lofty, as he noted in a report that he hoped to create a 'tolerable fishing village'. The harbour was a thing of some beauty, though: sturdy and offering haven at every stage of the tide and, while it is still very much the heart of Roundstone, there is now a series of shops, colourful houses and hotels stretching away up the hill. There are also – dotted throughout the village like shimmering oases for the parched traveller –

several pubs.*

As I drove into the village, I glanced down at the harbour, the stone walls protectively cupping several fishing boats that rocked gently alongside the weathered stone of the sea wall, halyards clinking against their masts in that most evocative of sounds. It was the noise of countless childhood holidays and adventures. As I drove past in the Land Rover, a lone drinker outside O'Dowd's bar raised a laconic pint in greeting, waving it in my direction, blissfully unaware of his role as my official reception committee to the village and indeed my summer in Ireland.

Beyond the harbour wall, I could see the stretch of water over to the island of Inishnee, a tidal channel dotted with moored boats and plump buoys. On the island sat the cottage I was renting for the summer, just back from the shore on a green headland. From here it glowed eerily as it caught the last of the evening sun, a snowy white beacon leading me home. I turned the Land Rover and RIB around at the head of the village, a ninety-seven-point turn that drew an appreciative crowd from the pub, and trundled the last few miles to the cottage.

It was late April so, as I crossed the bridge onto the island, my progress was followed by a succession of limpid brown

---

* Roundstone has a population of approximately 300. And – including the hotels – six bars. That's a bar for every fifty people. Considering that a fair few of the villagers are kids and not allowed to drink, that means here is a place that has a singularly democratic approach to having a beer. If each pub has forty feet of bar, a not unreasonable estimate, that makes a total of 240 feet. Let's say that a third of the village don't drink, that means that every single person in the village has about a foot and a half of bar specifically dedicated to them – just about shoulder width. How immensely civilised.

eyes and ludicrously cute faces: a series of lambs, calves and foals, all gambolling and frolicking in the approved manner. It was the golden hour before the sun dipped below the horizon, causing the fields to glow an iridescent green, and it struck me that if ever there was a good time to arrive in Ireland this was it – a glorious evening in late spring when the fields around me seemed to be a festival of life, a riotous celebration of rebirth as the land itself emerged from another brutal Atlantic winter.

I passed a number of small houses as the road twisted and turned along the coast towards my cottage. Many of these had trees in the garden, their branches sculpted into trailing limbs by relentless winds. It was an eerie sight, a freeze-frame of a force twelve, and one could almost feel the fury of the storms that had turned them into arthritic still-life sculptures as they had grown.

The track snaked its way over humps and dips corralled by dry-stone walls, until I finally crested the hill before the cottage. I stopped the Land Rover and peered at my new home, chin resting on my hands atop the steering wheel.

It stood foursquare and solid, a bungalow with white walls, a bright red door and a slate-grey roof. I liked it immediately, deciding it looked unassuming and welcoming. It stood on a flat gravel platform with undulating green slopes leading to the shore, a perfect vantage point to view the channel and village beyond. The hill on which I now sat in the Land Rover protected the cottage from the open sea, nestling as it did in the lee of the slope, tucked away and hidden from the ferocity of the open ocean.

Reuben is a discerning judge of a seaside cottage, and I turned round to ask him what he thought – we were in this together after all. But Reuben wasn't looking at the cottage. He had other, more pressing matters on his mind. He was staring straight out of the side window, eyes fixed and tongue lolling. As I turned he emitted the briefest of whines, glanced at me, then turned back to the window.

I followed his gaze to see hares. Hares sitting upright on tussocks. Hares running. Hares feeding. Hares boxing. Great twitching, lolloping, floppy-eared, warm, furry packs of them. This is an animal that is rare in England, and now I knew why. It turned out they are all on Inishnee Island off the village of Roundstone – I made a mental note to tell someone important.

As Reubs stared at the hares, bewitched, I drove the last few yards to the little cottage perched on a slope running down to the sea on a tiny island on the westernmost edge of the European continent. This was to be our home for the next six months, a base camp for forays into the adventures on our doorstep. Roundstone sat at the base of the mountain across the sound, dark waters rustling past as the tide ebbed in the gentle light of an oceanic dusk. There is something intensely evocative about sounds travelling over water and, as I sat reflecting on my luck, I heard the echo of a distant voice, a door closing, and the low hum of a car engine, the sounds dissipating into the hills and across the sea, lost on the breeze as it drifted and spun into the wilderness that surrounded me.

The interior of the cottage resembled the saloon of a small ship – all dark wood and neat cupboards. Although it had that slight musty smell after an uninhabited winter, nonetheless there was an underlying whiff of wood and peat. The central room acted as a combined kitchen, dining area and lounge, with two comfortable old chairs pulled close to the fire. The floor was an incongruous mottled stone – the famous Connemara marble – meaning that I would begin every day by striding over 600 million years of history, the ancient heart of the land on which the cottage sat. It is said to bring serenity to those close to it, although this was somewhat lost on me as I skidded and slipped my way through the room, loaded with bags. Through the doors at each end of the kitchen were two neat bedrooms, one of which instantly became my kit storeroom, the other a jumbled pile of shoes and clothes as my exuberant unpacking style kicked into action. Adjoining this bedroom was a small bathroom, which Reuben briefly explored before showing his approval by taking a long and noisy drink out of the toilet.

We were old hands at making ourselves comfortable, although this particular arrival was different to so many others in that I had a profound sense of purpose as I unpacked. This was no idle stroll through a distant land, it was a statement of intent. I was here to work, to learn about the dolphins, sharks and whales that sculled through the channel and the open sea that stretched away in the moonlight. I was nervous, excited and energised at the thought of the challenge that lay ahead.

An hour later there was a semblance of order, with bags crammed into cupboards and the bed cleared of debris. The excitement of the day, the long journey, and the crisp Connemara air combined to have a profoundly soporific effect on me, and at last I yawned and stretched my way into the bedroom. Reuben stalked to the foot of the bed, circled three times as was his custom, and slumped to the floor like a puppet whose strings have been cut, giving a brief muffled sigh as he buried his nose in his tail. Dusk had settled into night, with a brisk sea breeze buffeting the cottage, testing the locks and causing the roof to gently moan and creak. I drifted off to sleep, my new home redolent with the smell of dark timber, lulled by the groan of the wind and the rustle of the waves. My dreams were of the sea.

2

Reubs

Reuben had become a totally integral part of my life since the days when we spent a summer shivering together in the bothy on the west coast of Scotland. He was now fully grown – fifty kilograms of sleek muscle and luxuriant black coat – and we had bonded utterly, an unbreakable link forged on many a hill and wild coastline. As we sat in the Land Rover surveying our new home, he was approaching the prime of his life, and I wondered how the hare population would react to the abrupt introduction of a shimmering jet-black timber wolf into their midst (although I had a fair idea). Wrestling matches between Reubs and me were now a forgone conclusion, and when he collided with me at full tilt – which he seemed to do with alarming frequency – he would poleaxe me completely. No dog will do this on purpose; however, he was still coming to terms with some complex physics relating to momentum and mass, and although he would clamp the anchors on at what he thought was the appropriate time, occasionally he was marginally out, resulting in me sitting on my backside reflecting on why I hadn't got a poodle, and him bounding round in delight that I had come down to his level.

A particular favourite on longer walks was to find a really hefty bit of driftwood. Using those great muscles of his neck and jaws, he would carry this piece of timber absurd distances, but there was an ulterior motive. When the moment presented itself – ideally when I was a good distance ahead and my concentration was elsewhere, he would juggle the wood in his jaws and break into a canter. He could get a fair lick of speed up, and would carry the wood at the precise height for it to connect vigorously with the back of my knees, causing me to crumple to the ground in an amusing manner. I know this may seem absurd to anyone who knows anything about animal behaviour, but the tremendous excitement this generated in terms of bounding about, tail wagging and delighted barking convinced me that Reuben thought this terrific sport. This scenario would be repeated a number of times on a walk, meaning that I frequently returned home feeling like I had been interrogated in a Turkish prison.

Another display of what I was beginning to think of as a well-developed sense of humour – in the Carry On / Keystone Cops genre obviously – came on a walk in Bristol. I was buying some dive kit at a local shop, and noticed a canal running alongside the car park. It was a hot day and I was reluctant to leave Reuben in the Land Rover, so I thought I'd take him for a swift ramble along the canal path. This would be combined with some stick chasing and a swim, and would hopefully result in a wet, happy dog to leave briefly in the car whilst I indulged in buying diving trinkets like the cheap trollop I undoubtedly am.

Eyeing one of the larger sticks on the bank, I picked it up and whipped Reubs into a pre-swim frenzy. There was the full repertoire of fake throws, tug of war, and lifting it out of his way just as he jumped at it causing his jaws to snap shut on thin air with a theatrical clump. Tail wagging furiously, he finally backed off to allow me to hurl it into the canal. There was, it has to said, a glint in his eye at this stage, and it dawned on me that perhaps I had overdone the pre-match entertainment.

With a grunt I lobbed it mightily into the distance. Reubs was already in mid air, legs pedalling prior to impact with the surface of the water. He landed like a depth charge, and was immediately in overdrive, tail acting as a rudder, the muscles of his shoulders bunching and pulsing and an impressive bow wave causing old coke cans and other detritus to surge against the canal walls.

Reaching the stick, he clamped his jaws around it and negotiated a difficult turn, employing bow thrusters and stern kicks, before snuffling and snorting his way back to me. Reaching the steeply sloping bank, he planted his two front feet on the slippery mud and lifted the stick (more of a log actually) towards me. I leaned over and grasped one slippery end, preparing for another few throws to thoroughly wear him out before returning to the car.

It may sound strange, but it suddenly dawned on me that Reuben had me in a somewhat compromising position. I was leaning towards the fetid water of the canal, balanced on my toes on a slippery slope, one hand clasped around a greasy log the other end of which was firmly in the jaws of my dog – the same dog that I had spent the last ten minutes winding up.

A look of complete understanding passed between Reubs and myself at that moment. A moment that saw him brace those spade-shaped paws in the mud, lean forward slightly, then heave backwards on the log to which his beloved owner was attached. I slid immediately past him into the canal, like some liner being launched into the Clyde. There was a certain degree of futile scrabbling in the initial stages of the short journey, and a final reproachful glare at Reubs as I skidded past him, before I slipped beneath the foul, evil-smelling gloop that is a city-centre canal in Bristol.

This was – certainly as far as one of us was concerned – absolutely the greatest thing that had ever happened anywhere in the history of everything. I surfaced to find Reubs still standing on the slope, half in and half out of the water, barking delightedly, the waters being thrashed into foam by a wildly wagging tail. As a rule, me entering the water was a sign for alarm bells to sound and an immediate rescue attempt to be launched. This was apparently very different, and I wouldn't have been too surprised if he had ducked me once or twice as I climbed out. As an example of one-upmanship it was impressive, and we returned home in silence with me gently steaming (in every sense) in the driver's seat, and Reuben curled up in the back sighing contentedly.

As with most dogs, he had mellowed considerably since his younger days, when he was a fearsome blend of exuberance and the occasionally misguided desire to be with me at all times. I first learned of his innate urge to accompany on any walk – particularly on a seashore which, as far as he was concerned, was littered with hazards for the inattentive human – when I left him in the Land Rover whilst gathering razor clams on a stormy beach in the Outer Hebrides.

This was plainly an unacceptable situation. Suppose my wellies filled up and I drowned? Suppose I was dragged into the sand by a massive and aggressive clam? There was only one thing for it – eating his way through whatever lay between him and the myriad hazards that surrounded the boss. If that happened to be the interior of the Land Rover, then so be it.

When I returned half an hour later, cold, wet but happily clutching a bag of clams, Reuben was sitting on what remained of the driver's seat, wagging his tail delightedly and attempting to spit out a frayed chunk of seatbelt. With a groan I looked at the explosion of foam and cloth that had been my headrest, and then counted the frayed ends of the seatbelts. There were seven – the grand slam of seatbelt destruction, as not an intact belt remained. It seemed that Reuben was desperately concerned about my safety on a beach, but plainly didn't give a damn about my wellbeing on the road. Glancing sideways at the door, I could see that he had just begun to work his way through the door panel, exposing the complex innards of pulleys and wires. He nuzzled me contentedly throughout, eyes inches from mine, occasionally raising a paw to check that it was actually me. I had made it back, he seemed to be saying, and just in the nick of time.

After this same scene was repeated about two weeks later (with a completely new set of seatbelts), I approached a local crofter to see if he had a solution. The crofters of the Outer

Hebrides knew more about dogs than I ever would, as there are very few who would work a flock of sheep or a herd of cows without an attendant collie.

'Aye, well,' said Donald MacDonald as he thought it through. 'I do have a solution for ye. It's a bit radical, mind. Always seems to do the trick for me, though.'

'Anything, Donald. I'm a desperate man.'

'I coat my seatbelts in Tabasco sauce. One whiff of that and they'll stop their chewing for sure.' He chuckled and shambled off, his own dogs leaping and spinning around his feet.

It would be harsh to say that revenge was at the forefront of my mind as I slathered the new seatbelts with Tabasco; however, I did feel it was time Reuben learned that there are times when I draw the line. The fact that the line happened to be a thick layer of monumentally fiery pepper sauce just added that extra edge – one lick of that and all would be well when I was one side the Land Rover door and he was the other.

Several days later, I parked the car at the top of a dune to investigate rumours of a whale carcass on a nearby beach. Dogs shouldn't be allowed near decomposing whales – or whales generally now I come to think of it – as they carry some nasty pathogens that will make a dog or indeed a person very ill indeed. I slammed the door triumphantly, barked a command to stay, and marched off onto the white sand.

I returned an hour later after a fruitless search, and found Reuben looking thoughtful in the back of the car. Four seatbelts hung in ragged strips, and Reubs glanced up at me through red eyes. Every now and then, he would rub his tongue over his teeth in a contemplative manner, before sighing deeply and curling up on the back seat. From his perspective it seemed, I had not only thoughtfully provided a seatbelt buffet, I had also added a touch of seasoning.

We drove home in silence, although I must confess to a disgraceful moment of satisfaction when I heard a slight whine of complaint the next time Reuben went to the loo.

His apparently insatiable need to make mischief aside, Reuben's gentle nature - so apparent in the bothy in Applecross - had remained his foremost characteristic. I had simply never seen him riled, even under the most extreme provocation. Children would tug his ears, smaller dogs nip his knees, or beery regulars accidentally tread on his vulnerable soft bits in the pub, and yet he never, ever retaliated.

Perhaps the ultimate test of his unbounded gentle nature came in the Outer Hebrides. I was raising two pigs for slaughter, and had decided on Gloucester Old Spots. This most benign of pigs is a great traditional breed, and used to be known as orchard pigs as they would happily snuffle their way through great drifts of windfall apples. My two piglets were christened Smoky and Streaky, and released into a large enclosure next to my bothy.

Reuben and the piglets bonded immediately. To them he must have appeared a giant, a dark protecting presence that would gently sniff and lick them, nosing them round their pen and watching over them. To Reubs they seemed to be small, rather odd smelling dogs, and it was a delight to see the three of them running and bouncing through the long grass of a Hebridean summer. I would throw a stick in for Reuben, and he would pick it up to have the two pigs chase him furiously round the enclosure, more out of curiosity than excitement as whatever he was holding in his mouth was plainly worthy of further examination.

This touching scene was repeated on a near-daily basis until Reuben made the somewhat unwise decision to roll onto his back with the stick clenched between his jaws. I had seen him do this many times before when we had been out on walks together, with the idea being to get a firm purchase before setting off again. With all four paws pointing skywards, he mouthed and juggled the stick with complete concentration.

What he had temporarily forgotten were the piglets in hot pursuit. Both had only recently been weaned, and plainly retained the memory of suckling from their mother. Both were also in possession of needle-sharp teeth, akin to those of a puppy. Both were also moving at some speed. Both spied what they took to be the milk-dispensing attachment at the same time, and both launched themselves into a frantic final leap before clamping on with the commitment and determination of any hungry young animal.

The only slight snag in this scenario is that Reuben is a boy dog. The noise he made as Smoky and Streaky latched on to somewhere deeply personal was very similar to the noise I would have made in the same circumstances. He leaped to his feet, turning a complete circle in mid air, and landed trembling on four paws, staring wildly about him at the now rapidly retreating piglets. If ever there was a moment that he could have thrown off the shackles of civility and become the ferocious wild dog of his genes, I do think it's the time when two of your best friends bite your wedding tackle for no apparent reason. Instead he looked reproachfully at me – supporting myself on the fence and gasping for breath – and stalked off. Later that evening I would see him periodically stare into space, before shaking his head, whimpering in disbelief, then gingerly curling into an even tighter ball in front of the fire.

He had only been with me for two years, but in that time we had become inseparable. He had been by my side as we explored many a hill, swam together in freezing loughs, huddled side by side in the rain, and sprawled on numerous sofas watching bad television. When I was away for months on end, living in remote regions of the British Isles, he was my constant companion. There is something very primal about the relationship between a human being and a dog when alone in remote regions – you learn to rely completely on one another, mirroring a scene played out throughout our parallel evolutionary histories over the millennia. As the winds shrieked and roared in the darkness, rattling the shutters on icy Hebridean nights, I would huddle under my bedclothes and know that there was a great dark mass lying in the gloom at the foot of the bed, ever watchful. He was the first thing I saw in the morning, the last thing at night, my best friend, and my protector. Reuben had my back, I had his, and the thought of travelling without him was ludicrous.

Connemara could have been made for him of course, with an endless series of coves, bays and loughs to explore. As I drifted off to sleep on that first night in the cottage, I could hear him snuffling contentedly in the darkness on the floor by the door. He was inhaling the sea air, breathing in the scent of new adventures for him and his master in the days to come.

3

Master Chef

My first morning at the cottage dawned clear and bright, and I was awoken by the unmistakable sensation of seven stone of dog pogoing on the bed. Opening a bleary eye, I saw a delighted, jet-black hairy face pushed up to mine. Noticing I was awake – one of those happy coincidences he seemed to be thinking – he licked my nose and pawed me clumsily in the eye, a sensation akin to a grizzly coming through the back of your tent in Alaska. I concluded that attempting to sleep from this point on would be futile, so wrestled my way off the bed and clumped to the door.

Throwing it open, I could see Roundstone nestled at the foot of Errisbeg Mountain on the shore opposite, looking neat and compact. In the mouth of the estuary sat the island of Inishlacken, neatly dividing the channel as it widened towards the open sea. It was a beautiful day, with blue skies and limpid seas, the horizon shimmering in an unseasonal heat haze. I took an exuberant step forward into my new world, inhaling extravagantly to savour the early morning air as I did so. Sadly my new world had a very low door jamb, on which I cracked my forehead mightily, rather spoiling the moment. This led to a period of rocking back and forth on my heels, hands clenched around my pounding skull, with Reubs looking on in concern. After a short interval of muttered oaths and an examination of the weal that had risen on my forehead, I walked the few steps to the gravel platform outside the cottage and stood looking at the scene before me.

Inishnee – my island – stretched away to my left in a gentle hill of green tussocks and ancient stone walls. Before me, the ground sloped away to the shoreline, an impossibly rugged set of coves and inlets shining with the rich tawny brown of large piles of bladderwrack. A number of rocks broke the surface just offshore, around which the sea hissed and frothed. Picking their way along the tideline were oyster catchers and sanderlings, tiptoeing through the flotsam and jetsam of another falling tide. Beyond the channel, Roundstone shone in the early morning sun, the windows of the waterfront houses shining like jewels set in the green backdrop of Errisbeg Mountain behind. Looking out to sea, I could see the low island of Inishlacken, the ruins of old houses standing proud on the shoreline, a memory of a community dissipated by the currents of time. The beach at the head of the island shone brightly, the shallow water around it an iridescent blue as the sunlight reflected off the fine white sand of the seabed. In the distance was the great parabolic sweep of the dunes at Gurteen, a golden arc leading to a headland pounded by Atlantic rollers, their demise a series of explosions of foam and spray, a fitting end to a 3,000-mile journey.

Walking back into the cottage, I hastily made myself a cup of tea and ate a slice of toast as I dressed. I had decided that today would be given over to exploration, a bedding-in period whilst I prepared for the challenges ahead. I would simply follow the bonnet of the Land Rover all day, seizing any opportunity that presented itself.

It turned out that I didn't have to wait long. As I drove through Roundstone once again, I noticed a sign proudly announcing the Connemara Mussel Festival for that same day. Without a moment's thought, I spun the wheel and followed the coast road ten miles or so to the tiny village of Tully Cross. After a glorious forty-minute drive along a coastline burnished in gentle spring sunshine, with crystal-clear waves flopping lazily into a series of quiet coves and inlets, I finally rounded a sharp bend that led me into the heart of the village.

The Connemara coastline is not only a patchwork of different ecosystems – rugged bays, gentle rolling fields, white beaches and stark mountains – it also represents an array of cultures. Facing west, its toes dipped in the Atlantic, this essentially coastal community has always been a gateway to the New World, as well as a haven for buccaneers, mysterious olive-skinned strangers, and flaxen-haired raiders. It was therefore no surprise to pass a large replica of a historic longboat as I pulled into the car park next to Paddy Coyne's Bar. By the look of things the raiders had only just left, as the village had a post-apocalyptic feel. It reminded me of those disaster films where some pestilence wipes out the entire human race, leaving people draped over cars with crows pecking at their festering remains. But Tully Cross wasn't dead – it was hung over.

I was informed of this by a very red-eyed gentleman called Gerry, the amiable owner of Coyne's.

'Ah, a bit of a night of it last night,' he muttered, gesturing vaguely towards the series of shadowy figures hunched in the murky recesses of the bar behind him. 'But you're very welcome. Tell me, can you cook?'

'God no. I'm a bloody awful cook.'

'Aha, that's the beauty of the mussel, impossible to make a mess of it. I think we'll enter you in the mussel-cooking competition.' Gerry brightened considerably at the thought.

It was extremely important that this idea was nipped in the bud. Although I enjoyed cooking in a ham-fisted, hoy-it-all-into-the-pot-and-stir-with-a-massive-wooden-spoon-using-two-hands style, it was a distinctly personal affair. Cooking in front of a group of people was my idea of hell.

'Gerry, it'll be a shambles. I'll set Connemara cooking back several decades and ruin the reputation of your seafood for ever. Please don't do this.'

'Ah you'll be fine. Just fine.' Gerry chuckled, patted me on the shoulder and wandered off to find an extra apron.

Over the next couple of hours people drifted towards the pub until there was a goodly crowd at the bar. The volume gradually increased, pints were pulled, tales recounted sheepishly of the previous night, and life was mysteriously breathed back into the hollow-eyed cadavers in the corner. By the time the cooking competition came around, there were at least forty people crammed into the small marquee that had been erected behind the pub, and they were ready to be royally entertained. It had the feel of a hastily arranged lynch mob, or perhaps a kangaroo court. The nine contestants were duly wheeled out to be inspected, huddling together for protection like nervous penguins.

We were all here to celebrate the mussel of course, and soon great shining mounds of them appeared, carried into the tent in bulging net bags, their shells shining and dark. The humble mussel – as in so many marine animals – is worthy of celebration for its hidden qualities. It is, in dry scientific terms anyway, known as *Mytilus edulis*, and is a bivalve mollusc, about an inch long. But there we should abandon the arid plains of terminology and classification, and explore what this remarkable little animal can really do. The first thing that should get us all very excited is that it can't move. It just sits there, a model of immobility and, one would assume, inactivity. It is, however, filtering away furiously whenever covered by the tide, hoovering in sea water like a demented pool scrubber. It's doing so to feed itself, and will react to whatever is in the water around by producing enzymes to counter some of the nastier stuff. It is, in fact, a tiny little scientist working all hours of the day and night, a constant researcher, a terribly keen field operative. Find out what enzymes it is producing, and you'll find out what is in the water around it. And that has been precisely what American scientists have been up to – introducing a programme called Mussel Watch in 1986 that now covers 240 sites around the USA.

The mussel can also look after itself. Fixed in place, it relies on its tough shell to deal with most interlopers, but it faces real problems when a dog whelk hoves into view. The dog whelk has a radula – essentially a conveyor belt of teeth

– which it uses to bore into the mussel's shell and suck out its innards. Not the nicest way to shuffle off this mortal coil, but the mussel does have something up its horny sleeve. When stressed – and I imagine having your innards turned into jelly and noisily sucked out of a small hole in your back is quite stressful – they can produce small fibres called byssal threads. When under assault, these threads will be used to pin a dog whelk in place, and if you stroll along a rocky shore you will often see dog whelks lassoed in place, a predatory Gulliver defeated by a Lilliputian foe.

The festival had been created five years previously to celebrate the unparalleled quality of the local mussels. It had gone from strength to strength, and was now one of the highlights of the Tully Cross calendar. Glancing at the other contestants in the cooking contest, I could see we were a motley crew, although there was a whiff of competence amongst one or two of the others that I found thoroughly alarming. Gerry's brother Shaun was next to me, looking uncannily like Willie Nelson, complete with red bandana, silver whiskers, and twinkle in the eye. He leant over conspiratorially.

'I must say I'm a tad nervous,' he muttered, 'this isn't the first time I've entered the competition, but it's the only time I've been sober. They're a pretty rough-looking mob, aren't they?'

They were indeed. The front rank in particular were terrifying: a row of ladies of a certain age, well oiled and eyeing us with considerable relish. I stared at my shoes and shuffled to the back of the group. If they spotted me – a lanky Englishman called Monty – I was dead meat, a fatted calf offered prior to the main event. They could warm up on me before discarding my twitching, snivelling corpse to begin barracking the real competitors.

'Ah yes, the front row,' said Shaun, 'they can be quite . . . ' he paused to search for the right words, ' . . . robust in their comments.'

I was about to see a perfect demonstration of this, as it was time for the first three competitors to begin cooking. Three hotplates were arranged at the head of the marquee, and the first cooks lined up miserably behind them. They were introduced one by one, names drowned out in a blizzard of good-natured barracking and catcalls. Shaun was the last to be introduced.

'And Shaun, remember you've only got thirty minutes,' said Gerry, plainly enjoying his role as host and compère.

'Ah Jaysus, Shaun's never lasted thirty minutes in his life,' said a faintly terrifying-looking lady in the middle of the front row. The crowd liked this comment a great deal, giving a great gale of laughter and even an incongruous ripple of applause, as if they had just witnessed someone sink a tricky putt.

'Now Marianne, go easy on him will you,' said Gerry, as Shaun caught my gaze and raised a laconic eyebrow.

'Feck him,' said Marianne, with admirable brevity.

The contestants were soon swathed in clouds of steam, through which could be glimpsed flashing knives, gyrating whisks and herbs being vigorously shredded. The crowd had gone silent, like a predator crouched in ambush, waiting for a glimpse of pulsing jugular or soft underbelly.

Soon the first contestant emerged from the steam, pink-faced and shiny-cheeked, to transport a piled plate of mussels the short distance to the judges' table. Here sat three august connoisseurs, in the form of a local chef, a slightly bewildered lawyer who had been visiting the village and was deemed to possess the necessary gravitas to sit on the high table, and Mairin Ui Chomain, the high priestess of all matters pertaining to shellfish. I had enjoyed a drink with Mairin earlier in the bar, a larger-than-life figure with the warmest of smiles and the gentlest of accents – a combination of the lyrical Connemara burr and a dry Dublin brogue. She had presented me with one of her books, and we had snorted and giggled over a plate of delicious shellfish. At the time, I'd had absolutely no idea who she was, and was therefore delighted to see I had a fifth columnist for the fray.

The contest continued, with my turn to cook creeping ever closer. As the contestants took their places, so the barracking grew more intense, the beer flowed, and the language ripened.

'And now,' bellowed Gerry, 'we have our final three contestants.'

We had been standing in the corner, mute at the prospect of imminent humiliation, dumb with the bovine acceptance of culinary death.

'May I introduce our first contestant in the final group – Monty!' With a theatrical flourish, he waved me forward.

There was a moment's silence, as though the crowd couldn't quite believe their luck and needed to check the facts, then a blizzard of derision. I shuffled forward to my station.

'Monty represents England!' shouted Gerry helpfully.

I wouldn't have believed it possible, but the barracking increased in volume, interspersed with the rattle of a raspberry or two and the odd unmistakable hand gesture.

The front row weren't actually rubbing their hands together in glee, but looked absolutely delighted nonetheless, like a group of wolves that had just been presented with a colossal chop.

The two other contestants duly joined me, one a visiting American and the other a pretty younger girl called Davina – Marianne's daughter and very much the local favourite.

We began, and to my surprise the front row remained relatively quiet. Marianne was eyeing me with a measured gaze, quietly assessing my fumble-fingered attempts at chopping and shredding. After a few moments of observing my cooking, she slowly looked up, caught my eye, and with considerable relish, said, 'Monty, you haven't got a fekkin' clue have you?'

There must have been something in my cow-eyed response, a look of such transparent hopelessness, that she relented.

'Ah, go on, I'm taking a bit of a shine to you anyway.' She waved her hand lavishly in my direction, arched her eyebrows, and the crowd roared their approval.

This was, if anything, an even more terrifying prospect. Head down, I concentrated on the cooking like a man performing a tricky heart bypass.

Minutes later, I stumbled to the judges' table proudly bearing a plate of mussels cooked with onions and garlic, and liberally soaked in cider. The judges had by this stage consumed more mussels than a deranged starfish, and had a somewhat stunned look about them. Nonetheless they nibbled thoughtfully at my meagre offering and made careful notes.

There were some very impressive offerings indeed on

the table, with steaming mounds of mussels garnished with wild flowers, rich sauces sweetened with exotic spices, and exquisite aromas rising to mix in a heady cocktail in the steaming pinnacle of the marquee roof. The would-be chefs were assembled behind the cooking station, and Gerry stilled the crowd with upheld palms. An expectant hush fell as Mairin moved regally to the front of the marquee, and cleared her throat to announce the results.

'Well, it's been a wonderful competition,' she said, beaming at the crowd who applauded wildly in return. Mairin waited for the applause to subside, perfectly in control of the mob before her.

'Now, I say this with my hand on my Connemara heart –' more bellows and applause – 'that in third place, a surprise for all of us I know, was . . . Monty.'

Third place: the proudest (and only) result of my short-lived culinary career. Come what may for the rest of my days, I will always have come third in the Connemara Mussel Festival.

Marianne was delighted, and leapt up to envelop me in a beery bear hug. She then sat back down on the arm of her chair, forgot that she had just hugged me, so jumped up and did it again. There was a moment's silence and then Mairin cleared her throat once again.

'In second place is – Kevin.'

A large, moustachioed, benevolent-looking chap promptly turned beetroot and raised a modest hand. He was applauded to the rafters.

'And the winner, and this year's Mussel Cooking Champion, is . . . Davina.'

This resulted in a positive explosion of exuberance, a

wild standing ovation that went on for several minutes. Extravagant and alcoholic celebrations began all round, celebrations I had an inkling would run into the wee hours and beyond. My back was vigorously slapped, my hand shaken – some people even asked me about my recipe, and I found myself in the truly unique position of holding forth to an attentive group on precisely how much cider one should add to a bowl of mussels for best results. A pint was pressed into my hand, advice was passed back and forth, the air was thick with shouts of laughter and a general feeling of bonhomie, whilst pervading all was the lingering smell of cooked mussels.

Much later, having fended off many generous offers of drinks and dances, I climbed wearily aboard the Land Rover to begin the journey home. Behind me the first fiddle was being strung, the first dance contemplated, and as I drove past Coyne's Bar and pulled away, a great shout of laughter rolled out of the door. I had no idea of the source, but suspected that Marianne would probably not be a million miles away. I reflected that as an opening attempt to bottle the essence of Connemara, I could have done a great deal worse.

4

Testing the Waters

Looking out of my cottage door was to gaze on endless possibilities, my field of dreams for the summer. Although I was obviously keen to get to sea, I didn't want to pointlessly cruise the coastline like a tourist on an extended break. I was here to prove to Simon I could do a decent job, and that I could solve at least some of the riddles presented by the giant sea creatures that sculled past.

Perhaps the foremost amongst these was establishing if the dolphins seen regularly by the boats that puttered in and out of the harbour throughout the summer were indeed a resident pod. This would be a very exciting discovery, as there are only four recorded resident pods around the UK and Ireland. I would need to photograph the dorsal fins of any dolphins I encountered, so they could be studied by Simon. Each fin is a fingerprint, a latticework of scars, cuts and nicks that represent the tumultuous life of a dolphin in the wild. If I could prove that the same dolphins were using the same patch of water throughout my summer in Roundstone, if I could show that they were producing and raising young in the calm bays and sheltered coves along the coast, then measures could one day – perhaps – be put in place to protect them.

There was also the sinuous presence of several shark species – there are at least twenty-one different types of shark encountered in the waters around the UK and Ireland. Roundstone sat on the very doorstep of the Atlantic, an echoing void where many sharks – well, those that remain after man has reaped his appalling harvest over the last few decades – went about their business. There were, of course, thrilling rumours of great whites in these waters, with several encounters recorded by the press along the Connemara coast. Most of these could be immediately discounted as basking sharks seen by hysterical tourists, and yet every now and then a credible sighting would emerge around the coast of the UK and Ireland – a fisherman who knows a great white when he sees one, or an encounter of sustained length that involves the messy demise of a seal. It was ludicrous to expect that I would encounter anything quite so remarkable, but one of the joys of the ocean is to bob in a blue desert and have absolutely no idea what may be swimming in your general direction. It is this heightened sense of anticipation, the hypnotic draw of the unknown, that has lured men and women to sea since time immemorial.

Before I could go to sea, however, there was something else that demanded my immediate attention. Reuben presented something of a problem on the RIB. For a start he was rather large, and the boat was rather small. He would invariably try to accompany me when I moved around the boat – as was his way – meaning that a large black nose was never more than six inches away from anything I did onboard. Added to this was another, slightly more exhilarating, habit. Reuben enjoyed nothing more when under way than hanging his front paws over the side of the tubes and trying very hard to bite the sea as it sped past. I've absolutely no idea what ancient evolutionary purpose this satisfied, but Reuben took his sea-biting duties very seriously indeed. He would lower his head over the side, growling and glowering and, as the spray rose when the RIB gathered speed, he would begin to bark furiously. Once he had got the message across that he meant business, and had then decided that the sea was ignoring him and was continuing to heave and splash in a provocative manner, he would begin to snap at it. Frequently this meant shuffling his entire body onto one of the tubes, where he would wobble and tremble like a drunk dad on a bouncy castle. He had never fallen in, but there had been a few close shaves. I decided that Reuben was, at least for the time being, banned from the RIB.

But what was I to do with him every time I went to sea? One of the first people I had met in Roundstone was Lorna Hill, a friendly, wildly enthusiastic bundle of dark-haired energy. She had been suggested as an excellent contact within the community by a mutual friend, and we had chatted briefly by the harbour on my first day. She had said that I should call if there were any questions at all as I settled in. Now was the time to see if she was as good as her word.

'Hello, Lorna,' I said, pacing the kitchen in the cottage with the phone pressed to my ear. 'I was wondering if you might know someone who could look after a dog for a few days a week when I'm at sea.'

Lorna's boundless appetite for life meant that she tended to engage all the verbal equipment at her disposal a fraction of a second before the information she was trying to pass on had been processed by her brain.

'Ah, right, yes, no, hold on, a dog you say? Right, not a problem. Wait a moment. A dog, aha, no, I've got just the . . . ermmm . . . hold on, sorry. Right, got it, my mum can do it!'

'Are you sure?' I asked. 'He's a big lad, and can be a bit of a handful.'

She laughed. 'Trust me, when it comes to get up and go my mum will put anyone to shame. She runs a B&B called the Anglers Return – I'll see you there in an hour or so, if you like?'

The Anglers Return was a beautiful, powder-blue house about five minutes outside Roundstone. I remembered it vividly from when I'd driven past, a grand old building looking out over a dark, tidal lake that was bordered by whispering reeds. Behind the house was a wood leading up the hill, with carefully manicured gardens in the lee of the building itself. It looked timeless and tranquil, the perfect place for a quiet break. An hour later I pulled the Land Rover into the drive, tyres crunching on the gravel, and Reuben and I jumped out.

'Best behaviour, young man,' I said. 'You need to make an impression.'

This was a warning that – sadly – wasn't really heeded. Even as I approached the gate, a certain level of bedlam broke out, with a lean collie hurdling the fence and, much to Reuben's delight, presenting him with a ball which he immediately tried to pinch. There was a brief punch-up – more of a swift establishing of hierarchy than anything else – after which both dogs hurtled into the lush expanse of the garden chasing the ball and each other. As I glanced up to follow their progress, striding towards me was Lynn. She was smiling broadly, face framed by flyaway curls, and was wiping her hands on a cloth having been working in the garden. I opened my mouth to speak but she beat me to it.

'Ah, hello Monty! Lorna said you were coming, how nice to see you. The collie is called Bonnie and *loves* having a ball all the time, but does get a bit funny when other dogs try to steal it. Mind you, I suppose that's not that unusual, is it, when you have your own ball, although it looks like Reuben likes balls too. Is he a German shepherd? Then I suppose he's very good at penalties! Anyway, come on in and have some tea and some cake, you must be a bit frazzled after your trip.'

I remained rooted to the spot, slightly stunned, but Lynn was already heading into the house, the dogs now rolling and spinning round her legs. She looked back as I took in the scene, and then returned to usher me into the house, moving around the kitchen in a blur of motion to place delicious-looking scones and cake before me, all the while chatting away merrily. Lorna joined us, crashing through the front door with a cheery hello, the two of them combining in a kind of perfect storm of chit-chat.

The Anglers Return would become an absolute haven for both Reuben and myself. Lynn and Lorna were splendid company, with the hands of the old clock on the kitchen wall marching round unnoticed as yet another cake was pushed under my nose, or yet another cup of tea poured.

Lynn's zest for life was extraordinary, a dynamic force of nature that singlehandedly maintained a beautiful old house and a great expanse of garden.

I mentioned how impressed I was with the house and its surroundings.

'Well, I must say it's been a bit of a carry on, but I do enjoy it, although it's not something you ever get on top of, is it? Do you garden? I suppose you do with your lovely little cottage on the island? Lorna tells me you're looking at whales and dolphins here? That sounds really interesting. I used to dive you know, long time ago, though. Now, you must tell me everything about it.'

I left over an hour later, piled high with teetering mounds of scones and cakes, Lynn sprinting out after me to present me with a pot of home-made jam in case I became weakened by lack of sugar during the five-minute drive home. I could have quite happily spent the entire day in the warm fug of the kitchen, and in the months to come I frequently would, but today I was anxious to get to sea.

The one thing a very enthusiastic man in a fast inflatable boat needs when patrolling the hazardous shores of Connemara is local knowledge. A heavy hand on the throttle in these dangerous waters would inevitably lead to a mildly expensive metallic crunch from the propeller, or a very expensive rocky crunch from the bow. There was only so much that could be garnered from charts, whereas local knowledge allowed access to the hidden swirls of the tide, to shifting sandbanks and submerged hazards.

I asked Lynn who was the best man to act as a guide for my first trip.

'Ah,' she said, 'Martin O'Malley is your man. He knows these waters like the back of his hand – it's in his blood, you know.'

After depositing the scones and cakes back at the cottage, I called Martin to see if he could take me out to show me the ropes. We duly arranged to meet at the jetty for what would be my first foray into the wild waters beyond the mouth of the estuary.

Nosing the RIB around the harbour wall, I could see Martin standing at the edge of the slip. He was a compact, powerful figure, deeply tanned and smiling the broadest of smiles. He gave the impression of immense solidity, as if he was made from recycled teak decking, his blue eyes twinkling in a face creased and lined by the sea. He looked very much like he spent the vast majority of his time lashed to a mast whilst rounding the horn, giving himself the occasional thrashing with bull kelp to ensure correct skin tone.

As I manoeuvred towards him, he cast an expert eye over the RIB, nodding in approval as I brought the boat alongside.

'That's a nice-looking craft you have there,' he said. I beamed, and decided that Martin and I were going to get along.

He jumped aboard expertly and shook my hand, a calloused rasp beneath a powerful grip.

'I thought you might like to go out to Slyne Head,' he said. 'It's a cracking route and will take you through some of the more complicated reefs and shallow channels. Nice day for it, too, although we should probably get away pretty soon as we'll need a bit of tide for some of the shallower bits.'

Slyne Head is pretty much the westernmost point of

Connemara, a dramatic collection of sharp ridges and rocks that juts into the Atlantic. It has the air of a front line, a salient jutting deep into hostile territory, which given its geography may not be quite so unusual. Step off the headland in your speedos, start swimming, and a little while later you'd be huffing and puffing your way past the Statue of Liberty.

The route to Slyne Head from Roundstone looked pretty exciting even on a chart, a jumble of tiny reefs, shallow sand banks, and swirling tides.

'There are two ways we can get there,' said Martin. 'The rather dull offshore route, or the very exciting inshore route. You look like a very exciting inshore route type of man to me.'

I took this as a compliment, although I suggested that it might be better if Martin drove.

'Aha, I was hoping you were going to say that,' he said, sliding onto the seat and gripping the throttle. 'You might . . . ah . . . not want to look at the depth sounder on the way, it being your own boat and all.'

Having idled our way out of the estuary mouth, Martin gunned the throttles, the engine tone rising from a dark muttering to a full-throated bellow, and we were away. The low island of Inishlacken sat at the point where the estuary widened into the open sea, a natural barrier to the gigantic swell of the expanse of ocean beyond. As we motored past, I could see the stark ruins of old dwellings, sagging and sighing in the sea breeze, a memory of another time, lost to the rigours of the environment around it.

'It was a tough life on the island for sure,' bellowed Martin over the roar of our buffeting passage. 'I think the hardest times must have been those days when the winds howled and the storms raged, and yet you could see the lights of the village across the sound. It was a haven you couldn't reach. Perhaps that's what did it for them all in the end – the last couple abandoned the island in 1984.'

Now the jumbled maze of dry-stone walls and a couple of the houses that have been refurbished are the refuge of visiting artists and writers. It was easy to see why you could find inspiration here – an eerie collection of ruins, rocks, wheeling gulls, and a wild shoreline staring into the dark maw of the Atlantic.

'Just before I take you through these local reefs it's probably worth mentioning that us O'Malleys come from a long line of pirates and smugglers,' Martin said, white teeth flashing through the tan. 'We'll be all alone out there, don't drop your guard now.'

With this, he reached forward and pushed the throttles up against the stops, the engine went from a bellow to a livid howl, and the RIB leapt forward, causing me to grab hastily at a handle on the console. Glancing up through streaming eyes, I couldn't help noticing that we were hurtling straight towards what appeared to be an unbroken low reef, with a healthy closing speed of about thirty knots. Arrival at said reef would take place in about fifteen seconds, and would – it appeared – result in a James Bond-style fireball from which I would emerge, cartwheeling in mid air whilst shedding a limb or two.

My dilemma here is that I'm British, and middle class, and called Monty. I would therefore much prefer to be turned into a big meaty frisbee by what appeared to be a deranged piratical loon in a boat than make a fuss. So I satisfied myself with half closing my eyes, gripping the handle with knuckles that turned porcelain white, and attempted to mentally transport myself to a happy place.

At the last second a gap in the reef magically opened before us, Martin spun the wheel, and we roared through the tiniest of passages. The noise of the engine was amplified by the razor-sharp, barnacle-encrusted walls skimming past on either side, creating a cavernous, echoing howl that for one alarming moment I thought might actually be coming from me. The water under the bow hissed like a furious stoat, and the white sand beneath us, covered in a mere film of crystal clear Atlantic water, passed in a blur. Then we exploded out the other side into the open channel, Martin's shout of laughter echoing behind us, whipped away by speed and adrenalin.

'Great stuff, eh, Monty?'

This insanity continued for several miles, with our progress at breakneck speed through an impossibly complex honeycomb of hidden reefs and constricted rock passages. It was a display of knowledge and nerve, combined with exceptional boat-driving skills, that took me right to the edge again and again, convinced that this time – at last – he must have got it wrong and we were sure to hit a rock wall, only to find myself moments later very much alive – as alive as it's possible to be, now I come to think of it – ragged with emotion and laughing delightedly.

We finally slowed, drifting to a halt in a wide sweep of bay, with the ruins of a castle dominating the shoreline. It was a magnificent sight, standing alone just above the low, dark cliffs, a grand old building that still held an impression of power and wealth.

'That's the family seat,' said Martin, 'where Grace plied her trade. They were tough days for sure, but she certainly made her mark on this part of the world, and beyond that when you think about it.'

The Grace he referred to was Grace O'Malley, a pirate queen, a warrior, an unquenchable spirit, and a skilled diplomat. Her story has passed (quite rightly) into Irish legend – but this is no myth, no tale fuelled by alcohol and fabricated around sputtering camp fires. The extraordinary feature of the Grace O'Malley story is that it is corroborated in historical records. The blood of a truly remarkable woman ran in Martin's veins.

Grace was born in 1530 at Clare Island Castle, the daughter of Owen 'dubhdarra' ('The Black Oak') O'Malley. The O'Malley clan were already established as skilled navigators and sailors, with their motto *Terra Mariq Potens* translating as 'Invincible on Land and Sea'.

Grace's mother wanted her to stay at home and live the life of a noblewoman. Grace, on the other hand, wanted to follow the family business, which happened to be going to sea and vigorously engaging with anyone unfortunate enough to sail past, as well as plying traditional trade routes. When her father finally allowed her to sail with him as a teenager, she was under strict instructions to go below decks should the ship be attacked. The first time a fight broke out, Grace climbed the rigging and launched herself shrieking onto the back of the English pirate who was fighting her dad at the time. I can think of no more embarrassing incident for a pirate than being attacked by a furious teenage girl and, understandably distracted, the English ship was duly defeated.

She was married in 1546 to Donal O'Flaherty, the next in line to the O'Flaherty clan and high chieftain to the district of Iar Connacht. Although only 16, she swiftly established herself as a shrewd leader and became head of the clan's fleet of ships. It was said that she was so attached to her fleet that at night she would sleep with a strand of silk round her toe, attached to the main hawser that moored the fleet in place. Pinch one of her ships, and you'd also get a piece of string with a livid Grace in her nightie on the end. Ship theft was – understandably – fairly minimal.

The city of Galway was a trading centre for the British, and refused to deal with the O'Flahertys. This annoyed her (an unwise thing to do), so she took to pillaging trading vessels as they passed. This in turn got up the noses of the ruling classes back in England – Grace was making some very powerful enemies indeed.

After her husband was killed in a fight with a rival clan, Grace was denied her rights of inheritance, so returned to the O'Malleys with her three children and two hundred followers. The pillaging continued unabated, and soon she had amassed a fortune and five castles. The final castle she coveted was called Castle Rockfleet. Being a fairly forthright girl, she decided to take this one by hammering on the door and proposing to the owner Richard Burke. As a rule, when propositioned by a violent pirate princess with several hundred supporters in tow, it is best to accept. Burke thought about it briefly – very briefly I imagine – and said yes. Although the marriage was supposed to be only for a single year as a form of convenient military alliance, rather touchingly when Grace offered to release him after twelve months, he declined and they remained married until his death seventeen years later.

The English finally had their fill of Grace, and took her son-in-law as a hostage. She was made to promise to cease her all her activity at sea, and the English Governor – a particularly ruthless character named Richard Bingham – stripped her of all her cattle and much of her land, and forced her into poverty.

Grace was into her late fifties by this stage, and for the next few years had to make do with slaughtering passing Spaniards, mainly to protect what little land she had left. In 1593, Bingham arrested her son and her brother. Grace sent a letter to Elizabeth I to ask for clemency, didn't receive a reply, so – uninvited – sailed to England to have it out with the queen personally.

There was every chance that Grace would have been put to death or imprisoned the moment she set foot on English soil, but for some reason Elizabeth agreed to see her. A story from the court at the time tells of a proud, fierce, Irish noble woman who conversed with the queen in Latin. The transcript of the meeting notes that 'In the wild grandeur of her mien erect and high before an English Queen she dauntless stood.' During their meeting, Grace sneezed and was given a scented lace handkerchief by a courtier. She loudly blew her nose, then threw the handkerchief in the fire. The court was aghast, as this was a gross lapse in protocol, akin to burning a gift. The queen gently chided Grace, mentioning that she should have put the handkerchief in her pocket. Grace in turn noted that no Irish person would put a soiled article in their pocket, and therefore must have a higher sense of cleanliness than the English.

Grace O'Malley was, in short, my kind of girl.

The queen, perhaps recognising a kindred spirit, duly agreed to instruct Bingham to release Grace's relatives and restore her possessions. This remarkable woman died in her early seventies in Castle Rockfleet - her death coming in the same year as Elizabeth's - and her memory is revered and honoured to this day.

Having shown us one of Grace's homes, and so satisfied family obligations, Martin turned the bow out towards Slyne Head, its craggy silhouette looming in the middle distance. It was a beautiful day, with the sea shining in the sun and the horizon shimmering and pulsing. The headland looked dramatic and imposing, with the lighthouse at its head, a white pillar polished by the midday sun.

As we wove our way the last few hundred yards through reefs that circled still areas of water like vast rock pools, Martin pointed out various seabirds en route, wheeling and skimming over the water's surface or sitting plumply in the heat, rising and falling with the gentle swell. A razorbill, resplendent in its livery of black and white bib, was startled at our passing, attempting to fly off but instead cannoning off wave crests and into troughs. The sand eel had only just arrived off the coast, a bonanza for all marine predators and the clarion call for offshore species to move towards the coast and begin the feast. The razorbill had been dining royally, and was now attempting to flee with a full belly - a portly diner in black tie and tails waddling away from the dinner table. It finally got airborne, more through luck than judgement, and whirred off towards the distant coastline.

Soon the islands and bays of the Connemara shoreline were behind us, and nothing stood between us and the headland except the open sea. Martin gave a final burst of the throttle, the RIB scudding over water that was deep, dark and full of promise, and Slyne Head grew ever closer, rising from the waters of the Atlantic until it dominated our view.

Although the lighthouse had long since been automated, it still had an eerie, evocative feel – like someone had just closed the door to pop to the mainland. Martin manoeuvred the RIB expertly alongside the stone steps, bringing her parallel to the basic stone quay with a flamboyant burst of the throttle – a delightfully proficient aquatic handbrake turn. I leapt ashore and, with a quick wave to Martin as he reversed the boat away from the steps, walked towards the lighthouse, following a stone path that snaked over the rocks.

Reaching the lighthouse, I leaned on the wall that surrounded it, my back pressing against the cold stone as I craned my neck upwards and squinted into the sun. I was enveloped in that special silence that only seems to occur in abandoned man-made structures, the breeze drifting and switching around the walls and steps, contorted and shaped by right angles and acute edges, the mark of man. From behind the wall I could hear the sea murmuring and sighing along the rocks, a hollow buffeting sound that echoed and resonated off the main structure of the lighthouse. Despite the reassuring presence of Martin puttering around the headland in the RIB, it was a strangely melancholy place, full of lost memories and fading sounds – the ghosts of the lighthouse keepers who had gone before.

My strange feeling of disquiet may not have actually been that misplaced, as Slyne Head had indeed been the setting for a piece of skulduggery that could have graced any cheap detective novel. In September 1859, an Assistant Keeper was lost as he slipped off the rocks into the sea. The official enquiry simply noted his death as 'drowned', a not altogether unusual way to die if you were a lighthouse keeper in the nineteenth century. There were – however – more sinister undertones. This particular chap – John Doyle – had been hastily ferried onto Slyne Head as Mr Gregory, the resident keeper, had fallen ill. This did not, as it happens, go down well with Mrs Gregory, who felt that her son Mr Gregory junior should have got the job. In fact she was so miffed that she is said to have slipped some poison into the new keeper's cup of tea. As I stood alone on the windswept buttress of Slyne Head, the tower soaring above me, the buildings empty and staring out at an empty sea, it was easy to imagine the new man stumbling up the path in the darkness, with a cackling Mrs Gregory stirring some foul vial into his welcoming brew. He drank the tea, and then staggered back outside, doubled up in pain, to slip off the rocks and into a watery grave. Mrs Gregory was duly tried but never convicted – and no one apparently thought to ask how Mr Gregory became ill in the first place, which struck me as a less than ringing endorsement of nineteenth-century sleuthing. As the wind moaned and sighed around me, I thought what an ideal setting a lighthouse is for murky plots and dark deeds.

Turning to face the sea, I stood on tiptoe to look over the wall. It was a hugely evocative sight, the open ocean stretching into the distance alive with potential. The same thoughts that coursed through my mind, the same feeling of distant promise and the bounty beyond the horizon, had long drawn the people of the west coast of Ireland to

America and beyond. Emigration has always loomed large in the Irish culture, with the bereaved and bankrupt often taking to the sea as a last resort. The promise of new homes and unlimited prosperity has of course seldom lived up to expectations, with emigrants frequently ending up in slums or impossibly bleak mining towns. An eloquent letter home in the late nineteenth century spoke volumes for the shattered dreams of many who travelled in hope of a new life:

> A big number of our boys and girls died of a broken heart and lived to rue the day they abandoned their happy homes in old Ireland – poor though they were – for the chimera of the golden west.

Although individual cases were undeniably tragic, the real sadness, for me, lay in the ripping out of the heart of a nation. In the late nineteenth century, after the potato famine, the very lifeblood of Ireland haemorrhaged into the sea, dissipating on wind and wave never to return. Indeed the modern economic crisis faced by Ireland has seen emigration rear its head once again, as a new population look west towards the promise of distant shores.

Shaking off my somewhat reflective mood, I quickly snapped a few photos before walking briskly back down the path towards where the RIB once again bobbed at the foot of the steps. I jumped aboard and Martin reversed quickly away from the quay wall, anxious to avoid the swell that was vigorously attempting to push us into the rocks and add another notch to Slyne Head's impressive tally of wrecks. Even on a calm day like today, the currents and tide that snarled around the dark periphery of the headland created conditions all of their own, a mini-maelstrom to lure in the unwary mariner.

'There's one last thing I must show you before we head home,' said Martin. 'You're a marine biologist – it's right up your alley, I'd say.'

Steering the RIB straight into the heart of the network of tiny islands that surrounded the headland, Martin soon came to a halt in a shallow area of flat, calm water, surrounded on all sides by low rock walls. The water around us shone an iridescent green, the sunlight reflected off the white sand of the sea floor. Glancing over the side, I saw a powerful stocky form streak past, followed by another, twisting to look upwards at our boat as we hovered overhead. Looking at the water's surface, I saw a number of heads pop up, slick round orbs with glistening whiskers, staring at these curious interlopers to their world. Interestingly there were both grey and common seals in the group – the first time I had ever seen both species in the same location. The smaller common seals were distinct with their snub noses and Labrador eyes – neat, compact and, although my heart sinks at even contemplating using the expression, undeniably cute. The larger grey seals were more aloof, sculling back and forth in the middle distance, Roman noses creating a distinct bow wave. Occasionally they would bark in annoyance, spraying sea water from partially submerged muzzles. They looked – and once again I hesitate to use the expression – pug ugly by comparison. I could see why they were fairly averse to hanging round with their coquettish and appealing cousins.

Surrounded by seals, with the lighthouse a towering

pinnacle in the middle distance, I resolved to return with dive kit and camera gear. The waters of Slyne Head, where men once hunted gigantic sharks, where storms howl and rage, where currents and tides rolled and swirled, and where the bark of seals is lost on the winds that sweep out into the desert of the open Atlantic, seemed to me to be worthy of further exploration.

5

A Brief Encounter

I had yet to encounter my first dolphin in Ireland, and as the days turned into weeks I interrogated many a baffled local fisherman, who seemed to encounter them on a near-daily basis. These fishermen were working beyond the range of my coastal patrols, and I began to seriously wonder if gunning the boat towards the horizon was the best option. The vast open spaces were certainly intimidating, with the thought of chance encounters seemingly diminished by the immense blue sweep of the horizon. What was beyond doubt was that the deeper water off the continental shelf was the realm of the true oceanic monsters.

'Ah, you'd have a very good chance of seeing sperm whales if you stayed out there a couple of days,' said Martin one night in the pub. 'They patrol the edge of the shelf, you see.' He took a sip from his pint and then added with a chuckle, 'Let's see you stick a tag in one of those – you'd get a free ride to America. That RIB of yours would really fly then.'

Despite the lure of the horizon, I stuck to hugging the silver bays and dark coves, engine puttering behind me, my gaze scanning the blue expanse before me, back and forth over empty seas. This was mainly out of a very healthy respect for these waters. I was a tiny speck scudding along the edge of an island at the shallow border of a violent ocean. A spiralling low-pressure system, generated and fuelled by the very rotation of the Earth itself, could arrive at any moment, turning limpid coves into snarling maelstroms. The first indication would be a capillary ripple of tiny waves and a puff of wind on the cheek, a murmured warning of the fury to come. I was a newcomer here, and did not want to get caught in the wide open spaces, no matter how alluring they seemed.

It was therefore with a real sense of caution that I patrolled the coastline towards Slyne Head, nosing carefully between the smaller headlands and keeping a weather eye on the horizon throughout. Returning from yet another fruitless patrol in the middle of May, I was just turning the RIB into the channel between Inishlacken and Roundstone, the start of the final leg home, when out of the corner of my eye I saw a blast of white spray a few hundred yards distant. I slowed the engine to a muttering crawl and picked up my binoculars. And there, racing towards me at full throttle, was a pod of bottlenose dolphins.

It's very easy to get carried away at moments like this. So I did.

'Yeeeeessss!' I shouted, to no one in particular. There then followed the standard thirty seconds or so adopted by anyone who sees a pod of dolphins charging towards them. I attempted to simultaneously get my camera, my guidebook, and a good telephoto lens from different parts of the boat, all the while laughing out loud and steering with an outstretched foot. Having got my binocular strap caught round my chin, I then dropped the guidebook and took a photo with the lens cap on. I don't care who you are, where you come from or how grimly unemotional you tend to be, if you don't laugh out loud when you see dolphins you are – quite frankly – weird.

Fortunately by the time the dolphins arrived at the boat, something like order had been restored and I resolved to keep on a straight path and let the dolphins do their thing around the bow and in the wake.

There appeared to be about ten of them, and the first thing that struck me about them was their size. These weren't the quaint, doe-eyed dolphins of our imagination, they were grey bruisers, barrels of muscle moving at extraordinary speed. Simon had told me stories of harbour porpoises being washed ashore with raked backs and pulped innards. Bottlenose dolphins are famously intolerant of competing species, and to be under assault from twelve feet of muscle, teeth and ill intent must be a singularly unpleasant – but blessedly short – experience for smaller dolphin and porpoise species. There is a very good reason that only bottlenose dolphin vocalisations are recorded in the Shannon Estuary where Ireland's resident pod goes about its business – everything else is too terrified to go anywhere near the place.

The size of the eastern Atlantic bottlenose is thought to be an adaptation to the colder environment around them. This is a well-distributed, highly successful animal, with populations spread to all temperate oceans, yet we have the largest bottlenose dolphins on Earth on our own doorstep. I think this is splendid – we may lose out on the size of our buildings, have a tiny army, a wheezing economy, and cars with engines smaller than sewing machines, but we have the largest dolphins, which after all is what is important.

Although they tend to look fairly uniform and grey, there are actually two distinct types of bottlenose – an inshore version and a more robust (and all-round scarier if you happen to be a porpoise) offshore animal. I had absolutely no idea which type these were, all I knew was that they were very large, very close, and impressing the pants off me as they rode the bow wave of the RIB.

It's quite something to be in a boat that is twenty feet long, and have several sleek animals about thirteen feet long riding alongside. The dolphins had not only mastered the water itself – one would have rather expected that – they had learned the complexities of pressure waves and spreading wakes. They would power their bodies vigorously towards the bow, then hang in station, riding pulses of invisible energy, making small adjustments with their bodies and tail flukes to remain in position. They would even occasionally roll nonchalantly onto one side and peer up at me as I craned forward from the central console, eyeing me with passing interest before getting back to the serious business of bow riding.

By now I had motored past Inishlacken Island, the pod remaining with me, and I had not taken a single photograph, so I swung my camera from around my neck and began snapping away furiously.

The real life of these animals involves fear, injury, hunger and a constant battle to survive, a far cry indeed from the idyllic image we have of carefree frolicking in the wide blue spaces. We are talking about one of the real thugs of the sea here. I've personally been on the wrong end of a good ticking off by a male bottlenose dolphin, having followed it for slightly too long on a dive in the Bahamas. The animal suddenly turned, raced towards me, and delivered a powerful series of clicks at close range, complete with what I can only describe as irate body language and the underwater equivalent of a furious glare. I'm no dolphin expert, but I think I heard the phrase ' . . . or you'll get the kicking of your life, my son' at the end of the tirade. I meekly shuffled away from the dolphin, hugging the sea floor and trying to make myself as tiny as possible, whilst it turned back rather huffily to the business of looking for dinner.

Ever since that encounter I had always tried to stay out of the water looking in, an arrangement that appears to suits both myself and the dolphins just fine. This does mean that I have to photograph a speeding torpedo of muscle, one that appears and disappears in an instant, from a bouncing RIB that I'm steering with my knees. As such, I feel I have one of the finest collections of images in the world of large spreading pools of spray and foam where dolphins have just been, as well as more abstract lopsided shots of waves and blue skies. I am inordinately proud of my 'Big Splash Where a Humpback Just Breached', and as for my 'Big Pointless Bit of Underwater Nothing Where a Shark Just Was', I'm not sure there is a better expression of something recently very exciting anywhere in the genre of diving photography.

These dolphins were being obliging in the extreme, though, and, as I slowed in the shallows that led to Inishnee Island, my own cottage sitting proudly on the headland, the dolphins slowed with me. Their explosive jumps and dynamic spiralling around the bow was replaced by a leisurely rolling alongside, their broad, dark grey backs glistening in the golden light of the evening. This gave me ample opportunities to get some crystal-clear close-ups of their dorsal fins and, by the time they had decided that I was really quite dull and spun away into the open sea once more, I had their fingerprints in the bag.

These images would prove the first tiny piece of the jigsaw that might ultimately tell me if I was encountering the same dolphins again and again, and could even help me track their movements. The first evidence of the Roundstone dolphins had been collected, creating the opening page of a story I hoped to collate over the rest of the summer. And so – at last – my work could really begin.

6

Fruits de Mer

Walking out of my front door every day presented me with a rolling view of nature running riot. We were now edging towards midsummer, and everything that could possibly blossom, frolic, display or bloom was doing so with some gusto.

Directly opposite the cottage was a steep meadow, a multicoloured bank of flowers and grass. This looked and smelled fantastic, as well as performing the additional (and key) function of shielding me from the brisk Atlantic winds as I sat out in front of the cottage of an evening sipping a gin and tonic. Starbursts of yellow flag irises nodded sedately in the sea breeze, whilst the low green hedge abutting the cottage magically transformed itself over the space of a few days into a violent, vivid red as montbretia bloomed like fireworks along its length. Towards the top of the hill was a patchwork of yellow gorse and pink fuchsias, through which cows ambled as they feasted on the lush buffet at their feet.

The hill was bisected by an ancient dry-stone wall, weaving its way down past the cottage and towards the sea. A hundred yards or so on its journey, it sagged drunkenly into an area of bog and reeds, before rallying itself and twisting up a small hillock and then tumbling towards the shoreline. Here it disappeared into the ground at the tideline, the latter represented by a technicolour mass of old fishing nets, discarded buoys, and the inevitable plastic detritus of any shoreline in Europe. This was very much the end of man's tenure on the land, and the beginning of the territory of the sea, the border symbolised by numerous fence posts and twists of rusty barbed wire. As seemed to be customary in Connemara, where good land was at such a premium, the fences ran right onto the very edge of the shore, where they were duly smashed, uprooted and pulverised. It looked like the front line in a longstanding conflict, a no man's land of shell holes and twisted wire, which I suppose in a way it was. The people of wild Atlantic coastlines have always had an intense relationship with the sea. It provides their food, their transport and their communication with other towns, provinces and distant lands; yet it also takes husbands, sons, fathers and brothers. It is the great provider and also the great predator, and many of the songs along the Connemara coast are written when in the grip of grief and loss.

For now, though, I was happy. In fact there was every chance I was nauseatingly happy, all over-the-top waves and shrill greetings to bewildered locals. As I thundered along the narrow roads that led through the village, I could almost see the weary expressions that said, 'Ah, Jaysus, here comes that fekkin' simpleton,' before a polite arm was raised in greeting as I careered past, bellowing a cheery hello. I hummed to myself constantly, and talked incessantly to Reuben (who had adopted his own expression along the lines of 'Look, I'm a dog. Beyond "Reuben", "sit", "pebble" and "stay", you're talking to yourself, you moron.'). Nonetheless, I was blissfully content as I puttered about my work. This was the culmination of everything I had ever wanted to achieve – which is perhaps a slightly histrionic way of putting it, but true nonetheless. I was in a beautiful place, patrolling tracts of wild ocean in my own boat, looking for dolphins to photograph and basking sharks to tag. All my boyhood dreams had come true, and I tried to thrust aside my middle-class guilt at feeling good pretty much constantly. There were times when I had to pinch myself. I would be powering through oily swells offshore, the outboard shuddering and roaring behind me, cold ocean spray in the air and a warm summer wind in my face, with the coast of Connemara passing in a blur of green, slate grey and gold, when a sense of unreality would descend. It was as if I was living in a world I had fabricated for myself. I was keenly aware that I must seize the moment, and that time was slipping through my fingers, my brief stay in Connemara shortened by every tide that rose and fell and every day that passed.

My only frustration was in the immense array of possibilities on my doorstep, and how little time I had to exploit them. My work was taking me along almost the complete length of the west coast of Ireland and, within a month of arriving in Roundstone, I had towed my RIB nearly two thousand miles along potholed roads and twisting country lanes. The boat was collecting an impressive range of scars, nicks and cuts, as was I. It was exhausting work and, after responding to yet another call from some distant headland, I would arrive back at my cottage in the dead of night, stumbling through the door in salt-stained coveralls to crash onto the bed, dribbling onto the pillow and waking later with a thick head and dry mouth. Days were long and evenings were short, the latter consisting of me gobbling a gigantic plate of food, then passing out like a darted rhino.

(On one memorable morning, I woke particularly early to deliver the boat to a local man for some minor repairs. Never at my absolute best in the mornings, in my bewildered state I managed to get both feet down one leg of my waterproof trousers. This caused me to hop around the bedroom energetically for a minute or so, both knees wriggling as I tried to extract the offending foot, before I crashed into the side of the bed and fell onto the bedroom floor. As I lay there, one cheek scrunched up on the carpet and one eye squinting at a lopsided world, I seriously contemplated staying put and getting a few extra hours' sleep, as both feet were firmly wedged in place and both arms stuck beneath me. Reubs ambled over to nudge me in concern, and eventually a potent combination of shame and a full bladder saw me wriggle to my feet.)

Although I had ample opportunity to explore the coast further afield, I still felt frustration at not being able to develop a relationship with the tidal shore right in front of the cottage. I had been in the extremely fortunate position of spending much of my life along the shoreline of Britain and Ireland, and yet so much of it passed in a blur from the speeding Land Rover that I began to feel I was missing out. There is much to be said about the grandeur of the Irish coast, and yet there are also great adventures to be had on any fifty yards of a tidal shore.

When I trained as a marine biologist, we went on a field trip to the convoluted, rocky coastline of Brittany. This is influenced by the tide like few others, as it is a series of flat ledges, every tide bringing a new world of predators and a new series of dramas. A perfect place for a group of embryonic scientists to learn their craft.

We all filed out of the minibus at the head of the shore, and were duly presented with buckets, small nets and various sampling gear. Our lecturers, three learned and much-published marine biologists, eyed us severely as we stood in a colourful gaggle of cheap waterproofs and new wellies.

'Ladies and gentlemen,' said Dr Wigham, beard bristling for maximum effect, 'this is a serious scientific field trip. You are here to learn of the flora and fauna of a North-West European inter-tidal rocky shore. We will be watching you carefully – you are to fastidiously collect, and accurately record, any species you observe.' He paused for added effect, before peering over the top of his half-moon specs.

'We are not here to rock pool and gallivant like children. Is everyone crystal clear about that?'

Suitably cowed, we dispersed onto the platform of rock that stretched out before us, dotted with rock pools and all manner of exciting nooks and crannies. I was in the process of carefully measuring a whelk when I was distracted by the distinctive sound of a grown man running in wellies, a kind of wheezing, flapping noise. It was Dr Wigham, running towards the other two lecturers crouched in a rock pool about fifty yards away from me.

'Hey fellas,' he bellowed, waving one arm aloft, 'look at the size of this bloody crab!'

Dr Attril and Dr Rowden duly crowded round, and there followed a certain amount of laughing and excited shouting as the crab wriggled and nipped in the approved manner. Watching them from a distance, it was immediately apparent why they had become marine biologists, and very good ones at that. Send your offspring toddling off towards a rock pool and you just never know what may come wandering back. They'll depart children, and return marine biologists. Their sense of wonder is precisely the same.

I duly resolved to get to know the shore outside my Connemara cottage in more detail. I wanted not only to understand the biology – three years at university had presented me with a reasonably solid grounding in that – I wanted to understand it as a hunter-gatherer, as a pagan man walking the shore looking for protein. I wanted to go feral.

We are all hunter-gatherers. But for an accident of time we'd be out running down a mammoth or two and clubbing our dates into submission. Humans have endurance that almost no other animal on Earth can match – the reason Kalahari bushmen can run down a gemsbok over several days. We can cope with almost any environmental stress, go without food for days, go without sleep, and problem solve in a way beyond any other species on the planet, which means we can outwit any animal that is unfortunate enough to cross our path. We are all Kalahari bushmen, Aboriginal hunters, and Inuit travellers – we've just had one or two too many pasties and pints of Guinness. Come the Apocalypse, we'll all very swiftly be back down to fighting weight and foraging as though civilisation had been a mere blip in our development.

I therefore decided that not only would I explore the shoreline in front of the cottage, I would also forage from it. I would wake the next morning as man the hunter, employing all the ancient skills at my disposal. There was a new predator in town, and his name was Monty.

The first attempt at reaping the marine harvest was placing down creels. A quick chat with Bridie, my landlady and very much the matriarch of Inishnee Island, quickly secured the loan of four battered lobster pots. It was early in the fishing season, and having had a little bit of previous form when it came to not catching fish, I decided that the best way to get the pots baited and out was to buy fish locally. Sadly I picked the wrong shop, and as such my creels ended up baited with fresh trout and smoked haddock, which led me to believe that I would end up catching the more discerning and aristocratic members of the local crustacean community. The next day, with a great deal of grunting and swearing, I tipped them over the edge of the RIB in the small bay below the cottage, leaving the brightly coloured buoys to bob promisingly in the calm water. I went to bed that night dreaming of many-jointed legs, full of delicious white meat, stalking over the seafloor on their inexorable passage towards my dinner table. It's a strange thing to collect your own food, as not too unreasonably it doesn't know it's food until the moment it meets you. From being the big enchilada of the rock pool to being in a big enchilada on my plate – a disconcerting tumble down the food chain for an animal with even the most basic thought processes.

Having retrieved the creels after a few days and found them empty, I re-baited in a more traditional manner with salted fish and tried again in a slightly different location. I puttered out to the buoys three days later and, with baited breath, hauled in the first pot. And there at the bottom of the creel, carapace as dark as midnight, claws clicking and creaking, was a lobster.

The lobster is a very interesting animal indeed even by the high standards of a rocky shore, crammed as it is with gladiators, experts in disguise, masters of the poison dart and the ambush. Much the same as crabs, the lobster has one large, crushing claw, and one smaller pincer for more delicate work like feeding itself and close-point crochet work. The one staring miserably back at me from my creel was a relative youngster, weighing in at about a pound – large enough to eat but not a big fellow by any means. The largest lobster ever caught was a great, clanking, armoured monster, almost four feet long, that weighed nearly forty-five pounds.

A lobster will live for a very long time, and the one I was looking at was probably about ten to fifteen years old. I experienced a strong pang of sympathy for it, for the battles it had fought and the tribulations it had overcome. Unfortunately as far as the lobster was concerned, I felt an even stronger pang of hunger, so he was duly transported back to the cottage, dispatched with a strong knife through the carapace (*much* more humane than throwing the poor thing straight into boiling water) and messily devoured with garlic butter and lettuce from the garden. Such is the conversion of protein in the natural world, and although the lobster as a species has a battery of senses, fearsome claws and a tough carapace, it also goes rather well with a chilled Pinot Grigio.

It was a lovely evening as I polished off the meal, looking out over the water and the village opposite. The sun was just dipping behind the summit of Errisbeg Mountain, creating a backlit line of rocks that meandered through an indigo sky. The first lights were just coming on in Roundstone, and a snatch of laughter was carried to me on the sea breeze from the open horizon beyond Inishlacken Island. The expanse of the ocean beyond the island looked endless, dark and listless, full of the promise of encounters to come. I took another sip of my wine, Reuben stretched and yawned at my feet, and I gathered up my plate and crunched over the gravel back into the cottage, closing the door behind me as another day on Inishnee Island on the Connemara coastline drew to a close.

7

First Sightings

The calls continued to come in, with the milometer on my Land Rover clicking over in a blur of passing hedgerows and winding roads. The trilling of my mobile would invariably mean a journey to some far-flung outcrop of the Irish coastline, and it was always with a combination of excitement and trepidation that I would answer the phone. I became expert at hitching up the RIB and hurling my gear aboard, to roar off to a basking shark sighting or a rumour of a whale stranding. Often a drive of several hours would end in a vague wave of an arm over a vast expanse of ocean accompanied by a muttered, 'Ah, it was over there two days ago but it seems to have gone now.' The Land Rover and the boat became battered and bruised, picking up a network of dents that were testimony to many a crumbling slip and rutted track. I would return to Roundstone a red-eyed, yawning ruin of a man peering myopically through the windscreen in the darkness, yearning for the lights of the cottage to appear at the tip of Inishnee Island.

But it was good work, worthy work, and my reward was to visit some truly remarkable places along the Irish coast.

With local shark fisherman John Brittain, I travelled to the island of Inishturk, a tiny outcrop of rock that was a microcosm of Irish life, with green fields criss-crossed by ancient walls, quiet coves and beaches, and a community of seventy people living in harmony with the environment around them. John was a shambling bear of a man and, as is so often the case with the modern fisherman, was keenly attuned to the conservation issues that were now inextricably linked to making a living from the resources of the sea.

'We've been tagging the blue sharks we catch for a long time now, several years. It's developed into one of the most successful tagging programmes in Europe, and we're really keen to take the work on to the next level.'

John had been fishing these waters for over twenty years, and had seen a sharp decline in shark numbers in the deeper waters of the continental shelf.

'We used to catch bluefin tuna here as well, and there was a time I could stand on the cliffs and watch them feed. It was a marvellous sight, as they'd drive the bait fish to the surface and you'd see the water boil. In 2001, I watched hundreds of them working the bait shoals, then the next year there seemed to be only a few dozen, and the year after that there were hardly any.'

John had caught two of the bluefin in the early days of his fishing career.

'They were amazing animals,' he said, half smiling at the

memory. 'Eight feet long and absolutely solid muscle – they were entirely silver, like they had been gilded.'

He paused for a moment, looking thoughtful.

'I must say, I wish I hadn't actually caught them now, what with the terrible pounding they've taken. But there we go, you live and learn don't you?'

John took me to the gigantic cliffs at Inishturk, home to clamouring colonies of seabirds that eked out a precarious existence perched on ridges and folds in the precipitous rock faces. We stood at the lip of the cliff – both of us sufferers of vertigo – and peered timidly over the edge at a swirling tornado of life, a vortex of sound and relentless action. Although the activity of the birds appeared absolutely random and chaotic, the cliffs were divided into distinct neighbourhoods and districts. The fulmars were in one area, white dots on the vastness of the cliff face, whilst below them were the dark, hunched forms of shags. The green swards of grass that trembled and shook in the wind were home to puffins, their burrows small dark holes that were perfectly concealed. If I watched carefully for several minutes I would see a tiny body emerge and hurl itself into the void, tiny wings whirring in an adrenalin-fuelled blur. There was good reason to be afraid if you happened to be a puffin – a perfect small bundle of protein – as overhead were two wicked, arrow-shaped silhouettes that shrieked and darted with dark intent.

'Look at that,' John said, pointing directly upwards. 'We don't know quite where the peregrines nest, but I seem to see them every time I come out here. I saw one take a fulmar once – never seen anything quite like it. So unbelievably fast, and at the end an explosion of feathers and an audible thump as it hit the other bird even though I was a good fifty yards away. Amazing.' He smiled contentedly and edged slightly closer to the cliff edge for a better look.

In the wide open spaces beyond the limit of the colonies patrolled the great skuas and black-backed gulls, dark bombers ever vigilant for a bird returning from hunting at sea, or a youngster left unattended in a nest. At their approach the colony would strike up a chorus of complaint, hundreds of voices combining in a rising clamour of alarm that resonated from the walls around them. Hundreds of feet beneath, the swell surged and boomed against the rocks and coves, a percussive backing track to the bedlam above.

I gave a talk in the island school that afternoon. The school building was perched on the edge of a steep hill running straight down to the sea, the view out of the classroom window a glorious stretch of shimmering ocean, the dark land and blue sky combining in a scene that was an education in itself. The total population of the school was seven pupils, who listened in perfect silence as I told tales of whales, dolphins and sharks from around the world. Just as I was becoming slightly rattled by the sombre circle of small faces peering at me nodding sagely as I spoke, a tiny hand went up and a querulous voice piped up a question. This was the signal for an avalanche of queries, followed swiftly by their own observations on the sea around them. As they spoke I realised that these children – the sons and daughters of fishermen and farmers – were as keenly attuned to their environment as any I had ever encountered. Their playground was the beach and the rocky shore, their companions the dolphins and basking sharks that sculled past their doorstep. They also received individual attention at the school, and if ever there was a clarion call for smaller class sizes in schools generally, it was in the babble of questions and comments that saw an hour pass in an instant. Afterwards we played football in the yard, the ball sailing over the wall every few minutes to roll down the hill towards the sea, followed by a shrieking child who would huff and puff his way back to the school yard to recommence the game. Attuned to the environment around them, nurtured, valued as the future of their small island community, and as fit as mountain goats – despite all the arguments for development and expansion, I couldn't help feeling that these children's future was as bright as any.

In my quest to understand more about the movements of the basking sharks along the coast I visited Achill in County Mayo, the site of the last shark fishery to close in Ireland. Here I met an old fisherman who regaled me with tales of fighting four-ton monsters from a wildly bucking rowing boat. Michael Geilty was in his seventies, his face fissured and lined by a life staring towards a listless horizon, and yet he still talked animatedly of the great hunt for the sharks.

'None of us could swim, you see,' he said as we enjoyed a pint outside his pub. 'Our fathers were away working when we were growing up, and our mothers had a real fear of the sea, so we were taught never to go in. It's quite a sensation to battle a big shark from a canvas currach knowing that if you fall in you'll drown.'

'And how do you feel about it now? Do you have any regrets when you see the sharks offshore?' I asked.

Michael looked thoughtful for a moment, peering out to

sea, a fleeting shadow of regret passing over his features. After a beat of a few seconds he spoke.

'Ah, very sad. I was only young and didn't know any better. They're just big old beasts going about their business – it's a great pity we killed so many.' He took a pull of his pint and raised his eyes to mine, a smile deepening the lines around them. 'They're not like seals – now they're complete fekkers, if you ask me.'

Michael was a lovely man and, although he talked with regret about killing the sharks, his eyes shone with the strength of the memory as he told me the tales of many a battle. He became ever more animated, eventually offering to show me the beach from where the hunts were launched.

We drove down to a beautiful, tranquil crescent of golden sand cupped by glowering cliffs. As we twisted down the sinuous coast road, the cliff falling away beside us, I could see the shallows were crystal clear. A little further from shore they darkened as the water deepened, turning bottle green at the mouth of the bay, and then the rich blue of the open sea. Walking towards the beach from the car park, we passed holidaymakers ferrying multicoloured paraphernalia down the steep path as they babbled excitedly about a day on the sand. Toddlers paddled happily in the glassy surf that flopped lazily ashore, drugged by the heat of the day. It was almost impossible to imagine the scene of carnage in this same small bay as the shark hunters went about their gory business only a few decades previously. Michael had brought a model of a currach with him – a sleek rowing boat, created to skim over the Atlantic swells. Michael's model was a perfect, tiny replica of the vessel that epitomised this stretch of coastline, a design proven through

ABOVE: The cottage on Inishnee Island – the base camp where many an adventure was launched.

BELOW: Dawn from the cottage – a breathtaking start to any day.

TOP: The crystal-clear waters of Gurteen Beach.
ABOVE: The cookery competition at the mussel festival.
Note nervous smiles and palpable sense of fear.

TOP: Martin O'Malley – a man with the sea in his blood.
ABOVE: With Simon Berrow at what is unmistakably IWDG Headquarters.
LEFT: An adult bottlenose dolphin jumps beside the boat – an image to linger long in the memory.
BELOW: The first fin ID shot – and so the work began...

ABOVE: Flushed with triumph at my first lobster. INSET: A lobster supper in the sunset – some moments make it all very much worthwhile (although not perhaps for the lobster).

*LEFT: Returning a tagged adult blue shark a wild ocean and an uncertain future.
ABOVE: Tagging a small blue shark – John applies his considerable expertise and bul the task.*

ABOVE: Shark fisherman Michael Gielty back on the beat at the fishing grounds.

RIGHT: Looking confident before the one-man orruch race.

BELOW: Keem Beach – an unlikely site for the carnage of the basking shark hunt.

THIS PAGE: The stranded minke whale — an autopsy of muck and muscle.

ABOVE: The summer in Connemara was perhaps the most fulfilling period of my (and Reuben's) life.
LEFT: A compass jellyfish goes about its business.
BELOW: The seas off Roundstone are alive with all manner of mysterious life.

ABOVE LEFT: Marty Nee – one of the strongest (and fortunately the nicest) men I've met in my l
ABOVE RIGHT: Lorna and Reubs go exploring.
BELOW: With the diving team, preparing to tag some basking sharks.

many a snarling storm and pounding surf. He indicated the far corner of the bay where the cliffs plunged into the water in a spiked headland, a natural barrier for anything moving out towards the open sea.

'Ah, Jesus, it was quite something,' said Michael. 'We'd set nets at the corner of the bay, and then watch the sharks sweep towards them. My job – I was only a 16-year-old lad at the time – was to stand in the bow as the men rowed us out. I had a harpoon, and when we came upon the shark I'd stab it in the head as many times as I could. This was from a wildly rocking rowing boat mind you, with the shark thrashing and flailing, and blood staining the water around me. One flick of that tail and you were a goner.'

He looked out to sea for a moment, lost in the memory.

'I know it seems wrong now, but they were great times. When the shark was dead, we'd tow it over to the processing ship – and it's only then we'd get our money, mind you – then head back ashore. For me that was the scariest moment – the swell could catch the currach and tip her over in a flash. Surfing certainly isn't a new fad on this beach.'

He looked at the tourists and leant towards me conspiratorially.

'See these tourists . . . Well, even back in my day we'd still get a few down on the beach watching us work. I used to stick a pair of boots in the sharks' mouths, so just the feet would hang out when we hauled them onto the sand. Used to get quite a reaction that, let me tell you.'

He gave a brief cackle, and turned to head back up the beach. We passed an attractive middle-aged couple en route, strolling idly along the edge of the surf with stylish white linen trousers rolled halfway up their tanned shins. The lady eyed Michael's model currach with interest.

'And what is zis?' she asked in an elegant Parisian accent.

'Ah, this is a currach,' said Michael, 'and I'll take you out for a trip in it, if you like. As you can see, though, it's only small so there's no room for your husband.' He gave an extravagant wink and then a shout of laughter, a legendary shark fisherman of Achill Island intoxicated with the power of his memories and – temporarily at least – back on the beat.

Many of the more spectacular whale sightings seemed to take place from the massive cliffs of Inishmore – the largest of the Aran Islands. It was a relatively short visit which coincided with their annual regatta, with Inishmore in its Sunday best to greet the revellers and celebrate the very height of summer. The three islands of the Arans are an outpost for an Ireland of another time, with Irish still spoken as the main language on Inishmaan and Inishsheer, the two smaller islands. The same granite that creates a wondrous moonscape on the shore of the mainland opposite the islands plunges into the ocean to rise again offshore in a series of cliffs and crags that have made the Arans a kaleidoscopic mix of arid rock and sunbursts of colour, as wild flowers spring from every dark cleft. One of the reasons the islands have remained a bastion for traditional Irish life is that they were considered a low priority for the British as trade in Galway Bay decreased, and so were largely ignored. The red petticoats worn by the womenfolk of the islands are thought to be the only genuine surviving peasant attire in Western Europe.

Rock is the very essence of the islands, and has always been the main building material. All three islands are divided and criss-crossed by low walls that dip, climb and weave their way over green fields down to beaches and quiet coves. Some of the walls ended abruptly at the edges of towering buttresses of rock, a perfect illustration of erosion in action, with fields and buildings long vanished into the sea. The northern edge of Inishmore glowers defiantly at the Atlantic in an unbroken series of huge cliffs against which the breakers hiss and crackle. The sea is slowly winning a battle that has been fought over millennia, with the Iron Age fort of Dún Aengus on top of the cliffs slowly disappearing into the sea. No one really knows when the fort was built, although local legend has it that the Celtic tribe the Firbolg (I'm not making this up) created it as a show of strength and as a backlash against having their hair ruffled and being given wedgies by all the other tribes for having such a ridiculous name (all right, I might have made up that last bit). The chief of the Firbolg was called Aengus, hence the fort's name that survives as a monument to him. The fort is now only half of its original size, as the sea slowly claims the ground beneath it causing the rocks to crumble and spin into the surf three hundred feet below.

I had decided that the best way to gather information on the movements of whales, sharks and dolphins off the islands was to inveigle my way into the local fishing community. What better means of doing this than entering every event in the regatta that I possibly could? Foremost amongst these was the one-man currach race.

Historically, if ever there was a barometer for virility in a coastal community in Ireland, it was the ability to row a currach at great speed over great distances. This was the means of gathering food, of arriving first at passing ships to trade, of evacuating your loved ones in times of need, of reaching distant communities. I had known about the race on the Arans for some time, and had secretly been training like a demon.

In a neat example of ancient meeting modern, my training means had been a state-of-the-art ergometer. This apparently simple piece of equipment is akin to a medieval instrument of torture, a brutally efficient means of reducing a coherent, rational human being into a quivering, hacking, heaving, sawing mass of sweat and trembling limbs. Essentially it is a rowing machine, but due to complex connections to a wind turbine and an impassive computer that tells you precisely what a weed you are throughout, there is simply no hiding place during a workout. I had ordered one as soon as I arrived at the cottage, and a large and appropriately coffin-shaped box duly turned up. I assembled it – a workout in itself – and stood back to admire the gleaming collection of cogs, wires and sleek alloy before me. The first time I used it was the next morning in a truly spleen-busting workout. Watching me heave and gasp my way through the next ten minutes, Reuben became so alarmed he tried to climb onto my lap whilst simultaneously growling at the machine – not a problem I imagine Sir Steve Redgrave faced in his training sessions. I finished that first workout by rolling off the machine sobbing gently, feet still hooked into the straps, to lie in the gravel pawing weakly at my face whilst heaving in air with desperate, slack-jawed gasps. I had an inkling my heart would imminently burst like a balloon filled with jam, but somehow my body eventually calmed itself, although ten minutes later I was still lying there with Reubs licking my face and whining in concern.

But each workout had got better and better, and now I was banging out five kilometres in good form, all hissing exhalations and thighs like hydraulic rams. I therefore approached the row of brightly coloured currachs on the beach in Kilronan with some confidence, feeling like a cardiovascular miracle and thoroughly ready for the fray.

I spoke to Tony Gillian, the main organiser of the event, as he scuttled past on the beach with a clipboard under one arm and a loudhailer dangling from a wrist strap.

'Hi, Tony. Any chance I could enter the currach race?'

He glanced at me quizzically, pen poised over the clipboard.

'Ah, yes, my name. It's Monty.'

Tony's eyebrow, already in the arched position, now soared virtually into his hairline. If ever there was going to be a meeting of cultures, a tectonic coming together of two worlds, it could probably be neatly represented by a posh English chap called Monty settling his newly toned behind into a racing currach on the Aran Islands.

'You sure?' he asked genially. 'Well, if you like – I'm sure it'll be fun if nothing else.'

He scribbled my name on the list and pointed his pen at one of the currachs drawn up on the beach.

The racing currach is a will-o'-the-wisp craft, a feather-light amalgamation of canvas and tar designed to skim over the surface of the water, gliding along with the vagaries of the sea rather than battling against them. I climbed aboard and grabbed the oars, noting as I did so that they were skinny planks to their very ends. The currach wobbled alarmingly as I took my seat.

A middle-aged local man saw me climb aboard and ambled over.

'You'll need a push out. I'll be giving you a hand, if you like.'

'Thanks very much,' I babbled. 'Erm . . . any tips?'

'Yep, stay on the beach. Too late for that now, though. I can tell you some interesting trivia, though – did you know that *currach* is the Irish for "wobbly"?'

He smiled and took up his position at the stern, standing up to his knees in the clear water of the harbour.

I glanced across at my fellow competitors, all of whom sat stony faced in their own currachs. There was a reassuring spattering of double chins and generous bums, with the competitor sitting directly next to me taking a last-minute puff on a rolled-up cigarette, his belly spilling over the waistband of his shorts like the edge of a badly trimmed pie.

Tony's voice bellowed out a countdown in Irish, distorted by the loudhailer. The final command was clear enough, though, and my new friend gave me a mighty shove, followed by a bellow of encouragement and a cheery wave. And off I went. Sideways.

My first heave on the oars did two things. The first was to crack my knuckles together mightily, an audible clack of bone on bone that carried all the way to the beach. The second was to spin the currach on its axis, the boat setting out determinedly at a 45-degree angle. I hastily corrected, digging the oar in on the appropriate side, cracking my knuckles the other way round and skewing rapidly in the other direction. Everyone on the beach was enjoying this tremendously, and a ragged cheer went up from the small but appreciative crowd that had gathered on the sand.

By the time I had corrected, over-corrected, then re-corrected, the other competitors were twenty metres ahead. The currach bucked and skittered beneath me, trembling and tipping, a deranged colt with a ham-fisted rider hauling on the reins. At long last we seemed to be heading in something approaching a straight line, and I actually began to close the gap on the two competitors who lagged behind the others. By then, however, I had crabbed and drifted beyond the protection of the harbour wall, and the brisk wind that whipped the open waters into a series of small waves and white horses hit the side of the currach and whipped it round once again.

There was, I am ashamed to say, a fair degree of ripe language taking place in the currach by this stage. Each stroke went through a distinct routine of a painful knuckle crack, followed by an ungainly heave, followed by a wild slew to one side, followed by a bellowed oath, followed by a mightily hauled correction that dragged the bow round to vaguely the right direction.

By the time I had rounded the buoy and made it back to the beach, the other competitors were standing around exchanging polite chit-chat. Indeed, the winner had had enough time to visit the mainland, study for a degree, meet a girl, and raise a small family. Defeated, red-knuckled and chastened, I finally hauled the currach up to the beach, the bow whispering into the white sand amid a deathly hush of condemnation from the silent crowd. I walked back up the beach not meeting anyone's eye, my test of virility spectacularly failed. Any island girl unfortunate enough to marry me back in the mists of time would have had to get by on hermit crabs and the scabby bits in the bilges of the trading vessels. I was not what one might term a catch on the Aran Islands.

There had been a moment of magic out there though. A fleeting second when the currach had leapt forward, more through luck than judgement on my part. It was a strangely addictive feeling, a harnessing of the pull of the oars and the energy of the waves that created a brief and yet thrilling surge of speed. As I trudged up the beach, smiling sheepishly at the good-natured banter that accompanied my trudge of shame, I resolved that I would improve. There would be more regattas, more currachs, and – I hoped – more opportunities to experience the unique feeling of a currach coming alive on the sea.

And so my travels along the length of the Irish coast continued, with time and distance passing in a series of passing hedgerows, rugged inlets, tiny fishing communities, and an accumulation of knowledge of this extraordinary frontier. Here was a convoluted border between two kingdoms, both in conflict yet shaped and moulded by the other. The miles were many, and the rewards sporadic, but my nomadic search for answers was unquestionably one of the most fulfilling times of my life. And I was about to be rewarded for the long hours as, sculling towards the coast from all points of the compass, drawn in by an array of senses science is only just beginning to understand, was a dark fleet of giants.

8

The Leviathan
of the Sun

'Sole, Lundy, Fastnet, Irish Sea, Rockall, Malin . . .' The sonorous tones of the shipping forecast accompanied my youth, a roll call of adventure and mystery consisting of an impenetrable list of names, yet somehow stirring something deeply familiar. My parents – both shameless landlubbers – would always listen, the noise levels of the house dropping respectfully as the calm, measured tones of the announcer ploughed a steady track around the British Isles and Ireland. We are, after all is said and done, a maritime race living on a spume-blasted lump of rock in the Atlantic. Our primeval forefathers may well have trudged across land bridges, but most of us arrived a little later with the crunch of a wooden prow on a shingle beach, a hitching up of a leather skirt, and a thunderous run uphill to smite the resident men and snog the resident women. Perhaps that is the reason the shipping forecast cuts so deep, reaching a part of us that still yearns for the whiff of salt and creak of a mast.

It was with a distinct quickening of the pulse therefore that I heard the breathless words of Emmett Johnston on the phone one rainy evening in early June.

'Basking sharks,' he said, voice crackling with excitement. 'Masses of the bloody things. I've just been sitting on Malin Head, and I counted twenty-four at least. I'd get up here, if I was you; this could be your best chance.'

I had met Emmett at a basking shark conference in Galway a few weeks previously – a quiet, competent presence throughout the meeting. He was plainly an intensely practical man, offering advice and tips to counter the more theoretical approach of the assembled scientists. We were essentially planning to creep up on something the size of a respectably plump dinosaur, before sticking a pin in it. Emmett gently vetoed the more absurd concepts – including my own rather brilliant idea of doing it from a sea kayak. He was the nature ranger for the region around Malin Head, patrolling the land and sea with an enthusiasm born of a lifelong passion for the wild places.

Malin Head is pretty much the northernmost point of the Irish landmass – a nearby headland called Banba's Crown just sneaks in by a rock or two but looks far less impressive, so a kind of collective national decision has been made that Malin Head is a more appropriate choice. Whenever Malin is mentioned in the shipping forecast, it always seems to be experiencing apocalyptic weather conditions. The name – from the Irish 'Cionn Mhalanna' – evokes images of dark rocks and drifting trawlers, of foghorns and forbidding cliffs. It juts out of County Donegal, the least populated county in Ireland with only 150,000 inhabitants, which has a history of insurrection with a potent touch of sectarianism, as well as a fine tradition for the smuggling of poitín. It is a mass of swirling tides and craggy reefs, with a particularly low tolerance for small boats and big egos. It is also over 200 miles north of Roundstone, a prodigious distance to tow a boat along small roads of dubious quality. So, what's not to like? I hitched up the RIB, fired up the Land Rover, and rattled my way north. There was mischief afoot off Malin Head, and I wanted to be at the heart of it all.

Unbeknownst to me, excitement was brewing even as I drove. Whilst I concentrated on navigating my way through the valleys and towns of Connemara, Mayo and Donegal, the trailer was quietly getting on with the job of disintegrating behind me. In all fairness, it had never received a day's maintenance in its entire life, had been dragged in and out of murky patches of sea water on many a steep, rocky beach, and was now barrelling along at sixty miles an hour in the hands of a man blinded by the red mist of basking shark fever. My immediate response to one of the louder rattles from the rear was to turn the radio up, which neatly drowned out the clamour from behind me, although even I had to admit that it was not perhaps the most mature approach to mechanical issues. Nonetheless, it had stood me in good stead previously, so I relaxed as the damp air of Ireland's green hinterland barrelled through the window.

Emmett met me at the slipway, wiry red beard running amok, eyes shining with energy. He shook my hand, grinning widely and gesturing towards the sea with his other arm.

'Ah, Monty, great to see you. Let's get the old girl in, and I'll take you to shark country.'

The slip was steep, covered in green slime, and overlooked

by a group of surly fishermen – a potent combination that has historically led to some of my more flamboyant reversing displays. Emmett lent a hand, recruited two bewildered members of the audience to haul on ropes and heave on bits of the trailer, and within moments we were afloat. The trailer, relieved of its burden, quietly collapsed, an old warhorse having delivered its master to battle one final time. With a sigh, one wheel detached itself, flopping onto the road, leading the entire ensemble to lean drunkenly, utterly defeated after years of sustained abuse.

'Can you get that sorted?' I bellowed to one of the fishermen whom – Emmett had assured me – was the local mechanic. He opened his mouth to say something but, with cheery, triumphant waves, we gunned the engine and flew towards the open sea.

By now it was early evening, and the sea had that oily calm that only seems to come with dawn or dusk. The hull hissed beneath us, the outboard howled behind, and the dark cliffs of the headland grew closer on our bow, reliving their volcanic birth as they rose from the green water around them. These were not pretty rock faces and quiet coves – these were sharp and serrated, a hint of a monster beneath ready to devour the unwary. Even on this still, calm evening, the sea hissed and frothed at their base, tide and current meeting in a series of mini-whirlpools and torrents, unimaginable energy pulsing and contorting the water's surface where ocean meets land. In the gentle evening light three gannets flew low over the water, heading back to their nests far away on Scottish shores. It is not only people who venture to the deep waters and swirling currents of Malin Head to fish – birds and mammals are drawn there too.

'See that over there,' said Emmett suddenly, pointing at a stone tower that stood on the final green hillock before the cliffs – the last hill in Ireland. 'That's the tower that they used to send telegrams from. Semaphore was used to pass on ship movements from the smaller offshore islands, and then the tower would transmit them from there. Dr Crippin was caught thanks to that tower in 1910 as he tried to escape across the Atlantic. You can run from Ireland but we'll find you in the end.' He grinned wolfishly, raising his binoculars to scan the sea ahead in slow, steady sweeps.

'Breach!' he bellowed abruptly, turning to me with a shout of laughter. Gone was the measured, pensive man of the meeting, to be replaced by a wild Irishman with the wind in his beard hunting sharks off a dark peninsula.

Following his outstretched arm, I saw only calm sea, and then gave an involuntary shout as a massive body exploded through the surface half a mile away. It defied logic, a great dark shape akin to a missile hurtling upwards through the water column with such power and purpose that even the ocean could not contain it. As an expression of power it was breathtaking, with the percussive thump of the detonation of landing reaching us moments later, a roll of thunder carried on the wind. All that was left was a spreading pool of white water, and an image of the animal suspended in mid air, seared on my retina for ever. There is a theory that breaching may be used as a means of impressing other basking sharks, which makes sense as it certainly worked on me, doing my own basker impression with mouth agape as I sat at the helm of the boat.

'Good enough for you, Monty?' said Emmett, slapping me on the back and snapping me out of my reverie. 'Right, let's go and tag some sharks, shall we?'

With Emmett standing on the bow like Queequeg, harpoon in hand, scanning the water ahead, we motored slowly round the headland. At the tip of the harpoon sat the tag, wickedly sharp and trailing a bright yellow square of plastic emblazoned with the identifying number.

Tagging basking sharks is a unique combination of ludicrous amounts of fun and some rather good science. For some reason we have thoroughly dragged our heels when conducting research into the basking shark – this is perhaps due to its elusive nature, perhaps due to an element of fear as many a scientist back in the mists of time would simply flee on seeing that dark, sail-like fin materialise next to their boat.

'It's a bit like being a Victorian scientist,' said Emmett over one shoulder, turning back periodically to scan the water ahead. 'This is cutting-edge stuff, and we're doing it with bits of plastic and a large broom handle.'

A scientific paper produced in 2008 attempted to collate much of the data that exists on the basking shark. It is littered with deliciously vague and apologetic phrases – 'The number of female basking sharks in all seas in the world remains completely unknown.' 'The natural mortality rates for basking sharks are not known for any geographic region.' 'Comparatively little is known about courtship and mating behaviour in wild sharks.' 'The population abundance and density of basking sharks in any sea area of the world is not precisely known.' In other words, we don't know how they mate, where they are, how many of them there are, or how far they travel. When a satellite tag was finally fitted to a basking shark – in August 2007 – that shark was duly tracked for 9,589 kilometres from the Isle of Man to Newfoundland, reaching a depth of over a kilometre, blowing all manner of preconceived ideas about how deep a basking shark swims, and how far offshore they travel. Here is a creature that until only a few years ago was thought to hibernate in silt on the seabed, was mistaken for a sea serpent when it washed ashore, was shrouded in more myth and legend than almost any other visitor to our shores, and yet was seen every year, regular as clockwork, continuing its time-honoured passage through its murky inshore feeding grounds.

It's not as if our relationship with the basking shark is one of apathy – we certainly haven't ignored them. The old Irish name for them is *liabhan greine* – the leviathan of the sun – and up until 1984 there was an active fishing industry based around them. The oil from their livers was particularly prized, lighting the street lamps of Dublin for many years – a giant creature lured to the surface of the sea and a violent death by the sun, ultimately to provide light for man to go about his business in his cities after night had fallen. The fishery represented a neat encapsulation of mankind's approach to these things, with a short period of heady excess, followed swiftly by a severe depletion of stocks. An 1836 Fisheries Board report noted that the species was 'already in decline', and with additional fisheries appearing along the coast for the next 150 years, it is only now that we can begin to hope for a recovery of basking shark numbers along the coast of Ireland.

As I watched Emmett standing on the bow, knuckles white on the harpoon, it occurred to me how wonderful it is that two men in a small boat armed with some plastic tags and a pointy pole can still do some good science in this day and age. The previous year Emmett had counted over a hundred basking sharks on a single day, and as population estimates for the entire planet are in the region of 20,000, it meant that one half of one per cent of all basking sharks on Earth had been in his little bay at that moment. Great stuff.

The actual number of basking sharks out there in the wide open spaces of the oceans, however, is anyone's guess. The Convention on International Trade in Endangered Species (CITES) categorises them as 'threatened', although gathering data on the basking shark is bedevilled with problems. Any knowledge that is gathered on the sharks breaks new ground.

Tagging the sharks over a sustained period gives an idea of total population and of course their movements over months and years. If you tag five animals, and every time you see a shark for the next year it has a tag in it, then you can assume the population is fairly small and staying in the same place. Tag hundreds and never see one with a tag in it again, and you can fairly safely assume that there are a fair few sharks around and they move from place to place. Hardly rocket science, but then again I'm sure the Apollo programme started with the designers blowing things up in their garden sheds when they were kids.

'There we go,' shouted Emmett, interrupting my thoughts. 'Only a small fella but they all count.'

Sure enough, a hundred yards ahead, three dark shapes broke the surface. The nose led the way, a bulbous shape pushing through the surface as the mouth gaped beneath, the dorsal fin breaking the water six or seven feet behind, and then the tail sweeping slowly from side to side at the rear. Basking sharks are ram filter feeders, driving their body forward with their mouth agape, like an American at a buffet. The basking shark is the only ram filter feeder of any of the shark species – the rest are gulpers – and will comfortably filter 2,000 tons of sea water an hour, about the same amount of water as fills an Olympic swimming pool.

This shark was about thirteen feet long, and probably weighed about two tons, a mere toddler. He was pottering along very happily filling his belly without a care in the world, thinking his basking shark thoughts in his tiny basking shark brain, blissfully unaware that behind him were two men in a big inflatable boat sneaking up with dishonourable intentions.

Without looking round, Emmett raised his hand and slowly waved for me to slow down. I slipped the engine into neutral, and we drifted slowly forward, only ten metres from the shark as it cut a whispering wake through the still water. Emmett lifted his hand again and I gently idled forward once again – ten metres, now eight, now five, now three. He dropped his hand again, and I cut the engine completely. The shark was now almost under the bow, an immense dark shape, gill rakers distended and nose aloft, back as broad as a snooker table. The last distance between us closed silently, momentum taking us over the top of the animal. I had a sudden vivid image of the absurdity of it all – we were in a small boat hovering over the back of an animal the size of an elephant, prior to jabbing it vigorously in the backside. I saw Emmett cock his arm, tense for a moment, then drive the harpoon downwards where it connected with an unmistakable and audible *thunk* at the base of the swaying dorsal fin.

The animal beneath us transformed in an instant. Gone was the gentle leviathan to be replaced by a violent explosion of muscle and gristle. The entire body pulsed, with the tail driving violently to one side in a blast of water that drenched me at the helm, crashing into the side of the RIB and causing Emmett to grab a fixed rope to avoid pitching into the water. Then the shark was gone – from feeding to fleeing in a fraction of a second, a juggernaut with the acceleration of a Formula One racing car. For a fleeting moment, I remembered the breach, that great body launching itself through the surface, and shuddered at the thought of the immense power involved.

Emmett turned from where he had been thrown at the bow, sea water dripping from his beard, a grin plastered from ear to ear.

'Well, that's the first of the day. You can do the next one, I think. Now to record the details.'

He spoke briefly into a voice recorder, noting the time and place of the tagging, and a brief description of the shark. ('Rather annoyed' would be a fair reflection, I thought idly.) He then handed me the harpoon with a fresh tag attached, and I took my place on the bow trying very hard not to beam and hop from foot to foot like a 10-year-old.

And so the evening passed, creeping up on dark shapes in the water, every tag representing a little more knowledge, a tiny step forward in our understanding of these animals. As the sun sank ever further towards the horizon, it suddenly dawned on me that I hadn't taken any images of the sharks in the water – a longstanding ambition ever since I had seen my first-ever basking shark off Cornwall over a decade before.

Having climbed into a wetsuit – and with Emmett alternating between manoeuvring the boat and repeatedly saying, 'Are you absolutely sure about this?' – I waited until we were in the path of a large shark then slipped into the water. Sculling gently towards the fin I experienced a moment of disquiet – I was half a mile off Malin Head, in a hundred feet of dark water, surrounded by cruising sharks, armed with nothing more than a large camera. This sense of disquiet was heightened considerably as the fin slipped below the surface and the animal surged towards me, leaving only a swirl of icy Atlantic water. Something ancient and primal awakes in anyone at this point, even when perfectly aware that the shark before you is a filter feeder eating only tiny animals, and it took some discipline to drop my head into the water and peer into the gloom ahead.

The first thing I saw was the mouth – over a metre wide, like a gaping, white cavern moving slowly towards me. Then the water solidified behind it, and the animal itself hove into view, a submarine with eyes. I hung dumbly in the water, a massive lump of plankton resigned to its fate. Eerily, there was no sound, as my head was completely underwater and shrouded in a neoprene hood. As this gigantic animal moved inexorably towards me, all I could hear was the pounding of my heartbeat, a staccato thump like a movie soundtrack.

The shark spotted me, and gave a faintly comic start followed by a distinct gulp. The latter was something these animals did anyway as part of their feeding mechanism. What was more unusual was that I did precisely the same thing. Two animals meeting in the immensity of the ocean and both temporarily startled by the encounter. The basking shark then made a snap decision – very similar I imagine to the majority of decisions it made in life as these animals are not renowned for their intellectual capacity. In this case it plainly decided that I was nothing more than a particularly large piece of flotsam, and could be nosed aside. It even decided to continue feeding, opening that vast mouth once again and motoring serenely forward.

There couldn't have been more of a contrast between his decision-making process and my own. I had decided that pedalling backwards and sideways would be a good option, and was doing so with considerable enthusiasm, legs pinwheeling beneath me in a blur of adrenalin. There was actually some vague logic in my overriding urge to remove my brittle frame from the barrelling path of four tons of shark. Although a filter feeder and the epitome of a gentle giant, there was the occasional tale of basking sharks becoming somewhat miffed at the close attention of divers or boats, and circling them closely in what could be construed as a threat display. There is even a tragic story from Carradale, a small Scottish fishing port in the lee of the Kintyre hills, that in 1937 saw three people drown after their boat was sunk by a basking shark. A few days later a passenger steamer – the *Dalriada* – was entering Carradale Sound and was charged by a very large basking shark. This story is easy enough to dismiss as a one-off incident when reading it on dry land; it's another matter entirely when one's trembling fin tips are flapping in hundreds of feet of murky water off Malin Head in the face of a pale cavern propelled by several tons of muscle and an ounce of brain.

By the time man met shark, I had managed to move slightly to one side but was still close enough to feel the gentle buffeting of displaced Atlantic water, and could easily have reached out and touched the shark's bulbous nose and dark eye. That eye regarded me with interest as it swept past, a black porthole in a grey supertanker. I snapped away with the camera furiously as the broad flank drifted alongside me. The skin was crinkled and corrugated towards the head, becoming smooth and mottled under the dorsal fin, before the massive tail hove into view, sweeping majestically from side to side, driving that immense body forward. As I kicked backwards, I inadvertently tapped the side of the shark with my fin tip, causing me to catch my breath in anticipation. I wasn't disappointed – the shark gave a twitch, a massive pulse of energy swept through the body, and the tail swept mightily to one side. This came entertainingly close to my rubber-clad scalp, my body swept aside like the plankton it was in a sub-surface wave of buffeting water, a whirlwind of bubbles and energy. I spun around, clinging grimly to my camera with my eyes screwed shut, like a child on a fairground ride. When I cautiously opened them again, I was alone in a dark sea, the only memory of the encounter a pirouetting spiral of tiny bubbles and a spreading pool of hissing foam – the wake of a monster as it sank deep into the violent and mysterious seas off Malin Head.

9

Grow Your Own (or attempt to . . .)

The mild spring sunshine and occasional showers of May gave way to a full-blown, glorious June. The sun shone day after day, and the island, already green and verdant, surpassed itself in a riot of life. Ireland is said to be made up of eight shades of green, and it seemed that every one of them crowded up against the dry-stone walls of the road that snaked through the heart of Inishnee. The grass grew dense and lush, dotted by the waving yellow heads of flag iris, spreading like a virus through the low gaps in the walls and spilling onto the gravel edges of the roads. Connemara ponies and foals lazed in the heat, flicking their tails in irritation at the clouds of flies that constantly hummed and circled around them. The tiny coves and inlets shone at low tide, with bladderwrack and kelp in glistening, odorous piles contrasting with the brightly coloured currachs that swayed at anchor just offshore. The village across the channel shimmered and rippled in the haze, a mural of brightly coloured houses and shops pulsing in the heat, the only movement being the fishing boats puttering in and out of the harbour, long wakes scudding and rustling across the limpid waters of the estuary to lazily caress the rocky shore.

Inspired by the landscape around me, I decided that planting some vegetables would be a good idea whilst I stayed in the cottage. The land along the coastline was a combination of shallow, rocky soil and moist bog, so I spent an entertaining morning collecting old fish boxes from above the tideline. I filled these with rich, dark earth from the interior of the island, heaving bags of it into the back of the Land Rover before creeping carefully along the lanes back to the cottage. In doing so I was replicating – albeit with the assistance of an internal combustion engine – techniques used in Connemara for hundreds of years. The bane of life along the coast was harsh, rocky land abutting the tideline, completely unsuitable for planting and sustaining crops. People would clamber into the hills and return with soil carried in sacks on their backs, piling it into containers next to their homes to give nature a helping hand and sustain what could be a brutal life. Not for the first time, I reflected on how very lucky we were in the modern, western world, all rumbling wheels, comfortable seats and surround sound – I for one did not yearn for a return to what we nostalgically term the simple life, with its relentless toil, meagre diet and routines dictated entirely by the weather, the tides and the fickle course of the seasons.

Foraging along the seashore below the cottage soon produced some twisted pieces of driftwood, as well as a tangled web of old green fishing nets. I spent an enjoyable hour sitting in the sun slowly unravelling the net, and then pinning it inexpertly to the wood to produce a truly disastrous fence. This I placed around a larger patch of sloping land immediately below the cottage and – accompanied by Reuben – set about digging a series of neat rows. Reuben is something of an authority on digging, although his ability to plough a straight furrow leaves much to be desired. I appreciated his efforts though, and thanked him warmly as he looked up at me over a dirt-caked muzzle.

In this oblong of newly furrowed earth, I placed lettuces, cabbages, rhubarb and elephant garlic. The latter I had bought simply because I liked the name, although I imagined it would also prove useful for seasoning any elephants I caught during my time on the island. By the time the sun was setting over Errisbeg above the village, I had completed my vegetable patch and stood back proudly to survey the neatly cultivated rows of trembling greens and the wobbly fence that surrounded them. For me the latter was the very essence of the island – made up as it was of offerings from the sea, gifts from the open spaces of the ocean borne to my door by currents and time.

There were echoes in the soil I tilled, though – shades of a darker time. The land through which I drove every day still held the vivid memory of an agricultural tragedy on a scale that beggared belief. A combination of greed from the landlords, ignorance of correct farming techniques and several seasons of potato blight created one of the worst famines in European history, one that had shaped the modern landscape of Ireland in more ways than one.

In 1810 a new type of potato was introduced to Ireland

to replace the traditional Apple and Cup variety. Historical records tell us that the Lumper was bland and tasteless, and yet easy to farm, and soon it became the staple food of the poor tenant farmers who made up the vast majority of Ireland's agricultural output. At the time, Ireland was seen as a means of creating extra crops for England, and the vast majority of the harvest of vegetables and grain were sent directly across the Irish Sea. Prices soared and, by 1830, about three million people in Ireland ate almost nothing but the potato. It was an environmental and social disaster waiting to happen.

With all the modern handwringing over genetic modification of crops, it is sometimes overlooked that the Great Famine was created by a lack of genetic diversity in the Lumper. Developed from only a few initial imported plants, the potato that had become such a staple food in Ireland lacked the resilience that comes with variation to cope with disease. It was mankind's first – and perhaps most devastating – self-imposed genetic farming disaster.

The blight hit first in 1845, then again in 1846, 1848, and finally in 1849. Potato crops were turned to dark mulch, foul-smelling and totally inedible. A combination of a lack of infrastructure, political apathy, and ignorance of alternative farming techniques saw over a million people die during this period. A further million emigrated, with another two million leaving over the next two generations, halving Ireland's population. The spectre of the famine and the mass emigration that followed still haunts Ireland to this day, its memory encapsulated in the rough stones that make up the jetties and roads throughout the Connemara landscape. Many of these were created as famine relief projects, with the stones laid by hands that trembled with fatigue and grief, memories of unthinkable suffering entombed within. I found it almost impossible to imagine but even Roundstone itself – the very picture of latter-day tranquillity – became a grey, apocalyptic landscape. Thomas Colville Scott noted in his 1853 *Journal of a Survey of the Martin Estate*:

> In going and returning from Roundstone, I looked at many of the rude graves in the bogs, quarry holes and even in the ditches into which the unfortunate people were flung at the time of the famine of '47. The very dogs which had lost their masters and were driven by want from their homes became roving denizens of this district and lived on the unburied or partially buried corpses of their late owners and others.

The vivid green patches of grass along the roadside represent – or so I was told – the only memory of where the mass graves lie, an entire generation interred in the sod.

I never really shook the impression of the severity of the landscape around me, indeed it was part of its soaring grandeur. For my own brief time there, I resolved to carve out a small patch and see what I could grow for myself, without ever really forgetting the appalling history that had gone before. I was playing at it, and I knew it – I was entirely happy to dabble in producing my own food, but I was never more than a ten-minute drive away from the pub. Then again, isn't that what we all do when we have a supermarket down the road and our survival is assured?

Having planted potatoes, shallots, cabbages and herbs, I gave them a thorough watering and stood back brushing my hands against my filthy overalls. I enjoy gardening, although by no means know what I'm doing. I am, however, very much a product of the instant gratification generation. Returning to the fish boxes every fifteen minutes to see if anything had grown yet was a pointless habit but one I simply couldn't break. I would peer at the soil intently and tap my foot in frustration, before patting the surface and adding more water. It's a monument to Mother Nature's resilience and fortitude that anything at all grows under my care. An added hazard were the hares, foraging in the rolling fields the other side of the fence, and I occasionally had the impression that I was doing nothing more than laying out a vast salad bar for them.

With food in abundance, however, the hares continued to forage further afield, lazily loping from tussock to tussock whilst occasionally standing tall on their hind legs to eye the cottage and its new occupants with genuine curiosity. Reuben found this state of affairs unbearable, and would stand at the back gate hopping from foot to foot before circling back to me to nose my hand and peer up at me pitifully. Occasionally I would open the gate to watch him thunder through it to the fields beyond, a hairy missile intent on carnage, tongue trailing like a pink streamer, eyes wide, and legs pistoning as he hurtled towards the assembled floppy-eared masses. They would scatter in all directions, explosive acceleration taking them well beyond Reuben's initial headlong dash, and he would course furiously from side to side, chasing shadows and flickering bobtails that jinked and leapt in an evasive sprint perfected over the centuries. Reuben would finally skid to a halt, chest heaving and spittle streaking his head like slimy vapour trails, staring wildly around him at empty green fields. With a heavy sigh he would lope back to the cottage, where I would murmur words of consolation and pat his head. Closing the back gate, we would both look up to see fields already repopulated by the hares, and he would whine in disbelief, nosing the latch of the gate once again. I suspected some sort of canine nervous breakdown would take place well before the summer was over.

10

The (Exploding) Whale

It was in the midst of this rural idyll that my phone rang. I whipped off my gardening gloves and scrambled for my phone, catching the call on the last ring. It was Simon Berrow, and he sounded excited. This was a perfectly normal state of affairs, but this time his voice had that extra ragged edge that indicated something rather special.

'I've got a humdinger for you,' he said. 'An absolute belter. It's a young minke whale that's washed up in Doolin – very dead, I'm afraid, but well worth a look. We know very little indeed about what these young whales eat, and we're going to go and dissect it. You'd be mad to miss it.'

Feeling somewhat morbid at the sudden leap in my pulse and a rather ghoulish surge of excitement – this was after all a young animal that had just died – I gathered my wits and asked the first question that sprang to mind.

'Erm . . . great . . . What do I need to bring?' Not being

overly familiar with hacking apart several tons of cetacean, this seemed a logical query.

'What? Oh, don't worry about any of that, just bring yourself. You might like to leave your sense of smell at home, though. See you in Doolin.' He laughed, bade me a curt farewell, and hung up.

The drive to Doolin would take three hours, winding along some of the most spectacular coastline in Ireland. The Burren is a series of silver limestone hills that rise inland then slope in lines of terraces and cliffs into the Atlantic. The rock provides very few sites for agriculture but is a site of international significance for wildflowers. Numerous species of orchids rub shoulders with eyebright and primroses, starbursts of colour against the insipid grey of the rock. In the early summer sunshine, it seemed that every hollow, nook and cleft was filled with flowers of a different hue, a kaleidoscopic patchwork that defied the arid terrain from which it sprang. The cool shade of a rock cleft and the baking heat of an exposed face meant that plants from different climes flourish here, with Alpine, woodland and meadow species vying for space. The initial appearance of the landscape – barren and bleak – is utterly deceptive. General Ludlow, an officer in Cromwell's army, noted that there was 'not any tree to hang a man, nor enough water to drown him, nor enough earth to bury him', which gives you a fairly good idea of the priorities of the average military man visiting Ireland in the seventeenth century.

The sea hissed and surged against the buttresses of the dark rock where it plunged into the ocean, the waves shaping and smoothing the coast, creating vast cliffs that plunged into the waters beneath through a thrashing border of foam and spray. The towering walls of the Cliffs of Moher are perhaps the most famous, dominating the skyline as I drew into the car park at Doolin. They stood glowering and grand, defiant in the face of the great Atlantic swells that roared and heaved against their base.

I saw Simon's battered camper van in the car park, and hurried across to meet him. He glanced up as I approached, with what I noticed was a somewhat preoccupied expression.

'Ah, Monty, hello. Well, here's the thing, it's, um . . . gone.'

A whale carcass moving overnight might not be as unusual as it initially seems. The body of the whale would have floated in on the tide and of course could float away just as easily. In fact, as the internal organs decomposed and produced noxious gases, the body would become more buoyant, turning the whale into a gigantic, foul-smelling inflatable mass of blubber.

I actually fell into the body of a decomposing whale once. This is an event that tends to make a fairly indelible impression on a person and, as I stood in the car park fighting a sense of disappointment, I could clearly recall the moment the ground mysteriously gave way beneath me, swallowing me in dark slime so utterly fetid I carried traces of it for days. It was in South Africa, where a very large, very dead humpback had washed ashore on a tourist beach in the Cape. Not knowing quite what to do with thirty tons of decomposing meat, the authorities decided to bury it where it lay, covering it in heaps of sand. The southern winds then set about removing most of the sand, leaving only a thin layer: nature's perfect mantrap for the flip-flop-wearing tourist. I wandered past several days later, walking over what

I took to be a rather strangely shaped dune, only to have it subside with a malodorous sigh beneath me, sinking me up to my thighs in liquid whale flesh and congealed blubber. My friends were no help at all, occupied as they were with laughing helplessly whilst simultaneously dry heaving onto the beach several yards away. I extricated myself and squelched down to the sea, breathing through my mouth and attempting to look dignified, standing miserably in a slowly spreading slick of lipids and stench. It's an episode that I still recall from time to time, generally whenever I'm in a situation that demands trying to think how things could possibly be any worse.

Simon, seeing my crestfallen expression, rallied and – as was his way – suggested we set out along the coast to try to find it.

'It can't be far. It's been pretty calm, so I bet it's lodged in one of the coves up the way. Come on, let's have a bimble along the tide.'

We set out more in hope than expectation and yet, within only a few minutes, were rewarded by the sight of a crowd of curious tourists clustered around a tiny, craggy inlet. With our coastline so crowded, it struck me that nowadays the best way to find anything of real interest is no longer to follow the flocks of gulls as Victorian scientists used to do, but instead be led by the strobing of camera flashes and chatter on mobile phones. Approaching the crowd, we moved to the edge of the small cliff that led to a natural rock shelf about the size of a tennis court. And there, lying on its side looking forlorn, alone and very, very dead, was the whale.

The first thing that struck me was how beautiful it was,

even in death. It was a perfect replica of an adult minke whale, a masterpiece of design built to cruise the oceans filtering great gulps of water at a time, straining the sea of life in order to sustain its gigantic mass. The body was deep ochre on top, giving way to a perfect white underbelly. The pleats of the throat, designed to act as a bellows to ingest the water required to feed, ran almost halfway down the length of the belly, where the body narrowed to a powerful muscular waist just before flaring to the broad tail flukes. Even though the young whale was only about ten feet long, it looked like no other animal on Earth, and I felt a moment of melancholy as I looked in the eye staring glassily back at me, frozen open at the moment of death. Simon had mentioned that the whale had drowned after it became tangled in the lines of a lobster pot, a terrifying, convulsive death for a young animal only recently weaned from the great protective bulk of its mother.

'Great,' said Simon loudly, rather surprising the tourists gathered in reverential silence, several of whom glanced at him disapprovingly. 'That's absolutely marvellous. It's even belly up, so we can get straight down to business. Last one of these I did was full grown. Had to use two JCBs, it was a bloody disaster. Right, let's get kitted up and stuck in.' He grinned at me delightedly and set off back to the van at a near canter.

Moments later we reappeared, clad in bright yellow dungarees and carrying an array of sickles, tubs and bolt cutters. We looked more like tree surgeons than marine biologists. Simon leaped athletically down onto the rock ledge, hurling his tools down with a metallic clatter, causing one or two of the tourists to blanch visibly.

'Come on, down you come,' he said, gesturing to me. 'No good standing up there. Right, hold one end of this tape measure.'

He scuttled around the carcass, making meticulous notes in a bloodstained book, taking photos and peering closely at the whale from all angles.

'This is good stuff, you know. It's so rare that we get a young whale, let alone one as fresh as this. It's gone slightly off as you can probably smell –' I certainly could – 'but nonetheless this is a tremendous mine of information for us. Right, we need to get cutting. Oh, and by that I actually mean you need to get cutting.'

With a flourish, he handed me a wickedly sharp carving knife and stood back expectantly.

I'm not particularly squeamish – paddling in whale entrails aside – but just before I made the first incision, I stopped for a moment to study the whale. My first, and certainly closest, encounter with a real baleen whale. These animals use a feeding system that requires the inhalation of huge volumes of water, which is then strained through fibrous curtains hanging from the great curve of the jawbones. This filters out the foodstuffs within the water and is a particularly efficient means of feeding. It has led to the largest animals that have ever lived, the true giants of the sea, being relentlessly persecuted and hunted by man, chased to the furthest corners of the ocean, and only now making what any sane person hopes is something of a comeback.

Of all the baleen whales, the minke is the smallest. The fact that it reaches thirty feet in length and weighs up to ten tons – the equivalent of two double-decker buses – gives something of an idea of just how big these animals can get.

The doyenne of them all is of course the blue whale – 120 tons fully grown, four tons at birth, the largest animal that has ever lived.

The minke got its name from a short-sighted eighteenth-century Norwegian whaler called Meincke, who would bellow that every whale he saw was a blue or fin whale. The boats would surge towards the whale, expectant of a massive haul of oil and meat, only to find it was a small, fast-moving whale. These smaller whales swiftly became known as Meincke's Whale, which through the Chinese whispers of time has become the minke. It is not recorded how Meincke fared in his harpooning duties, but there's every chance he gave up his whaling career for something less vision-critical – a sniper or an air traffic controller perhaps. Nonetheless, the minkes that swim through the oceans of the world today mean that his immortality is assured.

The minke is the only baleen whale still legally hunted, and although the populations remain reasonably healthy at anything from 500,000 to a million animals, it still beggars belief that in this modern age, a time of chemical synthesis and molecular science, we still allow nations such as Norway and Japan to chase down an intelligent mammal in international waters, and fire an explosive charge into its body. All to support a tiny industry that employs only a few hundred individuals – I do wonder how future generations will view us as they study twenty-first-century footage of thrashing whales being hauled onto decks awash with their own blood.

Thrusting such thoughts aside, I positioned the knife close to the ventral opening of the whale – this young animal at least would not have died in vain, I thought, as I prepared to make the incision, a noble thought somewhat marred by the fact that I was squinting and gasping with the stench.

'Yep, that's great, just there,' said Simon, who I couldn't help noticing had positioned himself a few metres away from the proceedings. 'Can I suggest that you don't cut too deep? Right, off you go, there's a good chap.'

I sliced into the belly, the skin opening relatively easily as the gases within pushed against the outside world. The layer of blubber was about an inch thick ('A good healthy animal,' said Simon approvingly as the skin peeled back), and beneath I could just make out the bulge of the body cavity. Carefully continuing to slice along the belly, I stopped between the pectoral fins, stretched out as if in supplication at the moment of death.

Simon stepped forward cautiously and peered over the top of the carcass.

'Good stuff, well done. Right, I'll tell you a bit more about what we're hoping to achieve here.'

He stepped over to my side of the whale and gestured at the area of the stomach.

'You see, we know very little about what young baleen whales eat. The adults tend to be fairly selective, as they've learned to prey on specific species in specific areas at specific times. There's a theory that the young whales just swim around hoovering up anything in front of them as opposed to the adults who are far more selective, but nothing's been proven. When we look in this animal's stomach, we'll be very interested indeed to see what it's been eating.'

We were about to find out in the most dramatic fashion, as unbeknownst to Simon or myself there were some fairly elemental forces at work within the whale's body cavity. My cut must have released a pocket of gas, and directly next to us a piece of intestine the size of a space hopper was bulging out of the slit I had cut, visibly inflating in front of the rapt gaze of the appreciative crowd. None of them thought to mention anything by way of a warning, but then again in their shoes I'm afraid to say I probably would have done precisely the same thing.

The bulge finally reached some sort of critical pressure, and the gut wall gave way in a colossal explosion, akin to a meaty hand grenade going off next to Simon and me. We were enveloped in a hot gust of fetid entrails gas, a stench from the very bowels of Beelzebub himself. In response to Simon's earlier query, it smelled very much like the whale had been eating old cabbage, washed down with a pint or two of Guinness and some pickled eggs. Perhaps that's what killed it, who knows? A colossal animal polished off by a terminal case of flatulence. It smelled like roadkill, like a shrimp left on a radiator for a fortnight, like Portsmouth, like a skunk with appalling wind, like death – in fact very much like the inside of a whale left for a considerable period in the sun.

Simon performed a feat of some athletic note, leaping simultaneously upwards and sideways to land on a ledge several metres away. I simply stood, aghast, in the eye of the storm, holding my breath and peering around me through slitted eyes, anaesthetised by the horror of it all.

Mercifully the wind from the sea swept the cloud of fumes aside, and I could finally exhale, a desperate gasp of disbelief. Simon laughed and jumped back down from the ledge.

'Aha, I was kind of expecting that. How are you feeling?'

'A tad queasy,' I said stoically.

'Well, keep going, you'll soon get used to it.' He smiled reassuringly and once again we set to work.

We mined deeper into the body cavity, a dark cave of entrails and extraordinary organs. The heart was heaved out, the size of a sewing machine, with the kidneys looking like a massive bunch of grapes ('More surface area to filter sea water,' said Simon when he saw my quizzical expression), and finally, buried deep in the slimy loops of the entrails, the stomach.

Which was . . . empty.

'Ah. Bugger,' said Simon, pushing his glasses back up his nose with one gore-rimed glove. 'My guess is that the poor thing vomited just before dying. The question remains – yet another thing we don't know about these animals. Not to worry, I'm sure there's a lot more we can learn from this body – I'll send a bunch of samples off to be analysed. You can tell an awful lot from the blubber alone.'

By now it was early evening, and even the crowd of tourists had started to drift away. Simon took a number of small samples, then began the clean-up. A few minutes later, we were trudging back to the van, carrying reeking overalls and greasy buckets, chatting in the dusk. I glanced back at the whale, small body now cut open, and couldn't help feeling another pang of sympathy for a young animal that had simply made the wrong decision. The waves were already lapping at the edge of the body, lifting the strips of flesh that hung down from the alabaster belly, the sea quietly reclaiming its own.

11

The Pod

The work of patrolling the waters around Roundstone and Inishlacken Island continued unabated, with never a calm day wasted. I had a clear sense of mission – in itself a wonderful thing as there is nothing worse than aimlessly tracking the open sea whilst not being entirely sure what you're doing out there. I wanted to encounter the dolphins as often as possible, and continue to amass images of their fins as they sliced through the bow wave of the RIB.

For every three or so times I went out, I could be sure that at least once I would see that extraordinary explosion of foam and spray as the dolphins would race towards me. It was absolutely nothing to do with me personally, of course, more an interest in the noise I was producing and the waves I was creating, but nonetheless my heart would leap at the sight every time. There was one dolphin in particular, a great sleek fellow with a distinct nick in the dorsal fin, that always seemed to be first on the scene, and my library of images of his fin from every angle grew to impressive proportions. For them it was an occasional encounter of mild amusement and curiosity, for me a growing obsession. When I spent one afternoon with the pod and noted young animals amongst them for the first time (although they were too old to be born this season and were probably mothers and calves from another pod), I went home and felt rather like I should be smoking a cigar and ordering congratulatory flowers.

The unfortunate Simon had to deal with a steady stream of dodgy images and some fairly wild speculation from his keen new volunteer. Having been sent another fuzzy shot of precisely the same dorsal fin, the poor man finally buckled.

'Right, I've got an idea for you,' he said one day, voice crackly down a bad phone line. 'I'm going to bring up an acoustic pod. We can stick it next to Inishlacken Island, and then you can recover it at the end of the summer. I'll be up next week.'

I had absolutely no idea what an acoustic pod was, but it sounded exciting. The next week saw me waiting for Simon in Roundstone Harbour, the RIB bobbing alongside the jetty wall and a blustery wind dancing over the surface of the sea beyond the mouth of the channel. Simon arrived in his camper van, waved a greeting, and immediately began to unload yards of chain, coils of rope, two immense bolts, and a suspicious-looking tube from the back.

'This is the pod,' he said, waving it in my general direction. 'It's a permanent listening device for you in the waters off the island. All of this . . . ' he hefted the chains with a grunt of effort, 'is to hold it there. Give us a hand and let's get it out there, then we'll see if you've got a resident pod or not. Simple.' He grinned, and began to stagger down the harbour steps clinking like some operatic ghost in the process.

The pod itself consisted a grey cylinder about a metre long, the vast majority of which was made up of battery. In the midst of it all was a tiny memory card, very similar to one found on a mobile phone. This would record every beep, click, whirr and chirp in the water around us for the next four months – a constant scientist fastidiously noting the movements of dolphins or porpoises past Roundstone. When I came to recover the pod in the autumn, within it could lie the answer to the riddle of the resident group of dolphins.

Twenty minutes later we were bobbing in the lee of Deer Island, a low green summit of an undersea hillock three miles offshore, its shoulders sloping away into the water around us. Simon peered intently at the echo sounder, then gave a grunt of satisfaction.

'This'll be grand I think. You've got good coverage of the bay, and the acoustic pod will be reasonably protected here. Can't tell you how many of these things we lost in the early days – might as well have been chucking credit cards into the sea.'

After a great deal of clipping, tying and muttering, we hefted the entire ensemble over the side. There was an exhilarating moment when I found myself standing in a loop of uncoiling line, Captain Ahab-style, which would have led to me disappearing overboard with a mighty splash and a disappointed expression. Some nifty footwork saved the day, and moments later I was gunning the RIB for home, the pod silently hanging in the water behind us, the answers to so many questions soon to be lurking in its electronic innards.

12

The Incident of the Dog in the Daytime

Reuben's ongoing vendetta against the hares continued unabated, although by now he had modified his technique slightly and was hiding his substantial frame behind the wall that led to the back gate. He would peer slyly around the edge of the gate post, exposing one eye and half an ear to the assembled masses, before slipping back into cover to wait for the optimum moment. When he judged the hares were close enough, he would launch himself through the gate, executing a clumsy handbrake turn on the path, spraying gravel in all directions, then hurtling at full throttle into the field beyond. Invariably he would see only receding backsides and bobbing white tails, and would end up once again sitting on his large rump, panting heavily and growling in annoyance. He would then stalk back to his ambush position, settle once again and begin a new vigil.

It was during one of these headlong rushes that he misjudged his final approach slightly and, to my horror, crashed headlong into a barbed wire fence. I had seen Reuben take plenty of tumbles before, and had always been astounded by his physical resilience. He would disappear in a spiralling cloud of dust, tail, legs, snout and backside, only to pick himself up, give a brief shake of that heavy head, and trundle on unperturbed.

This time looked altogether more serious – I saw him rebound heavily from the fence then sitting unmoving at its base, looking slightly bewildered and stunned. Unbidden, I found myself sprinting over the fields towards him, every paternal instinct roused, a great ungainly gallop towards what I feared might be my seriously wounded dog.

To my relief, he looked up at me as I skidded to a halt beside him, and his tail gave a brief thump on the hard earth at the base of the fence post. Kneeling down, I scanned him quickly and could see no serious injuries, although he remained unusually quiet. I gave him a quick scratch on his belly, and he flopped onto one side – an ideal chance to inspect his flanks and the insides of his legs. As I ran my hands over his back right leg I felt a wetness beneath my fingertips, and he gave a small whine of protest. Parting the hair, I could see a deep cut about an inch long, the red flesh beneath exposed and shining slickly in the afternoon sun.

It was certainly a bad cut, but nothing like the mass of lacerations and pulverised innards I had been expecting. I examined the rest of him, and it seemed that he had actually escaped fairly lightly. I rose from my crouching position and called to him to come back to the cottage. He got up stiffly, heavily favouring the injured leg, and walked slowly back up the hill and through the front door, where he collapsed onto his bed. I called the local vet, trying (and failing) to keep my voice matter-of-fact and emotionless. After reassuring me that dogs injure themselves constantly, and that Reuben might actually survive a small laceration on his back leg, we agreed an appointment time for the next morning.

I am keenly aware that men tend to be slightly more histrionic about injuries than women. The finest example of this happens to be my mum, who ploughs on regardless of wounds, twists, operations, bruises, high blood pressure, spinal surgery and malaria. When I visit, she is invariably stirring a vast pot full of chilli con carne (Mum tends to cook for the entire village), the temperature in the kitchen is akin to working a deep seam in a South African gold mine, and weakness is not an option. She's the living, breathing explanation as to why we once had an empire.

Men, on the other hand, tend to enjoy sharing their suffering – a generous characteristic I've always thought. I had laser eye surgery a few years back and thoroughly enjoyed the resultant two-day wallow fest, lying in bed and bellowing instructions to my girlfriend downstairs who patiently ferried up drinks, audio books, soup and various obscure items that I felt would somehow speed up the healing process.

Reuben is, as it happens, a chap, and it may just have been my fevered imagination but over the next day or so he certainly milked the moment. Each time I walked past he would hold up his rear leg so I could examine the wound (which seemed to be healing at a remarkable rate), his expression a pitiful combination of laid-back ears, wide eyes and trembling muzzle – very similar to myself after eye surgery now I come to think of it.

The next day saw me lifting Mummy's Special Soldier into the back of the Land Rover for the short drive into Clifden. He curled up on the back seat and sighed heavily, a wounded warrior exiting the field of battle. Having rearranged his bed around him, I gave him a final quick pat and muttered a few words of reassurance.

As I drove gingerly over the Bog Road, the narrow bumpy track that snaked between loughs and tussocks towards Clifden, I felt a rising tide of apprehension. Strangely enough, this concern wasn't for Reuben, who even I was beginning to suspect would pull through. It was for the vet. The poor, innocent chap going about his daily business even as I drove, with absolutely no idea of what was rattling towards him like an approaching tornado of teeth and muscle.

Reuben has 'issues' with vets. This may stem from when I dropped him off at the vet in Inverness two years before, only to return forty-eight hours later to pick him up again and drive him back home. Reuben's concern was that we left his testicles behind at the vet's when we drove away, and he hasn't seen them since. If the same thing happened to me I would probably react fairly strongly every time I was dragged into a waiting room. Trips to the vet were always exhilarating affairs for all concerned, with a certain level of flashing teeth and low growling, and that's just from me.

This was something of a problem because his harum-scarum approach to life meant that he got injured fairly regularly. In many ways he reminded me of the marines I had served with all those years before. He was boundlessly enthusiastic, extremely fit, totally loyal, occupied a great deal of his time by getting muddy and wet, and frequently did things on the spur of the moment without fully thinking through the consequences. Much like every marine I had ever known, he approached any obstacle at full bore, charging into various unsavoury environments with a glint in his eye and tail held aloft, emerging on the other side tattered and scratched but eagerly seeking the next absurd challenge. He also had the same deep suspicion of authority and anyone with a hidden agenda, which is why vets – scurrilous, deceitful curs who lured you in with sweet talk and then cut your bits off – were public enemy number one.

We pulled up outside the surgery, a nondescript building next to a cattle market. Dogs monitor our emotions on a number of levels – through our body language, through the way we smell, and how we sound – and Reuben knew something was up the moment I opened the back door of the Land Rover.

'Here we go, Reubs,' I trilled theatrically, as if I didn't have a care in the world. 'Out we pop, there's a good chap.'

Reuben looked up through narrowed eyes, and dug in as best he could to the back seat, squirming his rump towards the opposite door.

'Come on, young man,' I said sternly, holding the door firmly ajar. He looked at me miserably, and shuffled slowly across the seat before flopping onto the pavement to stand with his tail tucked firmly between his legs.

Half walking and half dragging Reubs the forty feet to the front door, it dawned on me that his wound seemed to have abruptly made a complete recovery. His claws skittered on the tarmac and his rear legs suddenly looked as right as rain, a far cry indeed from the forlorn figure of the last twenty-four hours. With a considerable clattering of the door and vigorous heaving, I made my entrance, smiling slightly hysterically at the people sitting in the waiting room. I dragged Reuben across the shining floor, his backside on the deck and legs skewed in the emergency stop position, before breathlessly giving my name to the girl on the reception desk.

The staff at the surgery could not have been kinder. All three took the time to come out from behind the desk and meet Reuben, throwing a ball for him, offering him biscuits (which, I noted, he wasn't too traumatised to eat), ruffle his ears, and generally make a fuss of him. The vet – a young, capable-looking chap in a smart green sweatshirt sporting the logo of the surgery – came and sat with me, ignoring Reuben aside from giving him a friendly pat. A palpable sense of calm and order descended on the entire affair.

'You know,' said the vet, 'I think it's probably best we examine him out here in the waiting room, as he seems fairly calm now. Why don't you give him a scratch on his belly, and when he rolls over I'll take a quick look at the cut.'

A splendid idea. Reubs now seemed entirely relaxed, and was nuzzling my hand like the hale and hearty dog of old. I reached down and scratched his chest, causing him to sigh and drop to the floor, half rolling to wave a paw in the air whilst closing his eyes in contentment.

The vet quite rightly saw this as an opportunity to kneel beside Reuben and peer closely at the cut. This was the same man who had only moments before been stroking him and giving him biscuits. It was the same man, but regrettably it was a different dog.

I felt Reuben change under my hand. The gentle rise and fall of his chest was replaced by a low rumble, the ribs resonating like a kettle drum being played in a thunderous roll. As the vet knelt at his side, the growl became a snarl, and in one fluid movement Reubs uncurled like a striking snake, lips curled back to expose bared white teeth, ears laid flat, eyes narrowed. Even in a moment of mild panic for me, and extreme exhilaration for the vet, I felt the stirring of admiration for a symphony of power and intent, a glimpse of the wild animal beneath the civilised exterior. Reuben was at bay, and was going to defend himself against all comers.

The vet didn't, it seem, share my appreciation of the aesthetic appeal of fifty kilograms of snarling Alsatian attempting to messily remove his kneecap. In his own homage to ancient instincts, he leaped athletically across the waiting room and landed on bent legs, eyes scanning the room for potential exits with an involuntary 'Jesus!' escaping his lips for good measure. Reuben settled back on his haunches once again, having had no evil intentions other than defending his wound and possibly the ghost of his testicles, before looking up at me sighing in exasperation.

The vet was plainly a tolerant and decent man, and eventually we decided on a solution of me rolling the dog over onto his back whilst he examined him as best he could from a safe range. I actually offered him my binoculars to get a better look, but he simply looked at me like I was mildly deranged and said he could see perfectly well from where he was. He had a point I suppose – if a new client had come through the door and seen him standing with his back against the reception desk peering at my dog twenty feet away through binoculars, it probably wouldn't have done his reputation much good. He settled on peering at the wound from a reasonable distance, with Reuben watching him from his inverted position and periodically licking his lips to make his point. In the end the vet handed me a small phial of iodine lotion.

'If you can rub that into the wound every now and then, that'll do the trick.' He paused and eyed Reuben warily. 'It'll sting a bit so . . . ermmm . . . good luck with that.'

There was to be, however, a neatly ironic twist in the tale. The next day I examined the wound in the morning – Reuben as gentle as a kitten and nudging my hand with his muzzle – and decided that it was healing so well that there was no need for the iodine, although as a precaution I would leave his normal morning walk until that afternoon. The skin looked pink and healthy, and I figured that one more day's rest in the cottage would do the trick in virtually completing the healing process.

Come the late afternoon, Reuben was bouncing off the walls, desperate to get out into the remnants of a glorious day. He paced the cottage constantly, nudging my elbow as I attempted to type an article, stared out of the window, huffing theatrically, and even when sitting alone in the corner fixed me with a relentless stare that distracted me from my work. I finally relented, pulled on my jacket, and walked to the door. Reuben accompanied me, spinning, jumping and bouncing across the small kitchen of the cottage.

It was an absolutely beautiful evening, with the warmth of the sun still held in the grey Connemara stone around me, and the golden hour before evening, bathing the field leading to the sea in soft light. Roundstone glowed beneath the hill across the narrow channel, the low sun shining brightly from the windows of the cottages lining the harbour. There was barely a breath of wind, just enough to dance across the water's surface in a series of tiny ripples, rising up the field to me carrying the scent of seaweed and salt. It was an idyllic scene – a heady mix of sights, sounds, smells and sensations that typified the very best of a temperate summer.

Inspired by the view before me, and remembering my resolution to become something of a hunter-gatherer over the remainder of my time here, I grabbed a bucket from beside the cottage and marched down through the thick grass towards the seashore. Reuben charged ahead with just his tail marking his progress, a black shark's fin in a waving sea of green. I would, I had decided, gather winkles.

The humble winkle is a greatly overlooked source of food on our shores. There are twelve species that graze the rocks and gravel of a classic rocky coastline, gentle herbivores quietly minding their own business and staying out of trouble. What they lack in culinary excitement, they make up for in their rather eccentric sex lives, with all manner of peccadilloes and quirks. Some species change sex, some lose their penis on an annual basis, only to have it grow back the next year, some give birth to live young, whilst some lay eggs. The winkle puts the rock-and-roll into rock pool.

The one great advantage of winkles is that they are very abundant, and filling half a bucket takes only a few minutes. I splashed and squelched my way happily through several rock pools, bending down and flinging winkles into the bucket with wild abandon. Reuben followed closely behind, staring intently at my feet as I walked and trying to catch the glinting drops of sea water that were raised at every step.

The water was surprisingly warm, and it wasn't too long before I decided to go for a swim. I had by then a splendid haul of winkles, the sun was still on the back of my neck, and the sea beyond the edge of the rocks looked clear, deep and inviting.

I quickly pulled my shirt off over my head, set down the bucket, and walked to the edge of the one of the larger rocks. Glancing into the water before me, I could clearly make out the sea floor many feet beneath, a patchwork of dark kelp and white sand. Reuben bounded onto the rock with me to peer over the edge, tongue lolling and ears pricked.

This was obviously going to be a two-mammal leap, a glorious slow-motion arc through clear summer skies into the limpid pool beneath, a synchronised moment of aerodynamic perfection performed by a man and his faithful hound. Warming to the idea more and more, I gave a rather dramatic countdown from ten to one, Reubs glancing up at me between each number. At one we both braced ourselves, and with a shout of 'Go' we leapt off the rock together.

We hit the water side by side with a very satisfying explosion of foam and spray. The slight snag was that one of us had become a tad over-excited in mid air, and as the spray rose in a shining wave around us had concluded that the best thing to do was to bite it. This exuberant snap saw shining white fangs close not on foaming sea water but on quailing, pale flesh. Reuben, as I surfaced, was looking very guiltily up at me, whilst clamped unequivocally onto a mouthful of me. His jaws had connected just beneath my ribcage, and although he immediately spat me out, I could instantly feel that this was more than a slight scratch. We swam ashore side by side in a rather embarrassed silence (this being one of those classically awkward social situations), and I left the water to examine the impressive gouge in my side, which was already starting to leak blood that mixed with rivulets of cold water sluicing into the waistband of my shorts.

Some fairly basic emotions had kicked in with Reuben, who had after all just bitten the top dog in the pack, and was therefore fairly confident that a shoeing of some dimensions was imminent. He raced back up the hill towards the cottage, and by the time I arrived back several minutes later, was peering at me from under the Land Rover. I walked over to reassure him, kneeling down to see one dark eye looking at me from behind the front wheel. I called his name and he shuffled out, ears flat, an absolute picture of misery. Ruffling his coat and talking gently to him, I told him that it had been an honest mistake and in fact I had done something very similar to a friend only recently (not strictly true but I thought it might make him feel better), and that he shouldn't feel bad about it.

As I stood to enter the cottage I noticed the iodine still in its vial on the passenger seat, and moments later was daubing it on to the wound using the reflection of the side mirror. The vet was right. It did sting.

13

The Mussel
(Muscle) Farm

During the Mussel Festival back in the mists of time – had it really been two months since I arrived? – I had spoken to a stocky, powerful man called Marty Nee who had supplied the mussels for the event. Having heard that I was a diver, he mentioned that I was more than welcome to pop in and see his mussel farm in Killary Fjord, should I ever be passing.

Killary is one of only three fjords in Ireland – ten miles of shimmering water with a depth of 130 feet at its deepest point – and was on my route every time I drove north-east from Roundstone. The fjord and surrounding hills were tremendously dramatic, a deep green Alpine valley with dark waters at its base. The grandeur of the region was a factor not lost on the local people, who had created a bustling tourism industry with pretty hotels sitting in lush bays and a steady succession of snow-white cruising vessels steaming serenely at the head of widening arrow-shaped wakes.

The fjord had been a scene of some drama earlier on in the year, as the wild salmon returning from the sea to spawn had been trapped at the head of the system by low water levels. They needed just a few extra inches of rainfall to lift them into the rivers that fed into the fjord; until that arrived, however, they were hemmed in by the shallows on one side and the steep hills that closed in on either bank of the fjord, creating a vast, ever-narrowing fish trap.

The local dolphin population needed no second invitation and had pursued the salmon up the fjord. The result was carnage, with the salmon cordoned on three sides by dark glacial rock. Trapped above, below and all around, they had no choice but to try to evade the dolphins that lay in ambush in the deeper waters of the fjord. Hunting cooperatively, using all the skills honed by evolution, the dolphins tore into the salmon in a scene of pistoning tail flukes and silver bodies flashing in dark water. Sadly, I missed this tremendous scene of predatory action, as I happened to be rattling through some obscure corner of Ireland at the time following up a reported stranding (which wasn't there, I hasten to add). The locals told me it was an awesome sight. 'Once in a lifetime,' said a coffee shop owner helpfully as I stopped en route back to the cottage, causing me to briefly consider throwing my cinnamon bun at his head.

There were also disturbing rumours of fishermen shooting at the dolphins, acting out an age-old acrimony. These animals are not universally regarded with affection and reverence, and there is a perception amongst certain quarters that the only good dolphin is a dead one. Rivalry between the two sets of fishermen – man and dolphin – has been played out all over the world for centuries, the only snag being that the dolphins cannot shoot back, of course.

The mussel farm dominates the central part of the fjord, a long row of blue buoys snaking along the surface in neat rows. I would regularly see Marty's boat bobbing between the lines, and give a cheery toot on the horn as I sped past on yet another (generally futile) mission to investigate a sighting or stranding on the north coast.

One glorious summer morning, I decided that I really should go and speak to Marty, as his work required him to be constantly on the water in the middle of the fjord – a perfect viewing point for any dolphins that happened to be passing. Towing the RIB to the joyously large slipway at the edge of the fjord, I reversed in and gunned the engine towards the distant farm.

As I approached, I could see Marty's boat puttering busily between the neat lines of buoys. He gave a wave as I approached, gesturing that I should come alongside. Having tied up, I clambered aboard, and he walked towards me with a smile, tearing off one grimy glove to shake my hand with a grip of iron.

'Ah, nice to see you, Monty. Not a bad day, is it?' He pushed back his cap and gave a weary grin. He was spattered with the detritus of his work, with bits of shell and mussel juice liberally smearing his overalls.

Marty was probably the fittest man I had met in my entire life. He gave the impression of utter solidity, a Spartan physique honed not in some air-conditioned gym but in the uncompromising environment of the exposed surface of the fjord. Day after day he was out there, laying the lines, wrestling with buoys and retrieving ropes packed with dense bunches of mussels. He looked like an international rugby player, albeit one who had just had a freak collision with a giant paella.

Glancing round the boat, I could see that it was built entirely for work, lacking any fripperies or refinements. The deck was grey steel, dominated in the centre by the Jurassic shape of the main winch, looming over a spattered conveyor belt which itself led to a fearsome-looking mangle. The system of harvesting mussels is very simple – haul in the lines of mussels, stick them on the conveyor belt, and watch the arms of the mangle separate the small from the large, which are duly spat out at the far end into a vast bag. Using this technique, around 1.1 million tons of mussels are farmed around the world annually. Eat a mussel at a restaurant, and there is a sixty per cent chance it is farmed as opposed to naturally collected – not an altogether bad thing as the farmed mussels are carefully screened for pathogens, some of which will very swiftly see your messy and odorous demise.

It all sounded straightforward as Marty patiently explained it to me, but we were having this conversation on a mild summer's day, with a warm wind dancing over the surface of the fjord. Replace that gentle breeze with a howling gale shrieking in from the Atlantic, with ice-laden spume coating the boat and the thrashing waters all around inviting a swift and frigid death should Marty slip on the pitching decks, and then one gets a real impression of the brutality of the work, and indeed the calibre of the man.

'Do you want to have a go?' he said, half smiling in anticipation.

Over the years, I have learned to be somewhat wary of the Martys of this world offering me a chance to 'have a go' at their work, particularly when they smile as they ask you. But for some reason I always say yes.

'Yes,' I said.

'Good man,' said Marty, now positively beaming in anticipation. 'Right, all you do is get to the head of the conveyor belt and strip the ropes of mussels as they come over the side. That's the easy part – I'll drag the ropes in over the edge of the boat, which is a bit trickier.'

He started the conveyor belt which coughed into life with a splutter of mangled marine life, moved to the edge of the boat, and grabbed the top of one of the ropes.

'As the rope comes in, just grip the top of it, run your hand down it, and strip off the mussels so they fall into the mangle. Oh, and don't, whatever you do, put your hand in the mangle, not if you fancy playing the piano in the near future.'

With a quick swipe of his knife, he severed one of the ropes that dangled off the main line, and with an explosive grunt heaved it over the side, placing the top on the conveyor belt. The belt rattled and hissed, I grabbed the top of the rope as it came past, hauled mightily, and – aided by the conveyor belt – dragged it towards me with one hand whilst stripping the mussels off with the other. The ropes spend up to eighteen months in the water before they are harvested, so are clustered with sea squirts, sponges, small starfish and various other encrusting organisms, all of which fell away as I worked my way down the rope. The mangle went to work, sorting the mussels from the associated marine detritus, and spitting them out at the top of the belt where they fell into the waiting bag. No sooner had I finished one rope than Marty handed me another, and I once again went to work, eyes slitted against the shrapnel of exploding molluscs. By the end of the fourth rope, I was hauling ineffectually with wide eyes and a rubbery gurn of effort, my features liberally coated with recently shredded invertebrates.

The lines Marty was handing me weighed about sixty to eighty kilograms each. In other words, for eight hours a day, Marty lifts line after line over the side of a boat, with the equivalent weight of a small man on the end of every single one. He does this by hand before passing it onto the conveyor belt, in fact he does it with one hand, something I noted as he waved the latest rope in my direction, the mussels hanging off it like clusters of angular, dark blue grapes.

'Well done, Monty,' he said, smiling supportively. 'You're doing fine.'

This always happens as well – the kind words of encouragement from a chap who could effortlessly wrestle me into an amusing shape like a meaty balloon animal should the urge take him. There is a certain tranquillity and inner calm with people who work hard in the outdoors, a lack of necessity to prove anything about themselves. My vaguely hysterical thrashing at the head of the conveyor belt was, of course, a living example of the polar opposite.

Pausing between hauling the ropes, Marty told me about the dolphins he sighted regularly in the fjord.

'Oh, it's a wonderful sight – I never tire of it,' he said, the memory of it crinkling the corners of his eyes. 'The dolphins will work their way up past the farm towards the top of the fjord, particularly when the salmon start their run. They always seem to pop over to have a look at me and say hello – you know, it's times like that when I realise that I wouldn't be in an office for anything.'

As I left Marty to his work, my final glimpse of him a cheery wave and broad grin as he hauled in yet another weighty line of mussels, it dawned on me that so often contentment lies not in great wealth or personal promotion. So many of the most grounded, balanced people I have ever encountered seemed to work immersed in their environment, employing the basic tools of strength and ingenuity that natural selection has given us. My final glimpse of Marty was a lone figure in the immensity of the fjord, the great hills of the Maumturks behind him, a man forging his own path on the dark waters that make up the southern border of Connemara.

14

The Really
Rather Large Idea

As I drove through many a pretty, multicoloured village on my never-ending quest to find whales and dolphins, it was tempting to paint the landscape around me as an idyllic haven, the sleepy hollow of Europe. This concept of Ireland – the 'hey diddly dee' version as Lynn referred to it – was very far from the truth. The fact was that I was driving through a country in the throes of one of the greatest economic crises in its singularly colourful history. Ireland was stony broke.

There was a distinct feeling of a party interrupted, of half-finished business, a vaguely morning-after-the-carnival aura. In every district and province of the country, I drove past half-built houses, grand places that peered at me through the empty eye sockets of unglazed windows. New placards declared the completion of swish developments, announcing with more than a hint of desperation that prices had been slashed by ludicrous percentages, and yet the houses and warehouse conversions remained empty.

Ireland had been – certainly up until the 1980s – something of a slow developer, lagging behind almost every other European country. And yet in the 1980s and 1990s the EU gave £8.6 billion in grants, the government created tax breaks on new buildings, American companies invested heavily – drawn in by a combination of favourable taxes and a sentimental attachment to the old country. House prices went up by 250 per cent from 1985 to 2006, and the nation was awash with cash. The Celtic Tiger was created – a sleek, prowling, well-fed super predator, basking in the glow of international acclaim.

'We were giddy with it,' said a local lady who occasionally looked after Reubs when Lynn was otherwise engaged. 'After so many years of having nothing, we suddenly had everything. There was a builder down the road who owned an eighteen-seater helicopter! Madness.'

The pretty cottages that lined the harbour in Roundstone still retained the legacy of those heady days, with purchase prices of up to a million euros. Because of this headlong rush to acquire a home in an unregulated free-for-all, Ireland now had 170,000 families in negative equity, one in three people under 30 were unemployed, the Anglo Irish Bank had debts of €74 billion, and the spectre that has haunted the nation for much of its history had once again reared its ugly head: mass emigration. About 100,000 professional people were expected to leave for richer pastures over the next couple of years, leaving behind a nation potentially crippled by debt and uncertainty. As I trundled along idyllic coast roads past manicured houses, I was driving through the most indebted country in Europe, with a budget deficit of thirty-two per cent of Gross Domestic Product, and a government that was attempting to slash and hack its way out of trouble.

'Ah, that's our birthright,' said the local estate manager, Simon, one night in the pub. 'We get disorientated when things are prosperous. Give us poverty and conflict – it means we can all unite against someone or other who we vaguely decide is oppressing us, and what's more it means loads of great new songs and poems get written.' He gave a snort of laughter before continuing in a more thoughtful vein. 'We'll survive, you know. We always have done – if we can put up with the various calamities we've suffered throughout our history, I'm sure being short of a few bob for a couple of years shouldn't be too much of a drama. Another pint?'

What this did mean was that charities such as the IWDG were suffering as donations plummeted. Reflecting on this as I drove past yet another abandoned housing development, I suddenly had a splendid idea.

My contribution to the IWDG was – at this stage – limited to amassing data on the dolphins off Roundstone, energetically poking basking sharks with sharp sticks, and being a pair of willing hands whenever Simon Berrow needed heavy things lifting or amusingly explosive whales dissecting. I wanted something more though, a legacy, a solid contribution that would linger long after I had departed.

Simon had mentioned over a scone or two that there are something in the region of 150 whale and dolphin strandings every year around the coast of Ireland. The vast majority of these are already dead, washed ashore as victims of their violent life in the ocean, to either decompose gradually, be dragged away and buried by man, or lifted by the tide and swept away to a dark and watery crypt where they represent a feeding bonanza to all creatures great and small.

About twenty of these strandings are live, however. These are animals that may be ill, in poor condition or injured. Many of these cases will either die naturally or be put down by a vet. Some, however – a very few – can be saved.

Cetaceans inhabit a world of echoes and contours, of ancient routes and timeless trails along abyssal undersea mountain ranges. A wrong turn, a moment of inexperience or a violent blast of man-made sound can occasionally lead up a blind alley, with a gradual shallowing of the water until a sleek body touches sand or rock. The tide leaches away and the animal is marooned in a strange world.

There is only so much anyone can do to keep a whale or dolphin alive in these situations. Digging out the sand around the tail flukes and pectoral fins prevents injury and allows heat exchange, draping wet towels over the body prevents drying out, and keeping people away prevents stress. It is getting them back in the water, though, that creates problems.

This problem has been tackled with some ingenuity in New Zealand, where specialised pontoons have been developed. These are tremendously rugged affairs, strong enough to hold a thrashing whale, and yet have all manner of subtle design features to assist the transition from the shallows to the sea.

The main part of the pontoon consists of a large, whale-sized tarpaulin. Either side of this, bolted on with mighty D-rings, are two inflatable pontoons. The idea is that the tarpaulin is carefully placed under the whale or dolphin (no easy matter but possible with correct training and lots of volunteers), and then the tubes are inflated on either side. The end product is the whale or dolphin supported on the tarpaulin, suspended on either side by two inflatable tubes, being steered out to sea by volunteers using strategically placed handles of tow-points. Get to deeper water, deflate the tubes and the watch the pontoon sink and – theoretically – the animal will swim away. Clever stuff.

It is worth noting that this is a moment that lives with the rescuers for ever, a once-in-a-lifetime memory. I imagine the whale looks back on it fairly fondly as well.

In the entire length of the Irish coastline, there are only two pontoons available. This may mean a response time of several hours getting a pontoon to a stranded animal, hours when a life hangs in the balance. I knew the pontoons cost in the region of €5,000, and I knew there was a desperate need for an additional one to cover great tracts of the Connemara coast.

So here was my idea: I would suggest to Simon that we organise a festival in Roundstone. A great big belter of a weekend for the IWDG, with lectures, music, face painting, beach games, a hog roast and oodles of cash towards a new pontoon, which I would present to the IWDG at a final event before I left. The festival would be my fond farewell, a chance to meld together all the elements of Connemara that had bewitched me – the nature, the people, the heritage, the music, the beer and the chance to finally make a small mark for an organisation dedicated to the giant creatures that swam off its rugged shores. And so – with a triumphant crunching of gears between one rutted track junction and the next – the Roundstone Diving and Wildlife Festival was born.

15

Bedouin of the Sea

Midsummer passed, and with it the long, balmy days of the warmest June in forty years. Having shimmered and gasped in the heat for weeks on end, the landscape had become brittle and brown, desperate for rain. When it finally came in mid July, people weren't quite dancing in the streets, but it wasn't far off. Shopkeepers emerged from their doors along the Coast Road and beamed up into leaden skies, fat drops of cool rain dappling their features. Children shrieked and ran barefoot in gardens where khaki plants seemed to open their leaves and look to the heavens in relief after weeks of barren skies. As I drove through Roundstone, my tyres hissed on wet roads, and the gutters burbled in mini-rapids along which spun the debris of the holiday season.

The mood of the ocean itself seemed to change with the weather, the warm, moist air creating winds that spiralled in from the horizon, dancing and gyrating over the tops of the waves creating a short, vicious chop. Taking the RIB out on patrol became an obstacle course of short, steep seas, with the hull banging and thumping through the surface in a debilitating series of aquatic speed bumps. Spotting the dolphins was a case of peering around me through half-closed eyes, the hood of my waterproof gathered around my face. The few encounters I had saw the dolphins appear for only a few moments, a cursory inspection of the boat as they passed. They no longer needed my rather pitiful bow wave, and would surf gleefully at the face of the larger swells, effortlessly harnessing the power of the ocean as they went about their business, providing me with an exhilarating yet fleeting spectacle as I struggled to stay with them. Nonetheless, I had two or three encounters over the month, and steadily my photo database began to fill with images of speeding dorsal fins carving a foaming arc through grey swells.

It was as I was loading the latest encounter into my laptop, waterproofs steaming gently on the hook behind the cottage door, that my phone rang.

'Hallo, Monty,' said the unmistakable voice of shark fisherman John Brittain, my erstwhile guide on the island of Inishturk. 'I just thought I'd let you know that there are lots of blue sharks in at the moment. Should you have a chance, I'd suggest coming out with me and maybe we can tag a few? I'm around the day after tomorrow – do you fancy it?'

It's not every day that a renowned shark angler offers to take me out into the deep water offshore to catch and tag a mysterious shark species that epitomises the great empty spaces of the open ocean. So I said yes. Then chatted politely for a few minutes about the weather and how his boat was faring. Then I bade him goodbye, hung up, and did an excited lap of honour around the front room, dancing an impromptu jig of excitement.

I had never seen a blue shark, the most elegant and nomadic of any shark species. They are built for one thing – to cruise the immense sapphire void of the open sea, searching for food. They spend their entire lives in flight, with the long wings of their pectoral fins steering them through the water column, a gliding dart of predatory intent equipped with senses that put any of man's technological efforts to shame. They constantly smell, scan and electronically assess the environment around them, homing in on the slightest hint of food, following a minute trace of distant blood or the far off thump of a shoal of fish. They appear like wraiths from an azure horizon, feed with the bold purpose of an opportunistic hunter, then melt back into the ocean around them, a Bedouin beneath the waves.

In line with so many other shark species around the world, blue sharks no longer find sanctuary in the wide open spaces of the oceans. The quest for shark fin to feed the insatiable markets of the Far East sees well-equipped long-line vessels ply their trade in the most remote corners of the globe. Their baited hooks, on lines stretching in glittering necklaces of up to twenty kilometres, reap a terrible harvest. Estimates vary in terms of the total numbers taken, but most scientists and fisheries experts quote about seventy to one hundred million sharks being taken from the sea annually, with blue shark numbers down by about sixty per cent in the last fifteen years. In 1961, the Shark Angling Club of Great Britain recorded six thousand blue sharks taken from the port of Looe in Cornwall; in 2007, that figure was down to 142. It is an industrial-scale massacre of a vital apex predator, the garbage-disposal truck of the seas, and its eradication – for that is the sure end of mankind's present unregulated fishing spree – will have untold consequences. One of them at least will be that the next generation will never thrill to that dark shadow appearing at the edge of the reef.

Tagging programmes such as those conducted by John provide vital information on the movements of the sharks, data that just might result in at least some form of protection for the sharks as evidence emerges of mating aggregations and established routes. John was one of many shark anglers contributing to the programme in the UK and Ireland, poachers turned gamekeepers launching a desperate last-minute rearguard action to save an animal they respect and revere. The programme was introduced in 1970, and in the next thirty years there were 16,719 sharks successfully tagged, with one tag recovered after fifteen years, and another recovered after the shark had swum 6,640 kilometres from Ireland to Venezuela. From 2001, the numbers began to decline precipitously, a measure of the impact of the long liners, fishing vessels that lay lengths of line with baited hooks every few metres. Great schools that had gathered for millennia in the same stretch of the ocean were eradicated in a single month, leaving nothing but vast, empty echoing spaces.

On the appointed day, I parked the Land Rover next to the quay at Cleggan harbour and grabbed my camera gear and waterproofs. As I shut the door, I caught a distinct whiff of John's boat – bringing the sharks in would require setting a trail of fish oil and flesh that even now was being mashed and stirred prior to being loaded aboard. This evil fish pie – a nauseating collection of pulped innards and liquidised flesh – was being vigorously prepared by John's son, Peter, who glanced up at me and smiled from a face spattered with mackerel body parts.

John's boat looked powerful and businesslike, akin to the man himself. John exuded an air of quiet competence, the ideal chap to be wrestling large sharks into submission on a pitching boat deck prior to stapling a tag into a dorsal fin before heaving them back over the side. As I climbed aboard the *Blue Water* and we shook hands, I surreptitiously checked to see if he had all his fingers – and was reassured to see that they seemed to be not only present but also in the right order.

'Could be a bit lumpy today, Monty,' he said, 'but certainly worth a shot. We'll go out and catch a few fresh mackerel as bait, and then see how we're feeling before heading out further.'

I had a very good idea of precisely how I'd be feeling. There is a certain size of boat – strangely enough the exact size of the *Blue Water* – and a certain type of swell – strangely enough the exact type that was thrashing against the harbour wall – that makes me feel very ill indeed. I reassured myself that at least I would be adding to the chum slick and so would make some sort of valid contribution to the day, albeit in the form of a semi-digested breakfast. Feeling seasick is the most miserable sensation, invariably enhanced by the fact that there will be nauseatingly healthy and chipper people around you whilst you feel like death. Annoyingly chirpy enquiries about how you're feeling, peppered with homespun suggestions about what you should be doing, only add to the urge to hurl. It is said that the best way to avoid seasickness is to sit beneath a tree, but you don't see blue sharks if you sit beneath a tree, do you?

'I'll be fine, John,' I said with an optimism I absolutely did not feel, enhanced by the fact that Peter chose that precise moment to lower a bucket of mashed-up mackerel past my twitching nose.

Moments later, the engine rumbled to life beneath my feet, the ropes were cast off, and we headed away from the harbour wall. As soon as we poked our brightly painted bow out into the open water beyond the shelter of the quay, the *Blue Water* began to pitch and toss, the engine roaring and vibrating as we drove into the humped shoulders of the swells as they raced in from the horizon. She was a fine boat, built for the job, and came to life as she whiffed the wide-open spaces ahead, lifting her nose and squaring her shoulders at the day ahead. John lounged in his skipper's chair, twiddling knobs on the console in front of him, and Peter continued to mash fish in buckets, whilst I stared tight lipped at the horizon (yet another top tip to avoid seasickness that never quite seems to work) and clung on with white knuckles to the stanchion that rose from the centre of the deck.

After motoring for about forty minutes, we came to a halt in the lee of High Island, the last outpost before the Atlantic. It was blissfully calm beneath the cliffs of the island, cupped from the wind and sheltered from the swell. John strode purposefully out of the cabin brandishing a couple of rods complete with brightly coloured feathers fluttering prettily in the sea breeze.

'Right, mackerel,' he announced with his characteristic brevity, before handing me a rod and letting his own feathers snake down into the dark water.

Ever since I was a child I have loved fishing for mackerel. Most of us only know this fish from our holidays, where we lower a string of feathers on industrial-strength gear to duly winch in glittering strings of thrashing fish. The mackerel is so much more than this – a gilded dart ready to explode into action at the mere sight of prey, a great fighter capable of phenomenal bursts of speed, and one of the most successful mid-water species in temperate seas. If mackerel grew to 200 pounds, no one would ever bother fishing for anything else – hence the reason tuna have been pretty much wiped out. Sadly today we were fishing for bait, using stout rods and huge cranked reels, and yet it still gave me pause to see the mackerel drumming in their death throes in the fish box. It was an incongruous end for the silver ingot pulsing and gasping before me, defeated by a wisp of a feather and fifty-pound breaking-strain line without even being given the chance of a fair fight.

Soon we had a box full, and John returned to the cabin to fire up the engines for the last half of our journey. This would take us out into open water, a good ten miles offshore, into the realm of the ocean cruisers – the sapphire hunting grounds of the blue shark. I braced myself once again and tried not to think of breakfast. The chum swilled from side to side in the stern as we set out, a nauseating sludge glooping at the edges of the box, releasing a fresh wave of fetid stench every time it did so.

Later, with the land a distant smudge on the horizon behind us, John once again stilled the engines and marched out of the cabin. I self-consciously unwrapped my fingers from the pole, and followed him along the deck. Peter had been busy during the crossing, riding the deck like a gaucho as it heaved beneath him, and two rods had been prepared for the sharks. He now began to ready the chum bags – forcing the minced mackerel into meshed sacks so it oozed between the gaps. I looked away at this point, breathing through my mouth, fighting a grim internal battle with a northbound fry-up.

As soon as the bags were hung over the side of the boat, an oily slick was borne on the current, shining on the surface of the sea and snaking towards the horizon. This immediately attracted the attention of the gulls that had followed us out from shore, as well as fulmars which sat plumply on the water at the stern. There was a great deal of excited squawking and the occasional punch-up as a vague hierarchy was established, and then an expectant hush fell on the flock as they stared intently at us and awaited developments.

The shark-fishing gear was a very different matter to the mackerel tackle, with 250-pound breaking-strain steel traces and hooks the size of a crooked finger. John expertly filleted a couple of mackerel, leaving two flaps of silver flesh on each to wave enticingly in the current. Hooking the fish through the head, he clipped a red balloon to one line and a yellow balloon to the other, then dropped them both overboard. They bobbed in the swell, drifting quickly away from the boat, carrying the baits beneath them into the heart of the chum slick.

Wiping spade-sized hands on his spattered overalls, he glanced up at me. 'We use brass hooks because – God forbid

– should a line break then the hook degrades very quickly and drops out of the shark's mouth.'

'This all seems such a departure from the macho shark fishermen of old, John,' I said.

'Oh, it is, it is.' He nodded vigorously. 'The vast majority of fishermen now would be horrified to actually kill a shark. They're fascinated by the whole tagging process, and generally want to know a lot more about where the fish end up.' He smiled broadly. 'It also means you get a chance to wrestle the shark when you bring it in! With the bigger ones, it can be a bit of a carry on getting the tag into the fin, so basically you have to body slam them into the deck. Now if that doesn't get the testosterone going, nothing will. Anyway, now we wait! Cup of tea?'

Even weighing your catch is now frowned upon, as suspension from the scales is thought to harm it internally. For the shark angler keen to know just how big his fish is, there is a means of assessing the weight without hoisting it onto a scale (which can be distressing and damaging for the shark). All you do is measure the girth in inches, then square it, then times that by the length of the shark, then divide the whole lot by eight hundred. It's a lot simpler to get a photo and exaggerate wildly, which is what most fishermen tend to plump for.

The next hour passed pleasantly enough, with the chum slick glinting in the flat light of the sun as the sea heaved and surged around us. I became more used to the motion of the boat, and began to enjoy the spectacle of the birds hovering around the stern. There was a brief moment of excitement when a fulmar became tangled in one of the lines, which required John to haul it in and gently free it.

During this process it lay on the deck on its back, plump belly upwards, wings spread and legs waving comically in the air, glowering at us throughout. It shouldn't have been funny, but it was, with our laughter echoing across the water. John carefully returned the bird to the sea, where it fluffed its wings and paddled furiously back and forth at the stern, livid at the indignity of it all.

The gannets that circled above would occasionally dive for the baits, a silver javelin of fine bubbles knifing through the surface.

'That's the reason I have the baits so deep,' said John. 'Disentangling a gannet is an altogether different matter, and of course you certainly don't want to hurt them. The older ones would never take a bait anyway, being altogether too smart, but the younger ones are pretty dense and eat anything. Like all youngsters, eh, Peter?'

Tiny, black, will-o'-the-wisp birds darted between the wave crests, dabbling their feet on the water's surface, a scrap of nothing riding the force of the wind around them. Storm petrels – which also go by the name of Mother Carey's Chicken, for some baffling reason – live most of their lives at sea, only returning to oceanic islands in June to breed. In severe storms, they shelter in the troughs of gigantic waves, a bird of a few grams, riding the lethal, ship-smashing rapids of a force twelve.

John stuck his head round the cabin door and waved a brown folder at me, crammed with dog-eared bits of paper.

'Come and have a look at our tagging data, Monty,' he said. 'As you can see, I have a truly unique filing system, but there's some terrific stuff in here.'

I weaved my way into the warmth of the cabin and sat on

the threadbare bench next to John, who immediately began to place various crumpled bits of a paper in my lap.

'That's a really good one,' he said, jabbing a stained finger at a complicated-looking table of data, 'Basically a blue I tagged here in 2001 turned up in Newfoundland three years later – a journey of 2,000 miles! Oh, and here's another one, St Helena after two years, which is 5,300 miles.'

There is some evidence that the blue shark breeds in the western Atlantic, and then – for some reason still to be established – the females swim across to Europe and the west coast of Africa, whilst the males remain where they are. There are very few animals in the ocean as well equipped for this voyage as the blue shark – every inch of its body, every curve and every sleek surface, is designed for mid-water flight. A recent research project that explored the hydrodynamic efficiency of a modern submarine and compared it to that of the blue shark, found that proportionally the shark needed six times less power to propel itself through the water. It can accelerate to speeds in excess of forty kilometres per hour, and individual animals have been recorded as travelling over seventy kilometres in a single day.

Running down the right-hand column of every tagging record sheet was where the tag had been recovered, a list that exclusively read: 'Spanish Long Liner, Spanish Long Liner, Spanish Long Liner, Spanish Long Liner, Spanish Long Liner, Spanish Long Liner', the greatest predator the shark had ever encountered in its 400 million year history – ravenous, implacable, and one to which the shark simply had no answer.

I glanced up from the tagging data sheets and out of the

cabin window to check on the balloons as they bobbed on the water, and happily at that precise moment the red one twitched, shuddered and then took off in a determined fashion towards the horizon, scattering fulmars en route. A reel outside screeched in protest, and the most extraordinary surge of adrenalin coursed through my body. I might have wrapped up this entire trip in the packaging of tagging and conservation, but I was still a bloke, on a boat, miles offshore, with a blue shark running with bait into the deep sea and a reel squealing beside me. Something ancient awoke within me, and I couldn't wait to do battle.

John came charging out of the wheelhouse and grabbed the other rod, reeling in furiously to avoid the lines becoming tangled. 'Grab the other rod, Monty,' he shouted at me, 'and when you feel the shark stop running, tighten the brake and lean back. Then reel in like buggery.'

I picked up the rod with trembling hands, line spooling from the reel, and prepared to flick the lever to engage the drag and therefore set the hook. As I did so, the line went slack, and my heart sank.

'Ah, bad luck,' said John. 'It's important to keep reeling in, though – you never know.'

I cranked the handle furiously, feet braced on the deck. As I did so, John suddenly muttered beside me.

'I've got him on this one now!' he said, the tip of the rod bending into an impressive hoop and the line hissing through the water's surface. 'Ah, hang on, he's gone again.'

Once again I felt the same surge of crushing disappointment. Glancing down as I continued to reel in, I could see that my bait was almost at the side of the boat, flapping and twisting in the clear water. And suddenly, in clear view a metre or so behind it, appeared the shark.

It closed on the bait, great pectoral fins held out to the side, tail driving it forward, sleek nose perfectly level as it closed in for the kill. The gorgeous blue sheen of its back was almost lost against the water beneath, making it look as though it was part of the ocean itself. And then, in the blink of an eye, it was on the bait.

The rod bucked furiously in my hand, and the reel once again spun and shrieked. The line flew out, bar straight as it knifed through the surface of the water. I leaned back and braced myself against the initial surge of the shark, the tremendous power of its muscular body transmitted through the rod in a series of vivid pulses of energy.

'Wey, that's a big one,' said John delightedly. 'Brace yourself, stay in touch with the shark, and don't let the line go slack at any point. If it wraps around the tail, it's potentially very bad for it, and you may even lose the shark completely.'

Already my arms were burning and my lower back tensing. After the tremendous initial run, there was a period of stalemate, where the shark surged slowly back and forth about fifty metres or so out from the boat. Lifting the rod tip, I gradually began to reclaim the line a few inches at a time, feeling the shark occasionally shake its head in annoyance in the dark water off the stern. I was now very anxious to get the shark onboard as quickly as possible, get the tag in and return it to the sea. The longer the fight went on, the more exhausted it would become, and the less chance it had of making a rapid and complete recovery.

'Right, Monty, pump the rod and crank the reel, let's get this fella onboard,' said John, echoing my sentiment exactly.

I lifted the rod tip again and again, every motion gaining a precious few inches. The lactic acid burned in my forearms, my hands were losing their grip on the handle, and my feet slipped on the tilting deck. And yet, oh so gradually, the shark came ever closer. Eventually the top of the trace broke through the surface, the shark now visible in the water beneath us, a shadow twisting and turning in the water column. John leaned over the side and grabbed the wire with one gloved hand, heaving mightily to recover those last few metres and drag the shark onboard. As he did so, the shark surged away once again, immense power generated by a whip-crack of that lean body and broad tail. The reel screeched, the rod bucked in my numb hands, and we were all back at square one, the shark now thirty metres off the stern, coursing back and forth on deeper water.

By now though the shark was very tired indeed, and bringing it alongside again was a relatively simple process. Speed was now of the essence, and John quickly grabbed the trace, looped a rope over the blue bullet of the shark's head, and dragged it over the side. He unceremoniously dumped it on the deck, planted his considerable weight on its back, gripping the body with his knees and its head with his hands. The shark – rather sensibly I thought – decided that this particular battle was not going to be won and lay still, the white nictitating membrane flicking over its eyes in surrender.

It was absolutely beautiful. There was simply no other word to describe it – the dark blue of its back pulsed and shimmered in the weak sunshine, a deep, soft, cobalt hue perfectly suited to the sunlit uplands of the open ocean. The dorsal fins twitched on the deck, each ending in a perfect, elegant curve. The snow white underbelly was unmarked, looking almost artificially perfect, hiding the shark from view against the bright surface of the sea as it cruised overhead like a fighter aircraft appearing out of the sun. I had seen many sharks before, but nothing quite matched the classic thoroughbred before me.

'Right!' said John abruptly. 'Let's get the tag in this girl and get her back in, shall we? Can you grab the pliers, Monty? The tag is already in there, just squeeze them together at the back of the dorsal fin.'

I did this as fast as possible, leaving the bright yellow plastic tag planted firmly halfway up the fin.

'Well done. Now, let's get her back home, shall we? Give me a hand – she's over a hundred pounds if she's an ounce.'

John held the head just behind the jaws, whilst I grabbed the tail and, with a shared explosive grunt of effort, we heaved the shark onto the rail. John released his grip, and I held mine for a fraction of a second to allow the head to enter the water first, then lowered my arms over the side of the boat to drop the tail through the surface.

The shark hung still for a single beat of time, the gills gently pulsing whilst ancient internal systems whirred into life. She then righted herself, pointed that elegant head towards open water and, with one sweep of her tail, was gone, out of sight in an instant. The deep indigo of her back made it look as though she was absorbed by the ocean itself, melting into the water column like a ghost. Gone into a new ocean her species had never encountered before, where she would inevitably come across a long line of shining hooks on her travels, and where her decision to feed or not feed at that exact moment would mean life or death. The next pair

181

of human eyes to see the tag that even now was fluttering in the current at her back could well be those that hacked the fin off as she gasped and twisted on a distant deck, and one more shark would be lost to the sea and to us.

16

Simon

August came, and with it the tourists. Like some vast migrating herd, they hove into view, guided by ancient navigation systems and instincts that science can barely understand, somehow finding their way to the exact bed they slept in last year. Roundstone became a multicoloured, glinting car park, with traffic wedged between the shorefront cottages and the harbour wall in an immovable snake of parping vehicles. Added to the mix were a large number of camper vans, numerous four-wheel drives towing expensive looking RIBs, and – best of all – gigantic fifty-two-seater coaches attempting impossible three-point turns on roads designed for a horse and cart. The locals would settle in for the afternoon outside O'Dowd's, Kings Bar and the Shamrock, watching in delight as the sport unfolded before them. Puce fathers of four in gigantic off-road vehicles (which never seemed to have tow bars – always a dead giveaway) would make furious hand gestures at wedged motorhomes before them, whilst their children wailed in the back seat. At various junctures, when it looked as though proper middle-class fisticuffs were about to break out, a pint would wearily be set on a table, and someone would take charge, directing, cajoling, reversing and encouraging vehicles until the road was once again cleared. Towing the RIB through town became nothing short of epic, and it never ceased to amaze me how some plainly very successful, well-qualified and highly intelligent people became cackling loons when behind the wheel of a car on a hot day after a long drive. I tended to favour the steady advance in the Land Rover, a ton of gigantic black vehicle towing an additional two tons of shuddering bright orange boat bearing down on a gleaming new car. This tended to lead to some fairly wide-eyed reversing, and I would raise a polite hand as I swept past my hyperventilating opponent, their car wedged up the pavement at a forty-five-degree angle between Rosie's Gallery and the Shamrock.

There had been a set of temporary traffic lights installed in previous years, which apparently worked very well in controlling the bedlam. The only snag was that of an evening they would be mysteriously moved into one of the various pubs that lined the main street, initiating various complex drinking games based on their various phases of green, amber and red. I personally thought this showed tremendous style, but apparently the local council didn't agree and the lights were huffily removed, never to return.

The village rose to the occasion, and the mood was generally one of benign acceptance and indeed celebration at the brief tourist influx. The pubs spilled out onto the streets, the galleries and coffee shops were packed, and there was something of a carnival feel to proceedings as the summer reached its zenith. The weather did its bit, with day after day of glorious sunshine, and Roundstone - although bursting at the seams - was a happy, vibrant place.

Although I was keen to stay and enjoy the fun, I had not visited Simon down in Kilrush for some time. I had a new set of images for him to analyse and a host of questions that had arisen since my last visit. I also felt that I needed a touch on the tiller to ensure I spent my last couple of months in a constructive manner - there seemed so much I could potentially do, and yet I was not precisely sure where best to focus my energy. With this in mind I threw some kit into the Land Rover at a ludicrously early hour of the day, hitched up the RIB, negotiated the mean streets above the harbour, and drove round the corner of the coast road to start my journey down.

The man who came back round that corner two days later was older and wiser, and had a certain look of mental bedlam in his eyes. The Land Rover boot was caked in dolphin blood, and the RIB nowhere to be seen. That's what a couple of days in the company of the elemental force that is Simon Berrow tends to do to a chap.

It all started innocently enough. I wound my way in the dawn light along the gorgeous valley past Ballynahinch Castle, the river looking turgid and serene as it glided along beside me. A couple of days of rain the week before had filled it to the point that the salmon massed in the sea loughs had been able to complete their migration, and even as I drove I could see the flash of fish moving up dappled runs and babbling rapids. Simon Ashe, the young and annoyingly talented estate manager, had told me that over two thousand fish had moved past the salmon counter in the space of the last month, a wonderful indication of the health of the river and – perhaps – the beginning of a recovery of the population after their decimation by large-scale netting and the impact of salmon farming along the coast.

The first indication that something was not quite right was a distinct odour of burning metal and grease. This can translate very neatly as the smell of burning cash when towing a large boat, so I pulled into a lay-by to inspect the trailer. I'm no expert when it comes to trailers, but I couldn't help noticing that smoke was billowing out of both wheel hubs, accompanied by hissing, dribbling waves of axle grease. My trailer – upon which sat my boat laden with petrol – was essentially on fire.

Believe it or not, I actually knew why this was happening. The trailer brakes occasionally locked half on, creating prodigious heat as they ground against the wheel hubs. This in turn ignited the grease, which bubbled out of the hub, which meant that the wheels soon had no lubrication. The trick was to hit the metal bits of the wheel with a hammer to loosen the brake pads. If one lacked the foresight to bring a hammer (which I did) a rock from a nearby river would have to do.

Passing motorists were therefore treated to the sight of what appeared to be an escaped lunatic in a lay-by attacking a steaming trailer with a large stone. Each moment of impact saw water fly off the rock and create gratifying clouds of steam, and I would dance back before charging in again with a banshee wail, the resultant mighty swipe ending in a bone-jarring clang. The occasional car would slow down to offer assistance, then think better of it and speed up as I turned to look at them through billowing clouds of steam, spattered in axle grease and holding a rock with skinned knuckles. Having battered the trailer into submission, I limped the next few miles to the long-suffering Lynn's beautiful bed and breakfast. Leaping out of the car, I hammered on her door, babbled a swift explanation and abandoned the RIB in her drive, giving a brief thumbs up and smile through the driver's window as I sped away, the trailer and boat steaming gently beside her immaculately manicured garden.

It was annoying not having the RIB, but it had been by no means essential for the visit to Simon, and my progress without it was considerably more rapid. It was therefore only a couple of hours later that I drew up outside the brightly coloured façade of the Irish Whale and Dolphin Group's headquarters in Kilrush. I met Simon as he came crashing out of the front door laden with photographic gear.

'Ah, hello, Monty, hello, good to see you.' He pushed his spectacles up the bridge of his nose, and ran a hand through his hair. 'Blimey, loads to catch up on, hey? Let's talk about it on the boat, shall we?'

'The boat?'

'Yep, I've arranged for you to come out on a tour boat. I have to go out on at least ten per cent of the trips they undertake to keep an eye on their encounters with the dolphins, and of course it's a great way to gather images. They're really one of the best tools we have for regular sightings of the Shannon dolphins, and do wonderful work in collating data for us. Come on, the boat leaves in twenty minutes.'

I followed Simon's battered pick-up truck through twisting lanes to the tiny harbour at Carrigaholt, where a smart-looking blue and white boat bobbed gently alongside the jetty. We joined a queue of tourists filing carefully down the stone steps and being welcomed aboard by the skipper.

'Allo, Monty,' he said in a broad Lancastrian accent. 'Me name's Geoff. Good to 'ave you onboard.'

Geoff had come out to Ireland twenty years before, working first as a fisherman and then running nature tours with his wife. Who was from New York. I was an Englishman on an Irish estuary on a boat skippered by a Lancastrian who was married to a New Yorker surrounded by tourists from across Europe – such is the world we live in nowadays. I wondered idly what the people who built the ancient harbour in which we sat would have made of it all.

We nosed out into the great expanse of the estuary, pushing towards the open Atlantic through a rolling swell that caused the boat to heave and pitch. We massed at the bow, all broad smiles and looks of recognition in anticipation of a shared experience. Geoff's voice over the tannoy gently reminded us that large waves came over the bow occasionally, advice we collectively chose to ignore. Thirty seconds later we were sat in the stern, blinking water out of our eyes and wringing out jumpers and jeans. Geoff continued the commentary in precisely the same nonplussed tone, the only difference being that we all listened a bit more.

There was a tangible sense of anticipation as we scanned the horizon. There is a more than ninety per cent chance of encountering dolphins in the Shannon Estuary, a percentage unmatched pretty much anywhere else on Earth. The rail bristled with a buffet of ludicrously expensive zoom lenses and smart binoculars, guidebooks were being energetically thumbed, and there was a palpable sense of excitement all round.

An hour later and morale was low, bordering on non-existent. Most of the group were now huddled in the main cabin, with only a few redoubtable characters still at the rail. One of these – needless to say – was Simon. He looked like a man who was on the first dolphin sightseeing trip of his entire life, eyes shining with delight behind his specs, long lens at the ready. Occasionally, he would charge up the ladder to the top deck, peer about him like a meerkat, then return to the lower deck to pace between the bow and the stern. He had been intensively studying these dolphins for nearly twenty years, but without a doubt there was no one more excited and animated on the boat.

Inevitably, it was Simon who saw them first.

'Aha, dolphins!' he shouted triumphantly, which instantly led to a thunderous rush out of the cabin and twenty people crowding the port rail. The average tour boat must have some fairly robust seagoing qualities, given that it has several tons of meat charging from side to side every time something vaguely interesting appears at the water's surface. Geoff's voice continued unabated through the tannoy, although I thought I detected a faint hint of relief at the encounter.

For me, the real interest did not lie with the dolphins – although heaven knows it is always a splendid sight to see them in their natural habitat – but in the reaction of the tourists on the boat.

I had been listening to the myriad collection of accents as we had cruised the estuary for the last hour, and had identified French, Spanish, English, American, Russian and

Irish. There were grizzled greybeards, bawling infants, glamorous upper-class eco-tourists on blue riband bespoke holidays, and working-class families on a cheap local break. To a man and a woman, a boy and girl, they all laughed and pointed. A collective surge of exhilaration and adrenalin surged through the group, with great shouts of 'There!' and 'No – there!' Suddenly, in the space of a single encounter with a single species, what they had been beginning to think may have been the worst €20 they had ever spent became unequivocally the best. It's a wonderful thing watching people have an experience such as this for the first time, and I often think that the best thing to do at an international summit of world leaders would be to take them out in a boat and show them a pod of wild dolphins. 'There we go, chaps,' you could say. 'I think you'll find that's what it's all about.'

Simon rattled off shot after shot, each one a tiny part of a twenty-year project of amassing data on the movements of his beloved Shannon dolphins. I asked him if he felt any sense of ownership of the resident pod. He thought for a moment before answering.

'Well, no, actually. These are wild animals that were here long before I rocked up, and will be here long after I leave. I don't feel any sense of ownership or indeed kinship.' He paused for a moment and looked out at the dolphins as they rolled and splashed in the dark water by the boat. 'I do feel that we've created enough interest in them to get a real groundswell of support if they were ever threatened, which can only be a good thing. I actually get a bit miffed when people come in and try to claim they have a special relationship with them – but then again we all tend to get a bit carried away with dolphins, don't we?' He smiled at the irony of the words, and raised his camera to his eye once more.

After half an hour or so, Geoff announced that it was time we left the dolphins in peace. Half an hour that most of the people on that boat will never forget, and will recount to their friends and family when they return home – spreading the word of the Shannon dolphins to far-flung corners of the globe.

Back at the office I had arranged to meet an old friend who was travelling in Ireland. Dan Stevenson is a stocky, swarthy figure who just happens to be one of the best deep-water cameramen in the UK. He is never happier than when crawling through the innards of a stricken cruise liner at 300 feet in pitch blackness, and he does this with a whirring, beeping set of electronics strapped to his back – a diving rebreather that means he can stay down for a very long time indeed – and pushing a camera ahead of him that is the size of a chest of drawers. He's a man entirely in his element when wedged under a twisted metal plate at six atmospheres of pressure in zero visibility with a conger eel tangled in his crotch strap. When he's not actually diving, he's talking about diving, and only stops doing so when there is a regulator in his mouth (and sometimes not even then). I was intrigued to see how Simon and he would get on – a kind of critical mass of enthusiasm meeting in a seismic event of arm waving that might well result in both of them becoming airborne.

After making the introductions back in the office, Simon and I at last had the chance to pore over the photographs

I had been taking over the last month or so whilst Dan looked through some of the displays downstairs. Over several cups of coffee and the inevitable scones, Simon pointed out the nicks and scars on the dorsal fins of the dolphins I was encountering off Roundstone, even tracking one of them back to an animal seen off Donegal several years previously.

'This is great stuff, Monty,' he said. 'It looks to me like you are encountering the same animals fairly regularly, which is really good news. To be honest I have my doubts about whether the dolphins off Roundstone are a resident pod, but that's for me to question and for you to prove, of course.'

One of the photos particularly interested Simon. It showed a dolphin's back breaking the surface in an explosion of foam and spray, the golden sweep of Gurteen Beach in the background. Its back looked peculiar – a misshapen hump, malformed and lumpen next to the sleek, shining silhouettes of its companions in the pod.

'Now this IS worth noting,' said Simon. 'This animal has got scoliosis – a severely deformed spine. It might have come from a difficult birth, but we don't really know to be honest. It's common enough in other mammals, but quite rare in dolphins. The reason is that most of them die quite young as they can't compete within the pod, but your chap here looks very healthy and sleek. I'd keep an eye out for him, if I was you.'

We chatted away for another hour or so, the afternoon slipping past until the first hint of dusk began to gild the horizon. Just as my thoughts had begun to turn to my hotel, or more specifically the bed in my hotel, Simon's phone beeped in his pocket.

He was - as ever - expounding on some wondrous characteristic of dolphins at the time, and had a brief fumble through several pockets before finding the offending phone. As he spoke his brow knitted, and he chewed his lower lip distractedly.

'Attacking people you say - bloody hell, that doesn't sound good. Right, I'm going to get out there and take a look at her - it's worth checking her out immediately, I'd say. I've got Monty and Dan with me so I'll drag them along. We can get some footage and underwater photographs, so we can check her condition from those. Thanks, Ken.'

He hung up and looked at me quizzically.

'Right, there's a dolphin that has been interacting with people for many years in a bay just down the coast, and now it sounds like we may have a problem with her. I try to stay away from this sort of thing as much as possible - quite frankly I think swimming with wild dolphins is pretty selfish, as it always seems to be the dolphin that suffers in the end. That call was from a friend who encounters her fairly regularly, and he's heard that she's being aggressive to swimmers. That's not good at all - she might be pregnant, suffering from lesions, or just feeling a bit grumpy. I think we should check it out. Are you and Dan up for it?'

This was an entirely rhetorical question, as we were moving out of the building and into the road as we spoke. Dan had overheard the conversation, and was actually ahead of us by this stage, tinkering with his camera housing in the boot of his car and beaming in anticipation. I was in the grip of forces I could only begin to understand, a bewildered cork bobbing along in the foaming rapids of Simon and Dan's combined get up and go.

'Good stuff – follow me as I'll be towing my RIB. It's about an hour or so.' With that, Simon strode off, specs glinting and shoulders squared at the challenge ahead.

Dan already had his engine running, and gave me a swift thumbs up from behind the windscreen, mouthing something I didn't quite catch, but was probably something to do with filming the entire thing in a pair of hessian swimming trunks with a herring under each armpit to try to get some real interest from the dolphin.

As I followed the RIB it was plain to see that Simon had a similar cavalier style to towing large boats to my own. There were several moments when impact seemed inevitable, but invariably he would hold his nerve and sweep past some cowering Fiat Punto with an inch to spare, giving a cheery smile at the cringing occupants. In his wake I got to see many an ashen face and white-knuckled grip on a recently spun steering wheel.

We finally arrived at our destination, the last recorded position of the dolphin. This was a tiny, nondescript harbour that was the launch point to a set of nearby islands, and as such was a streaming mass of holidaymakers returning from their day trip. Simon seemed fairly nonplussed at the approaching hordes, if anything subtly accelerating through their midst, scattering them like a plump, orange barracuda carving a path through a multicoloured fish shoal. I followed behind, and learned some new swear words in several European languages.

I just had time to clamber into my wetsuit as Simon launched the RIB. Grabbing my camera gear, I followed Dan as he stumbled along the quayside with a gigantic, metallic grey video housing.

He grinned at me as he jumped into the boat. 'Come on, my boy,' he said, looking very happy indeed. 'No time to waste.'

As if to emphasise the point, Simon started the engines. They coughed into life with a suitably dramatic cloud of fumes, before settling to a low mutter as they trembled on the transom. There was a storm gathering on the horizon, with huge, sooty black thunderclouds rolling ominously over churning seas. The RIB tossed and twitched at her mooring, like an animal sensing the chase ahead, returned to her natural element of a wild sea in the gathering gloom of an Atlantic evening. I jumped aboard, gingerly lowered my camera gear to the deck, glanced around at Simon and Dan, who were already in position, and nodded. Simon leaned forward on the throttles, I gripped the seat back before me, Dan grinned like a rabid hound that had just slipped the leash, and with a roar of horsepower and foam we were off, leaving only a faint whiff of testosterone hanging in the air.

Once out of the protection of the harbour wall we were instantly into some big seas. Happily Simon had learned his trade whilst working for the British Antarctic Survey in the southern ocean, so we were in very safe hands indeed. He surfed down rolling breakers, using the sea's colossal energy to drive us forward, see-sawing the throttle to keep the nose of the RIB pointed in vaguely the right direction. The cliffs of the shore passed in a blur of granite and dark fissures as we raced ahead of the weather, our wake carving a white scar on the sea's surface like the twisting tail of a comet.

After a roller-coaster ride of twenty minutes, we rounded a headland and entered the relative calm of a sheltered bay. The hush as the engine stilled was slightly eerie, with the only noise the slapping of small wavelets against the hull, and the moan of the wind across the surface of the sea. I glanced at my watch and noted that it was now 7 p.m. – if we were going to get a decent set of images of the dolphin, it would have to happen in the next hour or so or we would be defeated by the night. All three of us scanned the water ahead, looking for the tell-tale glint of a rolling back, or the explosion of foam that would mean a wild dolphin was sharing our small patch of the Atlantic.

'There, there!' shouted Dan. And sure enough, appearing wraithlike from the gloom beneath the boat, there was the dolphin. And it was huge.

As with an awful lot of wild animals, you simply have no idea of their size until you see them close up. And this dolphin was giving us a very good look at her indeed – sculling very slowly right up to the side of the RIB, almost on the surface, peering up at us with one eye and rolled on her side to display the grey of her flanks. We watched transfixed, struck temporarily dumb (and with Simon and Dan, the only alternative way to achieve that is some sort of horse sedative).

She was a good nine feet long – comfortably half the length of the boat – but it was her bulk that surprised me. She looked like a rather plump submarine, although there was nothing fat or spare about her. She was a dense cylinder of predatory efficiency armed with a battery of senses and supreme intelligence. Any thoughts of a benign, cute, Flipper-esque creature were immediately dispelled. I was looking at a great predator in her own environment, completely at home beneath glowering cliffs amid surging swell.

The wind whistled eerily through the superstructure of the boat, whilst the waves boomed and echoed along the shore, a Hitchcockian soundtrack to the encounter to come. The dolphin would periodically surface close to the boat, her breath an explosive hiss, making me jump and spin round to see her sleek, shining back roll beneath the water's surface leaving a spreading pool of agitated water in her wake. A few vigorous strokes of her flukes would leave a distinct energy bulge on the surface, a circular pool of transferred energy known – fittingly – as a footprint.

Dan lowered his camera over the side of the boat and instantly the dolphin levitated from the water beneath us, stopping with her beak an inch from the dome port. She regarded the camera intensely, head on one side, and I could see the turmoil of the encounter etched on Dan's face. This was unquestionably the best footage of a dolphin in her natural environment he would ever record; however, there was also the rather gripping fact that 300 kilograms of potentially hormonal female was staring directly at a glass port protecting thousands of pounds' worth of delicate electronics. He glanced across at me and smiled lopsidedly – something that was halfway between a grimace and a grin.

'Right, chaps,' said Simon. 'I'd like to have some shots of her in the water, please. Bear in mind, Monty, that this is probably the last dive you'll ever do, as you'll obviously be in intensive care communicating by blowing through a tube connected to a keyboard from now on. Any last comments? From my perspective, I'd like to ask if I can have your RIB, please? Oh, and your camera.'

He smiled at me, although it was a point well made. We

were here because there had been reports of this dolphin being aggressive, and Dan and I were about to slip into the water with her. This is an animal that could injure a swimmer very seriously indeed. A true attack would be over very quickly – perhaps a brief impression of a hurtling grey body, an explosive impact as the beak smashes into soft internal organs, possibly the fleeting pain of teeth raking across skin, and then nothing. The vast majority of aggression from these animals, though, is more of a gentle reminder of who is the boss out here, and that personal space should be respected – the cetacean equivalent of a tap on the shoulder.

Still, even a mildly irritated bottlenose dolphin – and let's face it we all get a bit grumpy from time to time – can cause considerable damage. A study by the National Marine Fisheries Service in the USA noted 'hundreds and hundreds' of negative interactions between dolphins and people. 'I literally ripped my left leg out of its mouth,' said one lady from her hospital bed – somewhat peevishly, I imagine. Never has an animal been so celebrated by people, fêted for what we perceive as a noble, compassionate nature akin to our own (an irony if there ever was one), and yet seldom has there been such a yawning gap between our perception and the reality. Although a 1994 study showed the injury rate is something in the region of one in ten thousand people who encounter dolphins, it still makes entering the water with one something of a gamble. There has only been one recorded death, in itself a neat encapsulation of our relationship with the sea and the animals therein.

Many years ago, a dolphin in Brazil had become accustomed to swimming with bathers off a particular beach.

One evening, a lone and slightly inebriated man decided to go for a swim with it. He frolicked for a while, then decided in that slightly drunk way that men have, to punch it. The dolphin punched him back. The man died in hospital a few hours later. These are not animals to be trifled with, even if you've had nine pints and feel fairly confident that you can take anyone or anything in a stand-up brawl.

Bottlenose dolphins in the Moray Firth in Scotland – possibly one of the most studied populations anywhere in Europe – have regularly been witnessed killing not only their rival cetaceans, but also the offspring of other members of the pod. Deeply shocking though we may find this behaviour, the same thing happens with lions and other apex predators. Cleansing the gene pool of anything but your own DNA is smart money if you want to be top dog.

This very dolphin had taken exception to a German cameraman several years before, and had given him a vigorous butt in the ribs to make her feelings known. He was subsequently taken to intensive care, and then airlifted home. As Robin Williams spluttered, leaving the water after he had been battered and bruised by a dolphin: 'Flipper – my ass!'

'It's one of those strange things,' said Simon as Dan and I shrugged into our kit. 'People do get terribly emotional about swimming with a dolphin. Invariably, people rattle on about how they had a mystical connection with the animal, but actually you're an object of curiosity and amusement – that's all. Habituating dolphins to people is also a very dangerous thing for the dolphin concerned: these types of encounters with lone animals seeking out people seem to end up with most of the dolphins being killed by boats or nets.

The two of us don't belong together, no matter how much we want it to be otherwise.' He leaned on the console of the boat, resting on his forearms and looking into the middle distance, before snapping himself out of his reverie.

'Anyway, let's get you in, and you can check this girl out. Any snags, just give me a wave and I'll come over and get you out of the water.' He chuckled drily. 'Or what remains of you, anyway.' His glasses were spattered with sea water, and the wisps of his hair skittered and whipped in the wind as the boat heaved and bucked beneath him. He looked very, very happy indeed.

'Oh, one last thing. She gets a bit funny about cameras.' Dan and I glanced up from where we were just making the last adjustments to our massive, shiny, cameras. 'No idea why. Good luck.'

Dan and I exchanged wan smiles, constricted by the neoprene of our hoods into a puckered gurn of anticipation. I nodded briefly at him, and we slipped quietly into the water.

As soon as we entered the sea, a heaving, bottle-green world of limited visibility and distant echoes, the boat slipped away from us, borne by wind and current. Very quickly we were alone, and instinctively moved closer together, scanning the water around us. It seemed absurd to feel nervous, and yet the entire reason we were there was because of reports of aggression from our companion in the water, who even now was sculling slowly in our direction.

Dan saw her first, which lead to a brief and undignified squeak of excitement through his snorkel. I turned slowly and watched her appear from the murk, a picture of elegance and poise, her bulk exaggerated by the magnifying effect of the water. The flukes of her tail moved slowly behind her, driving her forward, her head slightly cocked, closing the gap between us in a fraction of a second.

Dan and I spoke afterwards, and both said that we instantly felt reassured. It is well documented that dolphins communicate not only with audible signals, but also with body posture, and this animal just seemed the personification of laid-back amiability. It is said that vast amounts of our own communication still takes place through posture – a fact that tormented me on many a date in my younger days as I struck various louche come-and-get-it-I'm-SO-available poses – and perhaps something within us still responds to these signals from other animals.

The dolphin edged ever closer, until its nose was an inch from mine. She peered at me intently, the eye a tiny miracle of design – specifically adapted to low light, with excellent vision in air as well as water. After a moment where she hovered perfectly – swinging her head slowly from side to side to look first at me then at Dan – she gave a twitch of her pectoral fins, a swift flick of her tail, and accelerated smoothly into the jade backdrop of the deeper water.

The whalers of old used to say that if you looked into the eye of a whale you would lose your soul. I have my own half-baked theory about this, based on nothing more than intuition – that if anyone, no matter how inured to death, how conditioned to the gory business of whaling, looked into the eye of a dying whale, surely they would be profoundly affected and would never be quite as effective at the job again? A romantic notion perhaps, but you can picture the wise old lags telling the new apprentices to avoid staring into the eye as it frantically scanned a pitching deck awash with its own blood, desperately looking for any connection, any moment of mercy, as the flensing blades begin to descend.

For my part, I felt a vague sense of being studied, of being an object of idle interest, though little more. Dan seemed similarly impressed without being overwhelmed. I saw his eyes crinkle in appreciation behind his mask; he gave a swift thumbs up, and we got on with the job of filming and photographing the dolphin. Simon would analyse these shots back at the IWDG headquarters later, to check for scars, skin lesions, and signs of pregnancy. The sun sank slowly into a turbulent horizon, with the water around us fading from green to grey to black. The dolphin stayed close, a picture of power and poise, ever curious and watchful in the gathering gloom.

Finally the low light defeated the electronics of both of our cameras, and the time came to leave the water. Simon puttered over in the RIB, a shady figure silhouetted against the dying light of an ominously rolling black sky. I lifted my head partially from the water to check the position of the boat, and saw a final image – half scudding clouds, a towering headland, crackling surf, half dark water and a gliding, grey shape at my fin tips, turning on her side one last time to observe me as I left the water. A bottlenose dolphin very much at home as another night began beneath the mighty Cliffs of Moher.

The trip home was very entertaining indeed. As we rounded the headland, leaving the haven of the bay, we drove straight into the teeth of muscular swells generated by the storm on the horizon. Simon seemed to sprout horns and a forked tail, flying down the backs of immense waves and roaring his way up the steep faces of oncoming breakers.

His glasses became spattered with moisture, although it was impossible to tell whether this was from sea spray from the outside or the steam coming from his eyeballs on the inside. We all had a splendid time, and even glimpsed a very alarmed blue shark as it sped into the heart of a wave, running ahead of two tons of charging boat and its three cackling occupants.

We recovered the boat onto the trailer in the eerie calm of the harbour, and drove back to Kilrush through narrow roads as dark as black velvet, with villages that twinkled like jewels en route. Simon dropped us off at our bed and breakfast, where I finally staggered up the stairs and crawled into bed without even showering, a broken, bruised, shambling, ruin of a man – pummelled by the sea and replete with memories.

The next morning, over coffee and scones back at the IWDG building, Simon, Dan and I pored over the images and film footage. Somehow the wonder of the encounter seemed magnified by the clinical surroundings of the office. Watching the dolphin appear out of the green water drawing ever closer to the lens seemed faintly miraculous, and I struggled to make the leap of imagination required to accept that I was actually there throughout. It felt very much like watching a particularly pleasant film made by someone else.

'That's interesting,' said Simon, who appeared as fresh as a daisy and was well into his second scone. 'You can clearly see scars where she's healed really nicely. I've seen images of this animal with some terrible lesions on her skin, which must have been dreadfully painful.' He leaned closer to the screen and peered intently at the image. 'And I'm not sure she's pregnant. She looks fairly lean – by no means is this a big dolphin.'

I had a vivid moment of recall, recalling her sheer bulk in the water, and tried to imagine an animal even more rotund, even more muscular, even more intimidating.

'It was very interesting to see her close up, I must say,' chipped in Dan. 'You really don't appreciate just how impressive these animals are until you're nose to nose. She looked marvellous to me, although that's not based on even a modicum of scientific knowledge, I hasten to add.'

Simon nodded vigorously.

'Yep, she's in really good nick, if a bit thin. I'd say that sometimes these dolphins – the ones that seek out interactions with people – just need to draw the boundaries for the people in the water with them, so perhaps that's what was happening with the reports of aggression. You always get a few idiots, and a quick clout in the ribs does wonders as a little reminder of who is really boss out there. I'm still convinced that it's an entirely selfish activity, though – there'll only be one casualty in all this, you mark my words. And it won't be the people this dolphin chooses to swim with. It'll be her – tangled in a net or run over by a boat, perhaps. Mixing with humans is, I'm sad to say, a very poor career choice if you happen to be a dolphin. She's better off with her own kind.'

By now it was close to midday, and there were many more things to catch up on. The next hour or so was spent with Simon bustling around the office, rummaging in cupboards to present me with various scientific papers and bits of kit that he felt might help with my work.

Dan bade us a fond farewell as he needed to head north for some further work. 'Been bloody marvellous,' he beamed as he shook my hand. 'Bloody marvellous.'

By this stage, I was keen to get away myself, as I was fairly shattered. The previous day had been a good sixteen hours flat out – a classic Simon Berrow working day – and had involved several hours in the car, photographing dolphins from the tour boat, hurtling through Atlantic swells on the RIB, and swimming in frigid seas. I always loved visiting Simon, but sneakily I was looking forward to hitting the road for the two-hour drive home. But he was not finished with me yet – not by a long chalk. Having been Berrowed for the last twenty-four hours or so – and still managed to hang on in there – I was about to be re-Berrowed just to polish me off.

Simon's mobile gave a frantic cheep and, after the customary rummage through pockets and bags, was duly produced and pressed to his head.

'What? Nearby? That's great. We'll be with you in ten minutes.'

He turned to me, eyes glinting behind the specs.

'That was a local farmer. A dolphin has washed up where his land borders the banks of the estuary – let's get out there and we can get a look at it, maybe even recover it. Come on, don't stand there with your mouth open.'

I think SAS selection should end with a couple of days with Simon. Only the physiological elite would make it, requiring as it does sleep deprivation, clambering over obstacles, wrestling with large dead animals and generally showing maniacal focus. I sighed and followed him out to his car.

Ten minutes later, we were standing on a stony beach beside a medium-sized, very dead dolphin, fresh enough to still be burnished by the midday sun. The farmer stood beside us, chatting to Simon who was pointing out various bits of anatomical interest. The farmer's dogs sniffed warily at the body, baffled at this strange interloper onto their territory. Suddenly I heard my name being mentioned.

'My colleague Monty here will tell you the species, won't you, Monty?' He waved me over and gestured expansively at the dolphin. Somewhat startled, I turned my attention to the body at my feet, taking only a brief moment to glare at Simon reproachfully, who grinned delightedly back.

It was elaborately marked, with a dark back and creamy patches along its flanks. Needless to say, even lying on a beach, it looked sleek and lustrous, like a projectile fired from the sea to land on the shore. The farmer looked at me expectantly.

'Weeeeell . . . ' I said. 'It's not a bottlenose, that's for sure – too small and too well marked.' Simon nodded vigorously in the background. 'And I don't think it's a common dolphin either?' As those were the two species I could identify for definite, I was now in all sorts of trouble, and I suspected this could turn into a very long morning for all of us.

Simon sensed my disquiet, and bounded in to my rescue. 'Have a look at the eye, Monty – what do you see leading back from it?'

'A line?'

'Well done, well done! And what's the other name for a line?'

'A stripe?'

'Good, good.' He was now virtually hopping from foot

to foot. 'So, you have a dolphin, and it's got a stripe. What species might that be?' Even the dogs were looking at me expectantly by this stage.

'A . . . Striped . . . Dolphin?'

'Good man, good man! I knew you'd get there in the end!' He clapped me on the back, the farmer exhaled in relief, the dogs barked delightedly, and even the dolphin looked relieved. I basked in the warm glow of his praise and felt absurdly pleased with myself, like some 10-year-old who had just sung a song in front of his relatives. I could do handstands, too, and briefly considered doing one on the beach to hold everyone's attention.

'Right, let's get him into the back of my truck and have a look at him at the centre.'

We pulled on rubber gloves - dolphins and whales have some very nasty pathogens indeed - and heaved the body onto a tarpaulin. With a great deal of grunting and stumbling, and with the dolphin swinging against my legs leaving exciting-looking smears of cetacean blood on my jeans, we heaved him into the back of Simon's pick-up truck. I followed the truck back to the centre, a bizarre hearse with just the tip of a tail fluke peeking over the tailboard.

When we got back to the centre, Simon pulled back the tarpaulin to examine the dolphin more closely. He walked slowly around it, occasionally leaning forward, peering intently over the top of his glasses, before recommencing his steady amble around the back of the vehicle.

'It seems in great nick,' he said at last, 'so it's quite odd that it would strand. You can see from its skin that it hasn't been beaten up by the bottlenose dolphins here - that's a very common cause of death for any other small cetacean silly enough to wonder into their territory in the Shannon. It looks very healthy, actually – a couple of small tooth rakes on the skin but that's just day-to-day life, and they're not the big old lacerations you'd get from the bottlenose.

'I do have a theory about these white-sided dolphins, though. They tend to be a warm-water species, you see, and every now and then venture north to this coast – maybe a warm current or a bit of really good weather lures them out of their normal range – and then, when the water temperature returns to normal, they strand due to temperature shock. Just a theory, mind you, but we've had a few of these striped dolphins strand recently, so maybe that's it? Who knows.'

He looked thoughtful for a moment, then seemed to have an epiphany. 'I'd like to get this guy to the freezer in Galway. You're going to Galway on the way home, aren't you? Any chance of sticking this chap in the back of your Landy and you could drop him off? Ta, you're a good lad. Now come on, grab the head end, and let's hoy him in.'

As a consequence, the drive to Galway on the way back to Roundstone was somewhat surreal. Not only did I have all the windows open as the interior of the Land Rover was beginning to smell like a whaling station in South Georgia, I also had a dead dolphin staring reproachfully at me in the rear-view mirror. The boot – crammed with all sorts of gear – had proved fairly inadequate for the transport of dead cetaceans, so the dolphin had been wedged inexpertly up against the back seat, leaving its head propped up directly in my line of sight. I toyed briefly with giving it a hat, a pair of sunglasses, and even a pipe to lessen the impact on passing motorists, but eventually decided the best thing to do was get to Galway as quickly as possible. I drove with my head half out of the driver's window, breathing through my mouth, and hoped the police didn't stop me.

The freezer was located at the Galway and Mayo Institute of Technology, and it was with a feeling of considerable relief that I pulled up outside reception. Simon had called ahead, and a young Italian scientist called Allesandra was there to meet me. Together we hauled and wrestled the dolphin to the freezer around the back of the main building, an ominously humming white shed the size of a Portakabin. He pulled back the door, and there, arrayed on the floor, was a festival of dolphin death. Two common dolphins stared up at me through glassy eyes, whilst the mangled remains of another striped dolphin peeked out from under a bloodstained tarpaulin. We dragged our dolphin the last few feet, watching it slither across an icy floor to come to rest against one of its larger cousins, and then Allesandra pulled the door closed with a final grunt of effort. It was a sad sight indeed, but the dolphins would be used to train vets from the UK and Ireland about the anatomy of cetaceans, yet another of Simon's schemes, so perhaps these deaths weren't altogether in vain.

It was a slightly wild-eyed, pungent, bloodstained, shattered man that drove the last thirty miles or so to Roundstone. When I was reunited with Reuben – always the highlight of coming home – he sniffed my trousers at some length, whining and peering up at me with concern. As I wearily unpacked the Land Rover, pulling out salt-encrusted waterproofs, hydrophones and various new reading material – all lightly spattered with blood and giving off a faint, rancid whiff of death – I reflected on what a truly remarkable man Simon is.

Every now and then in life you meet someone profoundly driven, someone with such extraordinary energy that they carry just about everyone before them, and drag the remainder in their wake. Building up the Irish Whale and Dolphin Group was a remarkable achievement, the legacy of Simon's relentless efforts over many years. He was a tectonic force that moved ever onwards, a great example of what can be achieved with real purpose and application. To possess such drive must be a wonderful thing, and I was full of admiration for what he had achieved. As far as I could ascertain, he didn't eat at all, except for a scone every two days or so, and definitely didn't sleep – a luxury only for the weak and the decadent. Crawling under the duvet for an early night, my final waking thought was what a splendid chap he was, and a resolution to do my best to avoid him for at least a fortnight.

17

The Funky Chicken

Connemara boasts a gleaming network of rivers, streams and loughs, and in its damp heart – the great expanse of the bog – it is more water than land. Since the last ice age ten thousand years ago, the loughs have held great speckled, golden shoals of brown trout, as well as Arctic char and of course salmon. Driving past the loughs on a still day was to see their surface dimpled by hundreds of spreading rings of shining water as the trout made the most of the rich insect life around them.

The fishing in Connemara is very good indeed, and on any drive along the river past Ballynahinch I would always see hunched figures in dun-coloured clothing thrashing the water optimistically. They were after salmon, the king of fish, for many a lifelong obsession. The river was a perfect salmon habitat, with peaty water the colour of stewed tea chuckling over shallow stones, roaring through thrashing rapids, and moving serenely over deep pools fat with promise.

Although I was keen to try my hand at salmon fishing, for now I thought it best to concentrate on the trout. The salmon would have to wait until the tail end of the summer – something of a date with destiny for me. My father was a very keen fly-fisherman, and had caught a salmon forty years before, the only one of his fishing career. He was desperate for me to do the same, and I couldn't shake the faint and disturbing conviction that – despite a brief career in the Royal Marines and various expeditions around the world – I would only be a real man in his eyes when I finally caught a salmon on a fly.

There was really only one man in the village to consult about the murky world of fly-fishing on the local loughs and rivers. Ronan Creane was a lean, dark, sharp-eyed Pict of a man in his early thirties, all compact energy and enthusiasm. Chat to him in the pub about fishing, and you would end up learning about the biology and life cycles of the animals in and around the rivers, about the politics affecting the salmon run, and of his travels around the world seeking out the quiet valleys and dappled waters that sat in the ravines and hollows of many a distant mountain range. When Ronan wasn't fishing, he was talking about fishing, and when he wasn't talking about it, he was thinking about it, and when he wasn't thinking about it, he was dreaming about it.

'Aha, yes, of course I'll take you fishing, Monty,' he said over a pint in the Shamrock. 'Only one proviso, though. You have to tie your own fly. It's a great skill, and one that will keep you happy in your old age, which – let's face it – in your case isn't that far away. I'll pop round your cottage in a few days. If you get yourself into Clifden in the meantime, just go into the shop there and buy a cheap fly-tying kit, that'll get you going.'

Two days later I was unpacking my brand new fly-tying kit with trembling fingers on the table top in the cottage. Tumbling out of the box came the most wonderful array of feathers and fur, silk and cotton, glinting tinsel and bizarre-looking tools. I immediately resolved I would create wonderfully lifelike flies, uncannily reminiscent of the hatch of the day. I would stride sun-kissed riverbanks in my dotage, the air humming with circling mayflies that I would capture and replicate perfectly in a few moments of breathtaking dexterity. I would cast a nymph a hundred yards over a chuckling Wiltshire chalk stream to land on the nose of a plump two-pounder. I would stalk sea trout on their migrations up Cornish rivers in the dead of night, face smeared with burnt cork having tied mystical patterns that would become known simply as 'the Monty' by anglers throughout the country, patterns copied but never quite replicated. This was – in short – going to be great, and last pretty much for ever.

Before Ronan turned up, I had a chance to get a really good look at the contents of the kit. It was wonderful, a sensory assault of musty smells, glorious textures and vivid colours. Even the names on the labels spoke volumes – mixed marabou, bronze mallard, buck tail, golden pheasant, deer hair, pheasant wing, rabbit hide. I chose to quietly ignore the fact that I was looking at a buffet of messy mammalian and avian death, a kind of dressing-up box for those who enjoy murdering brightly coloured animal species.

The tools looked marvellous as well. I examined them

carefully, picking them up to turn them slowly so they glinted in the dull light of the kitchen window. There was a tiny vice, a bobbin holder, a dubbin needle, some hackle pliers and a splayed, spiky thing with stiff wire coming out at a series of right angles that baffled me utterly. I placed it reverentially on the table next to the others, the tools of my new trade, Mother Nature's very own watchmaker ready to ply his deadly business.

Ronan appeared a few minutes later, parking his van outside the cottage. This van was something of a legend locally, a TARDIS in which anything associated with fishing could be found. As Ronan rummaged in the interior, I had a glimpse of serried ranks of rods, boxes of flies, damp landing nets and hanging chest-waders. It was said that Ronan would sleep in the van whenever possible, resting a cheek on some wet mesh and occasionally licking a trout as a means of sustenance.

He wrestled a cabin trunk through the front door. It was the sort of size favoured by a certain type of Victorian lady for extensive travels through the Dark Continent.

'This is my fly-tying kit,' he said simply, throwing open the lid. Within the box was a staggering array of fur and feathers, all exotic colours and shimmering pelts. No one was a more ardent conservationist than Ronan, and everything in the box had come from entirely legal sources, but the clever application of dyes and judicious cutting and clipping made it look very much like a deranged ornithologist's collection box after six months in Indonesia.

'Right, let's have a look at yours,' he said.

He was very kind indeed, picking up what I now realised was a rather feeble set of beginner's tools and materials.

'There's some good stuff here, Monty; you can make all sorts of patterns with this. Let's get cracking, shall we?'

The next hour was wonderful, with Ronan showing me the essence of creating a fly from a bare hook. He did this by means of a short demonstration, a one-man master class in the art. After a blurred series of clipping, whipping, dubbing, creating collar hackles, palmered bodies and married wings, he gave the fly a final touch of varnish to hold it all in place. The final knot was tied with the shiny, bendy tool that had baffled me earlier ('If you get that right the first time you do it, I'll buy you five pints,' he said with a smile). The completed fly was a thing of great beauty, a tiny dandy in a multicoloured waistcoat, wings proudly held aloft, ready to wreak havoc in any river.

'Your go, Monty. I've got to dash, but I'll see you later at the pub and we'll head out to one of the local loughs. Take your time, remember the way I tied things, and most importantly the order I did it. You'll have a lovely little fly in no time, then we can go and catch something with it. There's no nicer feeling than catching a fish on a fly you've tied yourself. Good luck – see you in a couple of hours.'

And with that he was gone, leaving me with a host of beautiful tying materials, sweaty palms and absolutely no recollection whatsoever of where to start.

There is something rather commendable in the obsessive desire to create the alchemy of the perfect fly. Here's the description of tying a Tup's Indispensible Spider from the incomparably brilliant *Guide to North Country Flies and How to Tie Them* by Mike Harding:

The essence of this fly is the dubbing, which here is

a mix of pink and cream seal's fur and yellow sheep's wool. The original winged fly, the *Tup's Indispensible*, called for a mixture of fur, partly from a spaniel's ear and partly the yellow, urine-stained wool from round a ram's testicles. I would recommend that any fly-tying purist reading this approach the ram carefully, do not wear wellington boots and use very soft tweezers. I managed to get mine from a farmer at clipping time. As for the spaniel – give it a bone and ask it nicely.

It's all there, isn't it? A hint of boggle-eyed obsession, an admirable approach to detail, and a heady whiff of madness.

An hour after Ronan left, my thumb and forefinger were gummed together with varnish, there was a bit of golden pheasant tail stuck in my eyebrow, and the table looked as though a bomb had gone off under a parakeet. The final swearword was still hanging in the air. I had used just about everything in the kit, and before me was a monstrosity that resembled no living thing on God's green Earth.

Mashed and lashed to the hook was a bizarre collection of fur and feathers, held together with yards of cotton, several bits of tinsel and some loose strands of Reuben's coat. The latter was a nice touch, although Reuben was slightly miffed at this development and sat in the corner of the kitchen, eyeing the newly bare patch on his tail with a mixture of annoyance and disappointment at his master's irresponsible approach to pet ownership.

The fly was the size of one of the more immense Central American moths, the type of thing that invariably has the word *colossus* or *goliath* in its Latin name. Any trout watching this land on the water's surface above it would assume some freak kingfisher had been blown in from the Galapagos and would take cover under a rock for at least a week, traumatised and trembling.

The only thing missing was a name. After due consideration I decided to christen it the Funky Chicken. This was because a) it was the size of a respectably plump Rhode Island Red, and b) it was very, very funky indeed. I was inordinately proud of it. Cramming it into my fly box, I set out for the rendezvous with Ronan at the pub.

When he saw the fly, being a nice sort of a chap, he simply nodded sagely.

'Well done, well done, a very good first effort.' He picked it up and turned it in his hand, a bit of tinsel fluttering to the floor as he did so, before respectfully placing it back in the box like some delicate midge that had been tied by an old master. 'Your first tied fly is a very precious thing – let's see if we can go and catch a fish with it.' I presumed he meant a marlin or perhaps a ravenous cod, as anything else would simply lack the gape to be able to take the thing in.

It was a short drive to Lough Inagh, a picture-perfect natural lake cupped by green hills with dramatic plantations of pine forests clinging to their sides. The crests of the hills above were bare rock, another world from the lush valley beneath, stark and rugged as they tumbled across a powder-blue sky.

Ronan parked the van next to a small jetty and began to ready his equipment. The water stretched and shimmered before us, the surface ruffled by tiny waves. The reeds along the bank rustled and shivered in the wind, the breath of the lake cool and fresh against my face. The air smelled of water and peat, heady with a mixture of marsh gas and wet foliage.

The first stage of kitting up was Ronan donning a fearsome-looking waistcoat, from which dangled all manner of tools and mysterious potions. If it hadn't been dotted with brightly coloured flies, it would have been precisely the sort of jacket used by a member of a counter-terrorism force when storming an embassy overtaken by suicidal fanatics. It clinked as he walked, a dangling delicatessen of death. I discreetly studied it, lost in admiration, and resolved to get one of my own as soon as possible.

'Would you like me to tie on your leader and a good fly, Monty?' Ronan asked.

I had a faint feeling that there must be some sort of protocol about doing your own kit, but I was fairly keen to catch something so nodded and handed him my rod. I watched him expertly lash on a leader – the length of delicate nylon at the end of the heavier fly line – creating a dropper in the process, a smaller section of line that allowed two flies to be used at the same time.

Ronan produced a wooden box that looked as if it had once held colossal cigars, flicking a worn brass catch at the side to reveal massed ranks of flies, a veritable hive of feathers and fur, trembling drones awaiting their masters instructions. Strangely enough the flies all looked absolutely identical, layer after layer of them, all dun and sleek.

'These are sedges – I've tied a fair few over the years.' He glanced up sheepishly. 'It's a bit early for them, but I'll put one on the dropper and then we can have the Funky Chicken as the lead fly. A potent combo, I'm sure you agree.'

Ronan rowed our tiny boat out into the middle of the lough, all the while assessing the wind and peering intently at the reed beds along the banks. There was no sound save the gentle clop of the oars, the creak of the rowlocks and the wind tumbling down the green hills to coast along the surface of the lake. The morning sun warmed the back of my neck, and glancing down I could see the Funky Chicken trembling on the end of my line, a freakish praying mantis ready to pounce.

'I'd say over there looks pretty good,' said Ronan, gesturing towards a nearby headland. 'We can drift onto it, and I generally find I catch one or two as the water begins to get shallow. There are some pretty big fellas in here you know, up to ten or twelve pounds.'

As that was pretty much the same weight as the Funky Chicken, it struck me that it would be a fair fight. I picked up the rod and began to fish.

During my travels along the coast I had been lucky enough to bump into Jackie Coyne, the current fly-fishing champion of all of Ireland. He was a very friendly, wild-haired, garrulous fellow, entirely happy to chat about the black art of the perfect cast. He had kindly taken me dry casting over a green sward of lawn, talking me through the intricacies of the wind-up and the final delivery of the fly. Whilst explaining the minutiae of the arm action, he had paused thoughtfully, searching for a good description. After a few moments his face lit up as he found the perfect analogy.

'Imagine, if you will, punching a man vigorously and repeatedly in the face. Well, it's like that.' He looked delighted at the description, a quintessentially Irish means of describing the delivery of a tiny piece of fluff to a body of tranquil water.

Casting a fly is shrouded in mystique and folklore. Essentially the idea is to use the weight of the line to get the fly to the right place at the right time – i.e. touching down as gently as a falling snowflake directly over the dappled form of a cruising trout. It should replicate the gossamer arrival of something as ethereal as a mayfly, a tiny scrap of nothing barely breaking the surface meniscus.

My initial attempts created a mighty thrashing of the water's surface, with a casting action akin to a panicking driver of a runaway wagon desperately wielding a bullwhip at a rabid mule. The fly whipped back and forth overhead, breaking the sound barrier before touching down like a meteorite. Over time, however, I had become more refined and could now at least get a fly out on the surface of a lake without startling nearby herons into frantic flight.

I was retrieving the fly gently over the surface of the water as we neared the headland when the unthinkable happened. There was a brief explosion of foam, the line tightened whipping the tip of the rod round in the process, and I found myself fighting a small but sturdy wild brown trout.

'Aha, well done, Monty!' shouted Ronan, beaming from the stern of the boat. The trout leaped as it approached the boat, a bar of gold suspended briefly on glittering pillars of spray. Held in its mouth, the hook lodged in the fork of its jaw, was the Funky Chicken.

I manoeuvred the trout to the side of the boat, where Ronan scooped it up in the landing net. The net was a nice touch, as I could have lifted it fairly effortlessly over the side, but Ronan plainly felt that such a momentous fish – my first-ever trout on a home-tied fly – required a more dramatic arrival onboard.

I looked down at the trout as it quivered in the wet mesh of the net. It measured about ten inches from the tip of its jaw to the tip of its tail. Although the length and poundage would obviously improve both with time in the lake and also with how frequently I told the story, nonetheless I was looking at a neat, aristocratic predator, the heir of a family line that stretched back over ten thousand years in this very lough. The bronze of the flanks was dotted with vivid red spots, the tiny teeth set in the jaw that snapped and gasped on deck were sharp and vicious – a perfect hunter for the russet killing grounds of the lake floor. I quickly removed the hook, the Funky Chicken by now looking ragged and somewhat dog-eared, and slipped the trout back over the side. It was gone in a moment, vanishing into the waters of the lough to continue a fight for survival that had spanned a hundred human generations.

To my delight the Funky Chicken continued to catch trout, the zenith of the afternoon coming when two were taken on successive casts. Ronan continued to bellow encouragement from the bow, laughing in delight and shaking his head in bewilderment every time the water splashed and the line tightened. It struck me that this was the measure of a true fisherman, taking pleasure in the success of others – I'm not entirely sure I would have been so gracious if the roles had been reversed.

'You've created a sensation, Monty,' Ronan said as yet another trout slipped away into the deeper water. 'You'll come back next year and everyone will be fishing with

Funky Chickens, you mark my words.'

By now, however, the mighty Chicken was looking very threadbare indeed, having steadily shed feathers and fluff with each new cast until it was pretty much just a bare hook and a few strands of Reuben's tail hair, which stuck resolutely to the task. I began to wonder if it was in fact Reuben's contribution that had done the trick – he was after all the ultimate water hound. If this was the case, he was going to look very, very strange indeed by the end of the summer.

The fishing was so good that we barely noticed the day slipping past. Ronan caught a couple of trout – both of them considerably larger than anything I had taken – and a general air of contentment settled on the boat, both of us continuing to fish in companionable silence. The light slowly bled from the sky, touching the mountains around the lough with soft light and making the water appear bottomless. It was as the sun began to settle behind the crest of the highest hill that Ronan finally turned the boat for home. By then we had caught a total of eight trout between us, all returned to fight another day. As the comforting shape of the Lough Inagh Lodge appeared from the shadows on the bank – Ronan had declared that the only fitting end to a day such as this was a whiskey by a crackling fire – the rustle of our bow and gentle muffled swish of the oars marked the end of a classic few hours of fly-fishing. Our wake left a final, echoing note as it lapped at the foot of the mountains, the sound racing into the hills, leaving behind peat-stained water full of darting, speckled shapes with ancient memories in their bones.

18

Pirate Queens
and Indian Princes

With the frantic nature of the work it was several weeks before I could recommence my fly-fishing endeavours. The call though, when it came, was absolutely irresistible.

Simon Ashe had become a friend over the course of the summer, with our paths crossing regularly in the village. He was a tall, lean figure with a quick intelligence about him, a man of considerable talent and the youngest estate manager in the history of Ballynahinch Castle. As I drove down the road that snaked along the river, I would regularly see him in waders, raking the riverbed to create spawning grounds for the salmon or striding along the banks hacking at the rhododendrons that crowded the paths.

'Bloody things,' he would grumble in O'Dowd's bar. 'They're like a viral super plant. They were introduced by Ranji to add a bit of tropical colour, but it's like putting a lion into the environment of the hills here and expecting our native foxes and badgers to cope. The rhododendron is an aggressive plant and will very quickly outcompete any of our indigenous species. Their strategy is to very rapidly create a canopy that shades the ground beneath – anything trying to grow down there will get no light at all and die away. But we're winning – I'm sure by the time I'm ninety they'll all be gone. Bloody foreigners, coming here and nicking our sunlight.' He smiled at me and took a sip of his pint.

The Ranji to whom Simon referred was just one part of the extraordinary and colourful history of Ballynahinch Castle, an exquisitely beautiful country house that sat overlooking a wide, sweeping curve of the River Owenmore. Having heard a great deal about the castle, the first time I drove up the manicured road that led there I had set my expectations ridiculously high, but nothing could have prepared me for the timelessness and grandeur of the place. It stared out onto the river beneath, benign and tranquil, a grand old dame with history etched into every crevice of her timeworn face. The castle has been a fortress, an operating base for a marauding pirate princess, the birthplace of the world's most famous animal welfare charity, a haven for local people in times of great hardship, a home for an exotic prince, a retreat for the titled and the wealthy . . . Look up at the façade of Ballynahinch Castle, and seven hundred years of history is staring straight back.

Not too surprisingly for this part of the world, the history of Ballynahinch (*Baile na hInse*, meaning 'Castle on the Island') started with a monumental punch-up between the O'Flahertys and the O'Malleys in 1384. As a big scrap seems to be the starting point for the vast majority of

BELOW: Ballynahinch Castle – the realm of pirate queens, noble princes, and the king of fish.
INSET LEFT: About to start fishing with Ronan Crane – a man possessed.
INSET RIGHT: Raking the salmon spawning beds with the ludicrously talented Simon Ashe.

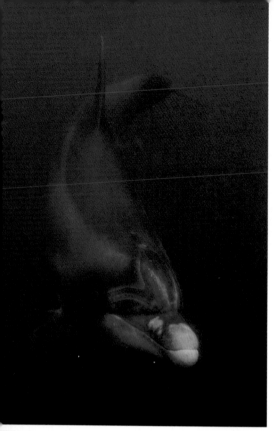

THIS PAGE
LEFT: A close inspection by several hundred kilogrammes of muscle and potential energy.
BELOW: A stranded striped dolphin – like a sle missile marooned on the beach.

FACING PAGE
LEFT: Moments before the hooker race commenced. Note the white knuckles.
RIGHT: Padraig stares grimly ahead as bedlan and anarchy approaches from behind.
BELOW: The calm before the storm as the hoo prepare for battle

LEFT: Connemara Ponies at home with the sea and mountains.

RIGHT: Tam – her Irish ancestry to the fore and the golden sands of Connemara behind.

THIS PAGE: The Aran Sweater – a dawn start, and an epic day ahead.

TOP LEFT: Paddy Shoulders – a living legend – and his nervous apprentice.
MIDDLE LEFT: A lonely man with a numb bottom ploughs inexorably onwards.
BOTTOM LEFT: A symphony of pain expressed with a gurn of emotion – nearly home, though.

ABOVE: Recovering the acoustic pod.
BELOW: Joanne arrives to open the magical pod.

ABOVE: The pupils of Inishturk Island School – and their erstwhile teacher.
BELOW: The magical moment of handing over the pontoon to Simon and the IWDG.

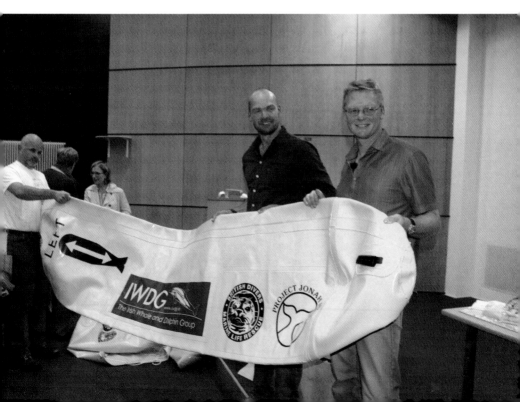

The cottage was a true haven, offering tranquillity amid the madness of the relentless patro

Connemara history, I'll move swiftly onto the years when Grace O'Malley – she of sailing-up-the-Thames-fame – lived in the castle and used it as her headquarters for piratical mischief. During the latter years of Grace's life, there was considerable skulduggery afoot from an English point of view as well, with 1584 being a particularly bumper year for caddish behaviour and everyone generally behaving like complete bounders. There were murders in the dead of night, the appointment of unpopular leaders by faraway British bureaucrats, a spattering of raids and a touch of kidnap and pillage. Quite frankly when you walk into the bar in Ballynahinch as an Englishman today, I'm surprised that you're not immediately punched on the nose.

After Grace died in 1603, the next notable residents of the castle were the Martins. The name might indicate a family that own a rather twee B&B outside Swindon, but actually they are recorded as one of the Fourteen Tribes of Galway after coming to Ireland in 1169 'with Strongbow' – a ringing endorsement of over-strength cider if there ever was one. The Martins developed the grand old house in the present location, and it was here that Richard Martin was born in 1754. Martin had two main hobbies in later life. The first was an abiding interest in and love of animals. The second was a habit of shooting anyone who didn't share the first.

In his capacity as an MP, he introduced Parliament's first anti-cruelty act in 1822 – the 'Ill-Treatment of Cattle Bill' – which in turn led to the formation of the Society for the Prevention of Cruelty to Animals in 1824. This in turn led to him becoming known as 'Humanity Dick'. His fondness for gunning down anyone who happened to be cruel to an animal – and, as you can imagine, in rural Ireland in the early nineteenth century that was a fair few bewildered and shortly to be deceased locals – led to him also becoming known as 'Hairtrigger Dick', which by a happy coincidence was also my nickname at university.

When not patting donkeys or blowing their owners' brains out, Martin had a lavish lifestyle which ultimately bankrupted the estate. It didn't help that, when his wife ran off with another man, Martin successfully sued for damages and was awarded £10,000 – a massive sum in those days. He duly had silver horse shoes created for his ride home, and instructed his coachman to hurl coins to the four winds for the entire journey until the money was gone. This showed a low appreciation for financial sense, but a high appreciation for letting your wife know that she had run off with a bounder.

Having been used as a haven for the victims of the Great Famine of the 1840s, Ballynahinch subsequently passed into the hands of the Berridge family, who restored it to something approaching its former glory. And here we come to the final part of the great dynasty.

In 1924 came a train through the wild country of Connemara, bearing none other than His Highness the Maharaja Jam Sahib of Nawanagar, better known as Ranjitsinhji, or simply Ranji. He had fallen in love with the region on a fishing trip, and so the castle passed into the hands of perhaps its most remarkable, benign and much-loved owner.

Ranji was also known as the Prince of Cricketers, second only to W.G. Grace as a batsman, of whom Ranji was a teammate. He still holds two English cricketing records to this day. Although cricket was his God-given talent, fishing for salmon was his abiding passion.

Leaf through the yellowing pages of his leather-bound fishing book, still held in the Ranji Room in the castle, and it lists day after day of classic sport, with his guests listed as dukes, brigadiers, princes and ambassadors. What days they must have been, with the river alive at the height of the salmon run, and the great and the good striding the banks in stout boots and tweed, the silver arc of two-handed salmon rods flashing soaring arcs in the Connemara sun.

Ranji was famously generous. He would purchase five cars in Galway every time he came to Ballynahinch in June and, before leaving in October to return to India, he would present them to local people. He would personally serve his staff at the great party held every year on his birthday, and the legendary gillie Frank Cummins – who only passed away in 1983 – spoke often of a pair of ruby cufflinks Ranji had given him. With the formation of the first Irish Free State overlapping with his time at the castle, potentially this was a very delicate time indeed for Ranji as a representative of the British Empire. Such was his tact and diplomacy that when he was tasked with the loyal toast to the King of England at the end of the annual workers' party, he would raise a glass to those present and announce 'To the Emperor of India', invariably to thunderous applause. The years that the Prince of Cricketers owned Ballynahinch are still spoken of with great affection, showing that the potential barriers of title, wealth and nationality are mere trifles compared to the significance of simply being a good man. Therein lies greatness.

I had driven past the river many, many times on my travels, and had always been impressed by its scale and grandeur. It was therefore a very big moment indeed when Simon had called me the day before and told me that the salmon were not only running, but that he had secured three of the very best beats for me to fish. The opportunity to cast a fly into a legendary river, standing in the footprints of royalty and rogues, was too much to resist, and I hastily rearranged my diary by lying my head off to everyone I'd arranged to meet (muttering things about 'crucial data assessment' and 'key logging of sighting matrixess') and scuttled off to the castle.

Happily for mortals such as myself, Ballynahinch is now a hotel, and before I met up with Simon I had the chance for a quick stroll through the corridors redolent with history. And so I stood in front of a portrait of Humanity Dick, leafed through the records of Ranji's great days as a fisherman and a cricketer, and raised a glass to the portrait of Grace O'Malley hanging over the bar – my latest and greatest crush.

Simon strode through the main reception area towards me, resplendent in a fishing waistcoat even more dramatic than Ronan's. In the interim I had purchased a waistcoat of my own, and sheepishly put it on feeling like a complete fraud. As is the way with fishing folk, Simon complemented me on my selection of flies, which now included various dog-eared and spiky affairs which I had tied myself during long evenings at the cottage. As is also the way with the real fishing folk, he quickly spotted that none of them would interest even a half-blind salmon maddened with hormones and hunger and, after rummaging in his pockets, produced a box of his own.

In the box were salmon flies. These were no delicate bits of fluff designed to fool a fickle brook trout, these were great, garish bold patterns aimed at goading the king of fish into an angry snap of silver jaws. When salmon enter rivers from the sea, they stop feeding, focusing every molecule of their being on driving themselves through cataract and pool, past every hazard and obstacle, to return to the precise patch of gravel where they emerged from the egg several years before. Any response to a lure is a combination of instinct and irritation, a fact that makes catching salmon a matter of good judgement combined with a healthy dose of dumb luck. Lacking both of these qualities, I had yet to create even a spark of interest from a salmon, although on this day, on this river, in this company, the odds were as good as they ever would be.

Simon lifted out a fly that looked like a bird of paradise on a kebab and carefully knotted it onto my line, chatting as he did so.

'Today, Monty, I've got you fishing on Beat One, Beat Three and Beat Four. Only an idiot couldn't catch a salmon with an array of water like that at his disposal.' He glanced up and smiled. 'It's a good day, the salmon have been running well, so let's see if we can break your duck, shall we?'

The day that followed was a delight, albeit a delight that didn't feature a salmon. We *saw* plenty of salmon, mind you – great silver bodies exploding from the river as it tumbled over steep rocks. On one heart-stopping occasion, a large salmon actually leapt over my fly as it landed on the water, causing me to take an involuntary step back and shatter the calm of the morning with a very rude word indeed, of which I'm sure Ranji would have strongly disapproved.

Simon was wonderful company, never too serious and yet steeped in the history and knowledge of the river system and the environment around him. Here was a man who had found an outlet for all his considerable energy and enthusiasm, a lifetime's work at his feet. He seemed serene and content, perfectly at home in the midst of the estate and yet keenly aware of the scale of the task that faced him.

'Oh, it's massive,' he said as he cast into yet another dark pool. 'There's major work here that'll comfortably outlast my lifetime, and probably the next estate manager after that. There's the spawning beds that need clearing, replanting to be done, I'm trying to restore the gardens to something approaching their original state, there's the work monitoring the salmon run, constantly assessing the health of the river, and then there's the bloody rhododendrons, of course.'

He showed me the salmon counter, a small stone building next to a steep run bisected by two white markers. Inside the building, incongruous against the backdrop of the river and the hills, sat a computer.

'I can monitor the movement of the salmon through this and count precisely how many fish we get coming upstream. I've got some great footage of an otter on here too as it sauntered over the markers one night.' He fiddled with the mouse, pressed a few buttons, and sure enough the unmistakable outline of an otter ambled through frame.

'It records the size of the contact as well – here's a real beast.' A massive dark shape moved up over the white markers. 'That'll be well over twenty pounds, that fish. Probably the only one we'll see today, the way you're casting.'

I asked him if there was anything really unusual he had seen on the cameras. He thought for a moment, before smiling and nodding vigorously.

'I came down one morning and the computer showed

two massive contacts that had moved through. It was really exciting – the return of the monster salmon to Ballynahinch. I checked the footage, a huge moment for me as estate manager, and saw a very nice, clear picture of my brother and his mate, naked, sliding over the rapids waving furiously at the camera. I think that was fairly unusual – does that count? Anyway, none of this is catching us our salmon, is it?'

The rest of the afternoon passed with Simon trying every fly in the box, and the two of us casting into every riffle and dark hollow, maddened by the constant activity of fish around us. Although frustrated, I was actually content enough. You have to earn your salmon, and my theory is that every cast brings me closer to the moment when the line will tighten and I at last feel the weight and power of that gilt body and spade-shaped tail. Such is the journey these fish make, such are the hazards and near-impossible odds they overcome, that I didn't begrudge them an uninterrupted final few miles. Should I ever catch one, regardless of size, I shall slip it immediately back into the water, one of nature's great survivors on one of nature's great journeys.

The end of our day's fishing was signalled with a mighty crack, the demise of the top section of my rod. To be fair, I had been clipping it incessantly for six hours with some fairly hefty salmon flies – the mark of an inept casting technique – and a final vigorous, agricultural heave saw the bright orange fake prawn smash into the delicate tip, shattering the carbon fibre in a glinting spray of rather expensive shrapnel. Simon didn't miss a beat and, as I stood in abject defeat with the ruins of my rod in my hand, he strode past and muttered a single word.

'Bar.'

Ronan had arranged to meet us at the end of the day's fishing, and he had already lined the pints up by the time we clattered our way down the steps into a welcoming fug created by the fire crackling in the grate. Lying on a dark wood sideboard as we entered was the only salmon caught that day, sightless and gaping, an animal frozen in time, still staring upriver towards its final goal. As I admired the fish and chatted to the triumphant and already mildly inebriated angler, I felt a moment's sadness for it – so near to its final destination of the gravel bed where it emerged, so many hazards overcome, and yet thwarted at the very last moment.

The real pleasure of Ronan and Simon's company – aside from the fact that they're very nice fellows indeed – is their depth of knowledge and passion about all things speckled that swim. As we talked, it became apparent just how much the waters around them had changed even in their own short lives, a single generation where netting at sea and fish farming had wreaked havoc on the already delicate gamble any salmon or trout makes as it noses its way from a home river into the wilds of the open ocean.

'Ah, it's pretty unequivocal,' said Simon, nodding to Ronan and waving his empty glass as he headed to the bar. 'I was here when the stocks crashed. Our anglers took ninety per cent less sea trout than the year before – this was just after the farms opened up in the bay. The salmon took a similar hit, a really catastrophic drop in numbers for a fishery. The young trout and salmon just get massacred by the sea lice they pick up on the way in and out of the river. We're fighting hard, and numbers are slowly improving, but it's an ongoing battle.'

'The irony,' said Ronan, 'is that the salmon farms directly employ so few people, just over a hundred and fifty in the entire country, whereas the game-fishing industry in Ireland employs thousands in hotels, as guides, and looking after the rivers. It makes no sense financially, environmentally, and in employment terms. But still it gets funded and supported by the government. It's all a bit baffling really – I wonder what old Ranji would have made of it.'

'It's a shame Hairtrigger Dick isn't around,' I said. 'I imagine he would have had a fairly robust solution.'

'Now there's a thought,' said Simon, sipping his beer and possibly briefly considering this as a genuine option.

One pint led to another, and the fire burned low in the grate. Outside, the wind had picked up, sweeping down the valley to buffet the walls of Ballynahinch. The lights of the great house smouldered in the forest that surrounded it as the river swept past in the darkness beneath, languid and timeless beyond the measure of the men who talked of its future, flowing inexorably towards the sea.

19

Red Sails in the Sunset

Whilst out in the boat, I frequently sighted elegant, dark-hulled vessels moving under ochre-coloured sails. They looked very much at home as they bustled through the swells, shouldering them aside with a long prow that led to a plump belly and neat behind. These were the famous Galway hookers, vessels synonymous with the west coast of Ireland, and in their own way little capsules of Irish history.

The hooker was developed to carry goods across Galway Bay and beyond. They are built very much for a job, all stout lines and robust fittings. The mast is a telegraph pole of dark wood, the boom a substantial log which shudders and groans under the immense strain of the sails. Back in the mists of time, owning a hooker was a passport to considerable social standing and potential wealth, although the key to maximising your income was to be out on the water in all conditions. Thus the hooker evolved over the years to become more and more stable in big seas, with a low cargo storage area, and a wide beam that saw her perfectly at home as she heeled over. The hooker is, for so many, the image of the West of Ireland, a source of misty-eyed nostalgia for the Irish diaspora throughout the world.

Whilst on patrol in the southern coast of the nearby Bertraghboy Bay, I bumped into Donal Greene as he sat on a quayside with a half-completed hooker sitting in the dock beneath him. Although only in his mid-thirties, Donal was a man of some standing locally, as he built hookers entirely by hand – no plans, no computer-assisted designs, just a steady touch and clear vision of how the final boat would look. He was eyeing the hull as I approached, doubtless planning the next stage, which would begin when the mood took him. He saw me walking past and beckoned me over for a chat.

He was a powerfully built man with a clear eye and a gentle smile. As we talked, he glanced frequently at his hands, turning an old piece of wood in them thoughtfully, the rough palms and strong fingers the tools of his trade. As the conversation developed, it also became apparent that he had a wicked sense of humour, laughing readily and frequently at his own mistakes as he had learned his trade.

'You know, it's a funny thing,' he said, after another tale of woe from the early days, 'building a boat for me nowadays is a mood thing. Suddenly the moment is upon you, and you know that all you have to do is lay the keel and the vessel will gradually emerge. Sounds a bit dramatic, but there we go.'

He told me how every aspect of the hookers – the basic

build, the rigging, the actual sailing – was always referred to in pure Irish.

'It's not snobbish or anything.' He glanced down sheepishly. 'It's just the way it's always been done. It keeps our language alive, though, which nowadays can only be a good thing, I suppose.'

We chatted for a while longer, before Donal finally hoisted himself to his feet and peered intently once again into the hull.

'Right, this young lady won't build herself so I should get on, I suppose. We're racing in a hooker regatta soon. Shall I give you a shout and you can come along – you could crew for us, if you like?'

This was a compelling invitation indeed, but there was one potentially terminal snag.

'But Donal, I don't speak Irish. How will I know what to do?'

He chuckled. 'Oh, you'll know, all right. You'll particularly know if you've done something wrong – it'll give you a great chance to learn some Irish terms when that happens, although I'm not sure you should repeat them in polite company.'

He bade me farewell and I left him as I'd found him, staring thoughtfully into the hull and tossing the piece of wood from hand to hand, consulting a mental blueprint that had been handed down through the ages in the lyrical tongue of the hooker men of Southern Connemara.

Several weeks passed, and I had almost forgotten about Donal's invitation when my phone beeped at me as I drove home one evening. Glowing on the screen was a message: 'In a regatta this weekend at Kinvara – you still up for it?' I certainly was, and I hastily called him. We arranged to meet at Kinvara the following Friday evening.

The week that followed was particularly busy, and it was a hollow-eyed and wildly ill-prepared man who rattled into Kinvara several days later. It was the eve of the main race, and the village was in its Sunday best, trim and neat in preparation for the festivities to come. Brightly coloured banners fluttered over the harbour, dancing in a brisk Galway Bay breeze, and the hookers stood in serried ranks at their moorings, ready to do battle. There was an air of expectancy over the entire scene, a hush before the gathering storm of competition.

Donal met me on the quay, extending a hand as he strode towards me.

'Ah, well done, well done, didn't think you'd turn up. Come in and meet the rest of the lads.'

We walked a short distance to where three very contrasting figures stood on the quayside. The first was a weathered older man, perhaps in his late fifties. He had an air of quiet authority about him; his lined face under a flat cap exuded confidence and serenity.

'Evening, young man,' he said, shaking my hand firmly. 'My name's Padraig, and I'm the skipper for tomorrow. You're very welcome onboard – we'll put you to work, don't you worry.'

Next to him was Joe, a tall, lean moustachioed figure with an easy rolling gait and a quiet economy of movement. When he spoke it was with a distinct American drawl, the result I learned later of a twenty-year stint living in Boston. He smiled warmly, and gave me a friendly wave.

The final man stood a little apart from the rest, quietly

coiling a rope on the quayside. He was a giant figure, massive across the chest and arms, with thighs like enormous hams wrapped in denim. He wore an Irish rugby shirt stretched tight across back and stomach, so tight that for a moment I thought I heard the seams squeaking.

'And this is Ronan,' said Donal, clapping the man mightily on the shoulder with a sound akin to someone hitting the back of a leather sofa with a cricket bat. 'He's very, very gay and a bit delicate, but we let him onboard anyway. In a way, I suppose, when we're nice to him it makes us all feel a bit better about ourselves.'

Ronan lifted his gaze, raising his eyebrows at me and shaking his head wearily as Donal chuckled at his own joke.

'Hello, Monty,' he said. As is so often the way with very big men, his voice was quiet and measured. 'Please attempt to ignore this idiot. It's difficult, I know, but try to think of him as a television that's always on in the corner of your front room. Mainly distracting and annoying, but when you want a few moments of zero mental activity you tune in – that sort of thing.'

Donal laughed delightedly, and en masse we turned to walk towards our boat.

All hookers are steeped in history and heritage, but our vessel for the race the next day had a particular poignancy. Built in 1924, she was called the *Volunteer*, a reference to one of the most turbulent periods in Irish history, a time of violence and tectonic political change. When I asked Donal about the origins of the name, he was – for once – serious and thoughtful in his response.

'Yes, it's an interesting thought, isn't it? Here you are – a

British ex-military man – on a hooker which was built to transport the young men who may well have fought for the Irish Republican Army.' He leapt aboard and began to rummage in the locker under the bow, talking over his shoulder as he did so. 'Apparently it was not uncommon that the hookers were used to move the volunteers – hence the name – in the dead of night from haven to haven, or meeting to meeting. I wonder if the men who built her would see the irony, but it's a very different Ireland now, of course.'

He smiled up at me, and gestured for me to jump down from the quayside. I landed with bent knees on the solid wooden deck and enjoyed my first good look at a traditional Galway hooker.

Glancing around I could immediately see that there was no question as to her heritage, apparent in a bulbous belly and immense shoulders leading to a bowsprit like a roof beam in a medieval church. Numerous ropes from the mast led to a bewildering array of block and tackle, cleats and strong points. The sails that Donal was dragging out of the hold were a gorgeous dark ochre, the colour of a fine red wine. Pervading all was a wonderful smell of sweet wood and canvas. We spent an hour or so preparing the *Volunteer* for battle the next day, and then – as tradition demands – retired to the pub for some pre-race carbohydrate loading.

Hooker racing is a very serious business, with rivalries between boats going back decades, even generations. As we chatted in the pub, Donal told me that there was only one other boat – the *Star of the West* – in our class, but that the race between them was due to be intense.

'We should be able to take them in a straight race – I

genuinely think we're a quicker boat - but then again on any given day one hooker can beat another. There aren't any bad crews out there - everyone knows what they're doing.'

'That's my concern, actually, Donal,' I said. 'I'm a bit worried that I'll be a liability and just get in the way.'

'Ah now, don't worry about that,' said Ronan, holding a pint in one mighty hand which made it look very much like a novelty shot glass. 'We've already had a chat about that, and you're in the "intelligent ballast" category. We'll tell you where to stand, and then tell you when to move. In the time between those two commands try not to touch anything.'

'It's a key role, that,' said Padraig wisely. 'Takes years of training to be intelligent ballast, you know.'

There was a great deal of sage nodding all round, and not even the hint of a smile (which was a good effort in the circumstances). I retired to bed secure in my role - essentially that of a large sandbag on wheels.

The next day was absolutely beautiful, with white clouds scudding briskly through blue skies and the surface of Galway Bay ruffled by just the right amount of wind. The boats nodded and twitched at their moorings, woken by the breeze and the wide open spaces before them. The morning passed in a nervous series of preparations and briefings, until - at long last - we boarded the *Volunteer* and lifted the anchor.

A Galway hooker is about the same size and weight as a train carriage. Imagine moving something of those dimensions around a tightly packed car park using just a scrap of sail and a series of subtle tweaks on ropes and pulleys. All with no brakes and twenty other carriages doing precisely the same thing. The air rang with ripe Irish phrases, near misses abounded, and I learned that a number of expressions do in fact survive translation. The air was filled with the thump of filling sails, and rustle of hulls sweeping through the surface of the water, and bellowed instructions within and between the boats.

The clock ticked inexorably down, and then – abruptly – the moment arrived, with the *Volunteer* and the *Star of the West* turned simultaneously towards the start line, our boat fractionally behind theirs. Padraig called instructions from the stern, the tiller nestled under one arm, Donal and Joe adjusted the trim of the foresails, and Ronan hauled mightily on the pulleys to tighten the main sail. The *Volunteer* pointed her nose at Galway Bay, lifted her skirts and hurtled after her competitor. She heeled over at forty-five degrees, harnessing the wind and pushing her belly into the surface of the sea, the water racing along the old wood of the hull and the wake rising behind us.

Everyone had a specific role, with mine happening to be standing solemnly in the one spot being heavy. Every now and then Ronan would glance up and nod his head towards another part of the boat, and I would scuttle into position, to stand once again thinking weighty thoughts.

'Well done, Monty,' said Joe, without a trace of irony. 'You're doing a fine job there.'

The really fun part was when we tacked, as it required me to duck under the boom and dodge from one side of the deck to another. The exciting part of all this was that Joe and Donal would simultaneously head with some determination in the opposite direction, trailing all manner of complex lines behind them. For a few moments, every time we tacked, my world was a dark cave full of flapping sails, a sweeping boom, thrashing ropes and two stout crew members heading briskly across the deck towards me. I would emerge wide-eyed back into the daylight with my woolly hat on back to front and my sunglasses dangling off one ear, to grip the side of the boat with white knuckles as the deck sloped away from me.

The route took us into the heart of the bay, a glorious scene of red sails and dark hulls, with the cliffs of the Burren as a dramatic backdrop creating a snapshot of living Irish history. The *Star of the West* remained firmly in our sights, the gap between us ebbing and flowing as both boats weaved their way into the wind.

After several miles of brisk tacking, the time came to round the buoy and race ahead of the wind back towards Kinvara. The *Star of the West* rounded the mark moments ahead of us, the *Volunteer* snapping at her heels, closing the gap the moment she caught the breeze on the downwind leg.

'This used to called the "gentleman's leg", Monty,' shouted Padraig, the glint of battle in his eyes. 'This is where the owners of the boats would take the helm as it was easy sailing. It's a flat-out race now, boy.' He grinned wolfishly and pulled down his flat cap into what was presumably a more aerodynamic position.

The crew began to ditch ballast for this final leg, emptying sacks of rocks over the side of the boat, the *Volunteer* hurtling downwind, closing the gap inexorably on the *Star of the West*, who hoisted every length of canvas in response. There was an expectant hush onboard, with Donal, Joe and Padraig watching the gap close, waiting for their moment.

Ronan was hurling stones the size of large watermelons overboard throughout. There was a distinctly nervous moment when he turned to eye me speculatively – a ninety-kilogram Englishman who had performed his role on the upwind leg, and was now essentially surplus weight – before giving a small shake of his head in a 'what-on-earth-was-I-thinking' kind of way. The relief was considerable.

Slowly and surely, we drew closer to the *Star of the West*, then level, and then crept in front. I was delighted, thoroughly infected by the intensity of the competition and the hard work of the crew around me, and danced a tiny jig of the excitement as we finally drew ahead. In the distance, directly on our bow, was a bright orange dot, the marker buoy that signalled the final turn for home and our inevitable triumphant entry into the harbour at Kinvara. The crew of the *Star of the West* had – not unreasonably – other ideas, and tucked in behind us, essentially harvesting our wind and staying within a boat's length of our stern. Padraig stared fixedly ahead, ignoring ten tons of charging vessel sitting virtually on his shoulder. There was a palpable air of tension as the final marker approached, with Padraig bellowing to our rival boat the traditional friendly notification of our impending turn to starboard.

'You feck off, this is our right of way!'

Still not deigning to turn round, he positively crammed his cap on, and stared fixedly ahead at the buoy. By now the *Star of the West*'s bowsprit was inches above his head, sweeping from side to side like an executioner's axe.

As should be very obvious by now, I know very little about hooker racing, but even I had a faint sense that something rather unpleasant was about to happen. I was not to be disappointed.

The *Volunteer* reached the buoy and turned sharply to starboard to begin the final run home. The *Star of the West* kept going in a straight line, arriving at the buoy with the momentum and enthusiasm only a hooker with a five-mile run-up can muster. Our belly was exposed, a pulsing bullseye that our opponent rammed at full tilt.

Lots of tremendously exciting things happened simultaneously. The first was that we were struck dead in the water, our bow spun round so the wind dropped from our sails. The *Star of the West* scraped down our starboard side, their boom acting as a mighty scythe to sweep our deck clear of people and intelligent ballast. The latter had taken cover on the deck, and watched several tons of potential energy sweep overhead from a prone position, with a deep sense of appreciation at his own ability to avoid impending disaster.

At the stern, more serious events were unfolding. A rope from the *Star of the West* had become draped over the helmsman's position, which at that precise moment, sadly but not unreasonably, was being filled by Padraig. This rope duly wrapped itself around him, and hooked onto the far side of our hull. Padraig now found himself stuck under a rope that was attached to another hooker, one which was already heading for home like a pony with the whiff of a warm stable in its flared nostrils.

Ronan and I spotted that our skipper was about to be divided like some flat-capped amoeba, and leapt to the stern to try to help. Our arrival coincided with a shout of 'Boom!' from Joe, who had spotted that the wind had suddenly filled our sail and was about to whip it across the deck.

The boom crashed across, missing the top of my head by about six inches. 'Blimey,' I thought. 'That was very close indeed.' In fact, I was so busy congratulating myself that I forgot about the thick ropes and tackle that connected the boom to the deck. These arrived on the scene moments later, picking me up and hurling me against the transom like a rag doll. There I lay for a moment or two, awaiting another beating from something traditional.

Fortunately Ronan had ducked and weaved his ample frame through all the chaos, and the combined strength of himself and Padraig lifted the rope away, meaning that we would return to harbour with five crew members after all, not just four and a half.

After a few seconds of stunned silence, followed swiftly by everyone swearing simultaneously, we set the sails and set off grimly in pursuit. Once again our downwind speed was superior to the *Star of the West's*, and we slowly closed the gap. Perhaps fortunately for all concerned, the finish line arrived before we could get really close, as I feared some sort of seaborne brawl in which I would have to throw several of my famously inaccurate haymakers. Hooker crews are tough, proud men, and I couldn't help thinking that me lying on my back snoring through bleeding nostrils after thirty seconds wouldn't contribute much to the honour of our boat. The fact that Ronan would be frisbeeing screaming opposition crew members into the heart of Galway Bay probably would have, though.

In the end, the matter was sorted by an affable judge on the quay who heard both skippers out, then poured oil on troubled waters by disqualifying both boats and telling everyone to get over themselves. I really didn't understand any of the process, involving as it did considerable hand waving and complex by-laws, although from a layman's point of view I did feel that trying to execute your opposition by using your boom as a great big scythe was probably not entirely cricket.

I left the crew in the pub muttering darkly and moving beermats around to show rights of way, with a peanut in the middle of the table acting as a temporary marker buoy. It had been a wonderful day. I had touched on a living piece of Irish history, I had sailed with a crew of genial and friendly Irishmen, and I had come close to having my head squashed like a satsuma. As I drove away, I reflected that any day when you are nearly but not quite killed is invariably a pretty good one.

But we definitely had right of way.

20

The Great Fest

I was now entering my final six weeks in Roundstone, and felt fairly satisfied with the way my work was progressing. I had reconciled myself to the fact that I wasn't going to break any new ground scientifically, but nonetheless my gradual gathering of images and data about the dolphins off Inishlacken Island were contributing to the bigger picture, and the tantalising question remained as to whether this was a resident group. I also had the acoustic pod silently harvesting the sounds of the sea just offshore. This would give me a very good idea of just how often the dolphins were appearing off the coast, and I looked forward to recovering the pod in the final week before I left for good.

Autumn arrived with an audible shriek one morning, with the cottage buffeted by a furious low-pressure system that rattled the doors and shook the windows in their frames. From the cottage, I could actually see the squalls approaching, a front of hissing water and rolling Valkyrie skies. Just before their arrival, I would batten down the hatches, throw some turf on the fire, and settle into a chair with my toes virtually in the grate. Reuben would curl up on the hearthrug, nose buried in the dark bush of his tail, snuffling and snoring as the storms swirled around us. The seasons were changing, and winter was on its way, crashing the party like a drunken uncle spoiling for a fight.

In the shallows, the seaweed began to die off in vast quantities, shedding oil into the water so a swim became an instant beauty treatment. The sea itself retained the memory of what had been a particularly fine summer, the warmth of the sun held in its surface layers. I would go swimming as often as I could, my skin prickling and taut, emerging into brisk breezes that saw me tiptoe hastily back to the cottage wrapped in a towel, gasping and spluttering.

Piles of dark wrack rose on the beach, washed ashore by grey waves and forming putrid mounds that marked the boundary of the highest tides. On land, the flowers that had coated the island in a nodding, multicoloured quilt through the summer were thrashed into green uniformity, shedding their bright colours to become stalks that whipped and twitched in the winds. The ponies on the island looked ever wilder, manes trailing and heels kicking as they raced ahead of the storms. The Connemara pony is a revered animal in the equine world, famed for its toughness and agility. It was only as the autumn flexed its muscles that the true heritage of these animals came to the fore, with the primped, high-stepping show ponies of the summer left behind to be replaced by the surefooted, resilient working animals that had carried turf over the rough Connemara ground for generations of man gone before. They stared into the squalls as they barrelled in off the sea and feared nothing.

Across the sound, the slopes of Errisbeg became purple with the winter heather, spreading tendrils of maroon into the yellow blossoms of high summer. Roundstone itself looked cosy and secure tucked into the base of the mountain, the lights glowing ever earlier as the evenings drew in and the clouds gathered.

It was time for some profound changes at the cottage as well, as Reuben and I were being joined by a girl for the last few weeks of our time in Ireland. Life on the road always makes it difficult to meet someone and, although I valued Reuben's company beyond all others, as a permanent companion he lacked certain qualities. For a start, he had a habit of losing interest halfway through some of my better stories, he occasionally nipped me when excited, he was a messy eater, and he chased squirrels in the park back in Bristol – four characteristics that were coincidentally shared by at least one of my previous girlfriends.

I had rather bravely decided to invite the girl I had met in England several months previously out for the remainder of the summer in Ireland. Even more bravely, she accepted, and one blustery morning saw her tiny car rattle its way down the track towards the cottage, where Reuben and I were standing nervously at the door in our best bib and tucker. Tamsyn Smith is a rather gorgeous, petite redhead with flashing green eyes that speak loudly of her Irish ancestry. Watching her climb out of the car and walk towards me was to see her coming home, framed as she was against the emerald backdrop of the island and the blue waters of the Atlantic.

Entirely of her own accord, Tam got stuck straight in at the cottage, which by now was showing distinct signs of being the long-term residence of two hairy bachelors. During the first bout of vacuuming, Reuben became very excited indeed, attacking the whistling tubes with some gusto as the cleaner swept up all sorts of interesting smells that he plainly felt were an integral part of his home. When Tam washed his blanket, it not only radically changed colour it also fundamentally altered texture, becoming less . . . crackly. Order and decency were established within days of Tam arriving, and life at the cottage became immensely civilised. To sit by the fire together of an evening became a real pleasure, and for the first time I began to feel thoroughly settled – rushing home at the end of a day's work to be together with her and tell tall tales of seeking out dolphins and tracking basking sharks.

Living together does highlight a person's little eccentricities of course. One morning, after a breakfast of boiled eggs and soldiers, I saw her carefully break the old eggshells that remained.

'Why do you do that?' I asked idly.

'It's because witches can use them as little boats,' she said, as if it was the most natural thing in the world. 'I thought everyone did it.'

Tam has a far more artistic side than me, and would return from walks along the seashore carrying pieces of driftwood bent and ravaged by the ocean. She would arrange these around the cottage, framed in the windows or propped against the hearth so their shadows would dance on the walls of an evening. Reuben was completely baffled by the entire thing – what's the point of a stick if it isn't

252

thrown and repeatedly retrieved? – but for me the cottage really took on the feel of a rather beautiful haven, precisely the sort of place I had always imagined but had lacked the artistry to create. Tam would also gather old shells from the tideline, scattering them on surfaces and in porcelain bowls, exquisitely delicate mini-sculptures that brought the tide into the cottage in their textures and their whiff of salt and chalk. Reuben was duly won over by some sustained tummy rubs of a morning, as was I. With Tam, the idyll was complete, and as time passed so we both grew ever more comfortable with the arrangement, each the other's reason for coming home at the end of a long day on the sea or walking the shore.

By a happy coincidence, Tam had worked as an event organiser of some note back in England and, having taken one look at the rapidly approaching administrative apocalypse that was the Roundstone Diving and Wildlife Festival, agreed to take charge and organise pretty much the entire thing for the IWDG. In this decision she encountered no resistance whatsoever from the event originator. Matrixes were created, complex spreadsheets produced, lists typed and phones manned. The Festival went from being a rather vague notion to a living entity in the space of a few weeks. Word began to spread, posters appeared in every shop window and coffee house in town, and local residents began to offer their encouragement and assistance for the event.

Gurteen Beach seemed to be the ideal venue – a long arc of white sand that cupped a shallow bay of shimmering blue water, with waving fields of sea grass showing as dark patches on the seabed. Sea grass is very interesting stuff indeed; it secretes a mild acid – zosteric acid – to stop marine organisms settling on its blades and therefore interrupting photosynthesis. This results in thick undersea pastures, and wonderful refuge for marine life. To dive through a bed of sea grass is to hover over a mini Serengeti, swaying pastures alive with tiny fish and all manner of scuttling, darting creatures. I could think of no finer environment to introduce new divers to the wonders of the marine world.

At the head of the beach stood a well-equipped caravan park, ideal for pitching the marquee that could overlook the beach and the sea beyond. After several weeks of frantic activity, the great day dawned. And it was raining. A lot.

This was of some concern to me as, by this stage, the IWDG risked being roughly €3,000 down on the event. I had become somewhat carried away in the run-up the Festival, and had decided that it should resemble a mini Glastonbury. We therefore had a hog roast, catering vans, two bands, a marquee that Billy Smart would be proud of, a mussel and smoked salmon cookery display, and a complete diving set-up on the beach. There's no sadder sight than an empty marquee on a rainy morning, particularly when it's you that's paid for it all, and I paced the car park muttering darkly and peering at the sky through slitted eyes. Tam bustled about completely unperturbed, secure in the knowledge that good administration and solid preparation would ultimately triumph.

Simon Berrow had agreed to come up and run a cetacean rescue course on the beach. He turned up with a squeal of tyres, his vehicle duly disgorging his entire family and a vast assortment of whale- and dolphin-related paraphernalia. As children scattered in all directions and Simon's wife Frances staggered past carrying the support kit required to maintain two small boys and girl on a beach for a day (akin to a Victorian siege-style expedition on K2), Simon strode up to me with hand outstretched.

'Ah, Monty, hello, hello. Looking good, isn't it?'

I glanced up at the sky and sure enough the first hint of blue was peeking shyly through a pewter sky.

'Where would you like the whale? I've brought the pilot whale along so we can try to get her into the pontoon for the demonstration. Two tons when she's full of water, great fun. Over here? Perfect.'

Simon rounded up his small army of helpers and charged off to inflate rubber cetaceans and lay out an impressive collection of dolphin skulls, a man in his element. If there was one thing Simon loved more than observing dolphins and whales in the wild, it was telling other people about observing whales and dolphins in the wild. With a potential audience of up to two hundred, all of whom were drawn here by their curiosity and a quest for further knowledge, he was positively rubbing his hands together in delighted anticipation. I left him vigorously pumping sea water into the flaccid body of the pilot whale, standing in the sea up to his thighs, brow furrowed in concentration.

A local man had agreed to do the hog roast for us and had secured from somewhere a colossal pig which was looking rather sorry for itself as it hung over a peat fire. Paddy McDonald was a dark, impish man, all suppressed energy and darting eyes. This was his first-ever hog roast, and he had cobbled together an impressive array of ironmongery to create a spit, the only snag being that he had to turn the pig by hand every fifteen minutes, something he had been doing since 11 p.m. the night before. As I passed, I could just make out a strangely hunched figure moving slowly through a fog of dense smoke, a figure that raised a grimy hand in greeting, peering at me through red-rimmed eyes. As the hog was being roasted, Paddy was being simultaneously smoked, and it occurred to me that if the pig wasn't ready in time he could potentially be on sale himself, thinly sliced and vacuum packed.

Tam saw me pacing the ground outside the car park, and came up to give me a quick peck on the cheek. 'It'll be fine,' she said. 'The sun will shine, the people will come, and you'll have a ball. Just leave the organising to me, and go and do your thing.'

'I'm not entirely sure I know what my thing is,' I said, managing to sound slightly whiney and petulant simultaneously.

'I believe it's meeting people, telling stories and playing with the kids round the rock pools. Off you go. It'll be a day to remember, just you see.' She smiled again, and darted off to multi-task, leaving me to meander and mix.

Lynn and Lorna turned up, as ever ready to plunge into the fray.

'Well done, Monty,' said Lynn, bounding up to me and giving me a giant hug. 'It'll be a wonderful day, you'll see. Now, what can we do?'

Soon they were both ferrying equipment hither and thither, cajoling favours and wheedling smiles out of even the most recalcitrant beachgoers. Where they went, things sprung up in their wake, and the event started to creak slowly into life.

Richard, Duke de Stacpoole turned up. I had heard a great deal about him in my time in the village, all of it good, and meeting the man at long last reinforced all of my preconceptions. Richard essentially held a title that ran back to the Battle of Hastings and lived in Errisbeg House, a particularly elegant building at the edge of the village. He was a slight, dynamic figure with a broad smile and a distinct twinkle in his eye.

He shook my hand vigorously, staring intently at me throughout. 'Anything I can do, Monty, anything at all, you tell me right now.'

I had never asked a Duke to do anything before, and wasn't quite sure what the protocol was. I simply said the first thing that sprang to mind.

'Well, the gas ring seems to be leaking. That'd be a top job to sort before the cooking display starts.'

I stopped, aghast. I wouldn't have been too surprised if the entire gathering had stilled, and then I had been violently ejected from the village to be pummelled vigorously in a ditch by the Duke's men. But this was no ordinary Duke, and no ordinary man.

'Brilliant,' he said, looking absolutely delighted. 'Point me at it and I'll sort it out, you wait and see.'

I saw him moments later, scuttling past waving a length of rubber tubing, and then later still with his sleeves rolled up, tongue out of the corner of his mouth in concentration, working it steadily onto the end of a gas tap. If I was ever a Duke, I would very much like to be one akin to Richard.

By now the sun was really doing its job, chasing away the clouds and drawing more and more people down to the beach. Curiosity led them to wander over to the marquee, with the smell of crackling and roasting pig keeping them there. Ticket sales ticked over steadily, each one decreasing the size of my debt, until we had a very respectable crowd indeed. There was one minor crisis when the cappuccino van failed to materialise; however, Lynn played a blinder by dashing into town to buy paper cups and a gigantic jar of instant coffee, and an unfortunate crêpe seller found himself in the position of supplying caffeine to a mob of hardcore addicts, with myself at the fore accepting a cup with trembling hand.

And so a wondrous day unfolded. First was local historian Michael Gibbons lecturing on the maritime heritage of Connemara. Here was a man with such a vast amount of knowledge crammed into his head that I'm amazed his skull didn't crack. Then underwater photographer Nigel Motyer showed images he had taken beneath the sea in Ireland, a dazzling array of shots, each more breathtaking than the last.

A steady stream of youngsters queued patiently on the beach for their first-ever introductory dive, waddling into the shallows accompanied by a bevy of instructors to emerge moments later with wide eyes and an expensive habit. Lorna had a go, having a conversation with a bewildered instructor as she stood on the beach in full dive gear about to head into the sea.

'Now,' said the instructor calmly, 'have you ever done this before?'

'Yes,' said Lorna firmly.

The instructor looked momentarily taken aback. 'Really? I thought we were only taking people in today who had never dived before.'

Lorna's face lit up. 'Oh, diving? No, I've never dived before. Nope, this is my very first one – very exciting.'

The instructor looked suitably baffled. Lorna smiled at him expectantly waiting for the next question.

A group – mainly of a certain, elegant age – accompanied me on a ramble along the shore, all floppy hats and walking sticks. They poked about in rock pools to bring me strange, clicking, slimy creatures to identify – children once again. They left with various new nuggets of knowledge, including the fact that the barnacle has the biggest willy relative to its size in the animal kingdom, and that weeing on a jellyfish sting is a good way to relieve the pain, but isn't quite so effective with – say – a grazed knee, although it would guarantee a tremendously exciting reaction from the patient.

I caught only occasional glimpses of Reuben as he dashed past in the midst of a group of shrieking, sand-encrusted children. Periodically, he would appear at my side to nose my hand and check that all was well, before heading back into the feral maelstrom that is a group of young people on the beach. By mid-afternoon, he was a ruin of a dog, lying flat-out in the shade of the marquee, covered in so much sand he looked like an angular schnitzel, a piece of seaweed draped over his muzzle and a faraway look in his eye.

Simon summoned the crowd to the whale rescue demonstration, with the star of the show now rolling in the shin-high surf looking very convincing indeed. Gathering us all together in a multicoloured gaggle, he bounded from spot to spot on the sand, telling tales of stranded whales in rocky coves. We listened in silence, rapt at the spectacle and the story.

'Above all,' he said solemnly, pushing his specs up his nose and pausing for a moment, 'it's about respect. Dead or alive, these animals deserve dignity and compassion when they come under our care.'

This was a good point and well made, but somewhat undermined by the fact that Ronan – Simon's eldest boy – was at that precise moment using the semi-inflated whale as a trampoline, bouncing up and down on it with tremendous vigour. All of this was happening about six feet behind Simon's right ear, until the smiles of the crowd caused him to turn and bark at Ronan, who sheepishly dismounted from his blubbery launch pad.

'Ahem. To continue,' said Simon, once order had been restored. 'I'll now show you how to refloat this whale using the rescue pontoon.'

He darted into the crowd and hauled out several bewildered volunteers, positioning them alongside the whale as it rolled and heaved in the shallows. The rescue pontoon was edged into position – a terrifically complex-looking series of clips, D-rings and valves – and the fun began. The idea was to gently roll the whale onto the tarpaulin, then clip on the inflatable tubes, then walk it slowly out to sea. As a vivid illustration of how tricky it would be with a live, struggling whale, it was excellent, and as pure entertainment it was outstanding. Simon was the maestro, darting from person to person, calling out instructions, cajoling and prodding, to ensure the whale ended up in the right position. There were several enormously exciting moments when the entire ensemble rolled dramatically to one side, causing the helpers to skip away before resuming their positions. These frantic, high-stepping withdrawals through the surf were greeted with a murmur of appreciation by the crowd, who were all secretly hoping for some sort of freak 'Man Crushed by

Rolling Inflatable Whale' incident. Simon orchestrated the entire thing flawlessly, however, and – to our considerable disappointment – the whale was duly floated out to sea, sent on its way by a polite spattering of applause from the assembled masses.

The afternoon passed in what was now blazing sunshine. As is the custom of the Western European male, several people decided to burn themselves to a crisp, essentially flaying their scalps to an iridescent pink.

One portly gentleman strode up to me and pumped my hand, thanking me profusely for staging the event. 'Fair play to you, fair play to you,' he said, over and over. 'It's been a grand day. A mighty grand day. Good man yourself.'

I would have basked in this praise if I had not been staring mesmerised at the boiled beetroot that used to be his head. His eyes peered out at me like ping-pong balls afloat in a sea of jam, and I had the strong urge to wrestle him into the marquee and coat his scalp in yoghurt. I satisfied myself with nodding meaningfully and advising him to move indoors.

'Ah, no problem there, the bar opens in a minute, I believe. It dulls the pain very nicely – I'll see you there, young man.'

He was right. A steady tide of bedraggled festival-goers was soon heading towards the marquee. Mary – the landlady from the Shamrock – had set up a very impressive bar indeed, and the noise level rose accordingly as her bar staff pulled pint after pint, stokers feeding a raging furnace. A beautiful day had become a glorious, sultry evening, with the sea rustling gently on the white sand of the beach. The sun sank slowly behind Errisbeg to the accompaniment of three local lads who played a fiddle and accordions, with one of them leaping up to dance an impressive jig on a table top that had been wrenched from its legs and hastily laid on the floor.

Paddy was still wrestling with the hog roast, although by now he was ringed by a salivating group of partygoers. He would glance up nervously every now and then, a potential prey item in an ever-decreasing circle of carnivores, occasionally prodding everyone back with a metal spike.

'Get back, now,' he would snarl, grimy face crinkling to show he meant business. 'It'll be ready in a minute, I tell you.'

The circle would briefly widen before steadily closing in once more, strangely silent and ominous. Paddy had a large thermometer that he would occasionally poke into the pig, reading the gauge with beads of sweat springing to his brow that had nothing to do with the heat. The hog – due to its immense size – was taking far longer than planned to cook through, and Paddy was under pressure.

It looked and smelled absolutely delicious, skin crackling and shiny, the smoke of the peat darkening the flesh. After another twenty minutes, Paddy finally emerged from under the belly of the pig, thermometer held aloft triumphantly and a minstrel's smile splitting his sooty features.

'Right, folks, it's ready! That's great news, so if you'd like to form an orderly qu–'

The crowd moved forward en masse, descending on the pig like ravenous hyenas. I waded into the mêlée, dishing out pasta salad and bread rolls in a desperate rearguard action, my world a waving sea of hands and leering faces glowing in the firelight – a pagan scene under the still moon on Gurteen Beach. The pig disappeared like some time-lapse piranha sequence from a nature documentary, with hunched figures disappearing into the gloom to messily devour their dripping piece of flesh.

Dinner over, the group moved back into the marquee to begin the evening's festivities in earnest, drawn through the doors by the irresistible sound of Na Ciotogai. I had first heard this band in the Shamrock and, once I had got over the shock of them all being so absurdly young, I had realised they were extraordinarily talented and had drunkenly booked them.

Surprisingly, after I had babbled effusively at them in the pub, they had still decided to honour their commitment for the evening, and played a mixture of traditional and contemporary tunes that struck exactly the right note with the crowd, who by now had as one moved onto the dance floor. Connemara folk never need an excuse to dance, and soon even I was vigorously jigging my way across the floor, swept along by Lorna and Lynn. Richard was in their midst, working up a considerable sweat as he threw various breathless partners around the floor, and weaving through it all was Tam, twisting and spinning with red hair flying and Irish eyes shining.

There was one surreal moment when the band stilled and announced that I would play a tune or two. This stemmed from the fact that I had mentioned to the guitarist during our earlier one-sided conversation that I was something of a player myself. This wasn't strictly true. Bono warbled once that all you need is three chords and the truth; well, I was one chord short of that, although I did have an overwhelming sense of my own latent genius when drunk, which more than compensated. Tragically for all concerned, I had consumed enough beer by this stage to actually believe I was something of a legend, and accepted the band's invitation with a lavish wave at the assembled masses. The guitarist handed over his beautiful instrument, the immediate problem being that he was rather small, and I am rather large. I lifted the strap over my head to begin, and found that the guitar was about level with my chin, a difficult and unconventional position to play. Not to worry, I thought, the show must go on.

The crowd hushed expectantly – the biggest gig of my life. I looked out over a sea of smiling, friendly, expectant faces and began.

Three minutes later, I was still looking out at a sea of smiling faces, although these were now of a more fixed variety. My version of 'Fisherman's Blues' – in the wrong key and hollered with emotion but not a great deal of accuracy – will I believe go down in Roundstone history.

'Were you there when he played "Fisherman's Blues"?' they'll ask in years to come.

'I was. I cried, you know.'

'So did I. So did I.'

The band took over again, and order was restored. Proceedings were interrupted for an auction, with local artists, hotels and shops having donated all manner of gifts. The crowd were now very well oiled indeed, and bidding was brisk and inebriated. A very hefty sum was raised, with Tam darting into the crowd to take names and details as evidence for the next day. Her red hair moved through the throng like a beacon as she cajoled and flirted outrageously to extract an extra penny or two.

Towards the end of the night, there was the obligatory fight, although this was more of a disappointing shoving match than a proper punch-up. I missed most of the action, but it seemed to follow the traditional lines of a bit of a ruck, a frisson of activity in the crowd at the corner of the marquee, and shouts of 'Ah Jaysus, now, come on, we've all had a few drinks.' The contestants were pulled apart and ticked off by everyone present, before the night rolled on in a more civilised manner. I finally wobbled off home in the wee hours, with absolutely no idea how well the night had done financially, but nonetheless suffused with a warm glow and a quiet conviction I was the new Michael Flatley.

The scene at the beach the next morning as I arrived for the clean-up was one of considerable carnage. I have always found the atmosphere after a large event strangely eerie, with the memory of the festivities still hanging in the air and the last echo of the night still resonating in the dunes. It's a peculiarly melancholy feeling, compounded by the fact that I had a pounding hangover and my tongue appeared to have been replaced with an old plimsoll.

As I walked amid the debris, stuffing discarded cans and cigarette butts into a bin liner, Tam was tucked away in the campsite shop counting the money. I would occasionally glance through the window to see her hunched over piles of coins and fluttering pyramids of notes, brow furrowed in concentration. She finally emerged after an hour.

To fund the pontoon we needed €5,000 and, with autumn in the air, there was now absolutely no doubt that time was against us. At my suggestion, Simon had already ordered the pontoon from an old friend in the UK. His name was Alan Knight, and he ran an organisation called British Divers Marine Life Rescue – made globally famous by their attempts to rescue the beaked whale that had found itself in

265

the somewhat dubious position of swimming up the River Thames several years before. With absolutely no money at all in the bank, ordering the pontoon was a bold move, and we were relying on the Diving Festival to raise a very substantial proportion of the total costs.

If we had only broken even, or made a loss, we were in real trouble. I watched Tam cover the ground between us as if in slow motion, my bin liner held slackly in one hand, breath foul and cheeks stubbly. As she came closer, she broke into a half-run, half-skip, and a full beam.

'We made €2,300 profit!' she said, giving another mini-skip for emphasis, before doing a tiny lap of honour around me looking rather pleased with herself.

The relief for both of us was immense. We were almost halfway to our target figure, and although we still had a way to go, this constituted a tremendous start.

I decided there and then that to raise the rest of the money I wouldn't indulge in self-aggrandising events – these funds would be created through well-researched, decent applications to relevant scientific and charitable organisations. If I was to be taken seriously as a scientist and a fundraiser, I needed to knuckle down and learn how to approach the relevant august institutions. The days of the cheap, tacky stunt were over . . .

21

The Aran Sweater

I thought the name for the event was rather good, combining the elements of intense physical labour, a classic piece of clothing, and the islands that loomed perpetually on my horizon. After a glance through the various funding forms from charitable bodies – meaty tomes full of impenetrable text – Simon and I had decided that the best way to raise the remainder of the money was obviously for me to row a traditional rowing boat, a currach, from the Aran Islands to Roundstone. I had three weeks left to plan and conduct the journey, which had never been done before as far as I could ascertain. There was probably a very good reason for this.

It's about twenty miles from the main harbour at Kilronan on the Arans to the harbour at Roundstone. That's twenty miles in a straight line mind you and, although I couldn't predict anything about the row, I could say with absolute certainty that straight lines would not feature strongly. I was what you might describe as 'game' when it came to rowing a currach, immense effort, gurning and swearing tending to feature strongly throughout. Getting the thing to go where I wanted was altogether another matter, and my erratic progress in various races throughout the summer had become something of a defining feature.

I still fancied my chances of making it, although the wind, the waves, the tide and good fortune would all have to be on my side. This reliance on serendipity, the thrill of the unknown, make such challenges irresistible. I set up a number of sponsorship schemes and websites ('You're doing what?' was the baffled response from one of my friends in England. 'Mate, much as I endorse conservation and all that, I can't see how knitting a big jumper will move the cause on.') Soon generous donations were trickling in, and with each one the pressure mounted to complete the challenge, an infinitesimal increase of tension that saw me become fractious and grumpy.

To undertake a mighty challenge you need a mighty man, and for me that man was Paddy 'Shoulders' McDonagh. Paddy had won the All Ireland Currach championship in 1964 and, although he was now well over 60 years old, his barrel chest and corded forearms were a testimony to the immense power and fortitude required to drive a currach through wind and waves over a distance of four miles, all the while locked in battle with the best oarsmen in the country. His boat had won the contest by half a length, a triumph of iron will as much as pure brawn. The race is talked about to this day, so it was with some trepidation that I approached Paddy about the challenge in the pub one night.

He looked thoughtful, then scratched his head and smiled.

'Ah, it's a good pull that. I thought about doing it myself once, you know.' He eyed me for a moment, internal cogs whirring, and then came to a conclusion.

'Right, I'll train you up – you'll have to be as fit as a flea, mind. I'd be out there with you myself, but I've had a few too many birthdays.' He smiled at me, looking very happy indeed at the prospect of the pain – my pain – that lay ahead. 'See you tomorrow down by the quay.'

The next morning I was down on the harbour early, bristling with isotonic drinks and beeping electronic navigation aids. Paddy rattled into view in his van, leapt out and walked briskly towards me. Following him out of the van was a much younger man, tall with dark hair and smiling shyly.

'I've brought my son along,' said Paddy, glancing in disbelief at my wrist-mounted GPS. 'Monty, this is Christopher. He'll give you some tips out there.'

Christopher raised his eyebrows and leaned towards me.

'He's brought us out here because he knows he can beat us both, and we can't have that, can we now?' He nodded towards the currach that bobbed in the harbour, and we climbed aboard.

This boat was an altogether different matter from the canvas currach I had rowed in the Aran Islands. This was a sturdy wooden vessel, beautifully constructed and lovingly maintained.

'Ask me how old she is?' said Paddy as he climbed into another, newer currach beside us.

'Paddy, how old is she?'

'She's 80!' he said, beaming triumphantly.

'Wow, that's only ten years younger than you.'

Paddy looked at me blankly for a moment, then gave a shout of laughter.

'Off we go, then,' he said, pulling on his oars. 'Let's see if you're still so chirpy in twenty minutes or so.'

The training session turned swiftly and inevitably into a race. There was myself – 43 years old, ex-marine, rugby player, gym bunny and avid runner – joined by Christopher, 22 years old, fit, lean and accustomed to rowing. And then there was Paddy – 66 years old, pulling the oars alone, with experience for him but time against him.

He was awesome. Face set in a grim rictus of effort, he heaved on the oars and defied the years. The blades flashed through the water, and the currach accelerated smoothly, responding immediately as Paddy eased her along, momentum and mass combining with explosive power.

'We're not having that,' grunted Christopher behind me. 'Come on, pull the oars, man. We've got to catch him.'

I thrashed mightily, increasing the cadence of the stroke, with Christopher hissing at each heave and my face turning an impressive beetroot as Paddy's boat remained resolutely ahead. After several minutes, the gap began to close, and at last we pulled level, two men against one, with Paddy finally slowing and leaning on his oars. He was smiling to himself, the memory of past triumphs in his racing heartbeat and burning lungs. It had been an extraordinary display of power and technique, and Christopher looked across at his dad with a shake of his head and a half-smile of pride.

'I knew it,' he gasped. 'I bloody knew it. There was no way he was going to be beaten by an Englishman called Monty.

Well done, Dad.'

Paddy looked delighted, and although I was very pleased for them both in what was a touching scene of McDonagh family bonding, the moment was somewhat lost on me as I was heaving air into lungs that were vibrating like old hoover bags whilst studying the decking at my feet with wide eyes. Plainly there was work to be done.

It wasn't so much a lack of fitness – the rowing machine had seen to that – it was technique. Whilst Paddy had been growing up on Inishlacken Island, the currach had been his only means of getting across to the village. It was his social life, his means of popping to the shops, and his cab home. His method of rowing was a series of short, sharp strokes to get the boat moving, then longer, deeper strokes to maintain momentum, the latter using his entire upper body as a pivot. This was basically the equivalent of moving steadily backwards in a seated position whilst vigorously doing press ups, throwing in regular sit ups for good measure. All for twenty-four miles. As an upper-body workout it was outstanding; as a means of passing a day it was horrendous.

Over the next three weeks, I met up regularly with Paddy for training sessions, the evenings now brisk and cold as I raced over water whipped by swirling winds coming from the open sea.

'Well done, Monty, very good. Fair play,' Paddy would bellow from the shore for hour upon hour as I thrashed past, a small figure hunched against the wind with his hands deep in his pockets. It was the equivalent of being trained by Steve Redgrave – a local legend pouring his knowledge into a stranger for no other reason than courtesy and

271

enthusiasm. I was profoundly grateful, and gradually under his careful tutelage my rowing improved.

There was also the route to plan. The eight-mile-wide channel between the Aran Islands and the mainland had the potential to be a vicious series of swirling tides and currents. I then had to negotiate the remaining fifteen miles of inshore reefs and islands, all crackling breakers and shallow coves. If I set out at the wrong time I would be a piece of flotsam at the mercy of wind and wave, spiralling aimlessly in the wrong direction whilst heaving pointlessly on the oars. I needed wisdom and experience. I needed a reality check with a touch of light abuse thrown in. I needed John Brittan and Martin O'Malley.

I met them at John's house just outside Clifden, arriving to find them poring over charts and tide tables in the kitchen. A stuffed gannet eyed me contemptuously as I walked through the corridor from the front door. The walls were covered with pictures of John holding specimen fish, a chronicle of his life as he progressively aged in each one as the hall lengthened towards the kitchen. They both glanced up as I walked in, Martin with a pair of specs balanced on the end of his nose.

'Ah,' he said, 'it's the condemned man.'

'You'd better check in the hospital if they do bum transplants,' said John, 'because the one you've got right now won't be much use to you at the end of this row.'

There was considerable jollity at this remark, and I sat down feeling out of my depth and faintly miserable.

'Don't worry, Monty,' said John, spotting my disquiet. 'We'll get you there. The right tide and wind and it'll be like riding a conveyor belt – trust me.'

And so fifty years of experience were applied to the task – better than any computer program or tidal chart. There was a great deal of muttering and pencil chewing, several comments about the state of my hands / backside / arms / lower back / brain at the end of the row, and endless cups of strong, dark coffee. By the end of the evening, the table was strewn with notes and charts, and we had a route planned and a time to leave.

'That'll fire you from the Arans to Roundstone, Monty,' said Martin, taking off his specs and stretching his back. 'Get that tide right and you'll have trouble stopping when you get to the harbour. You could sit back and read a novel through the entire thing.'

If the sea conditions were anything more than a force three, I was going to be wasting my time, so the next couple of weeks were spent scanning the forecasts waiting for the right moment. The ability of the Atlantic to change in the blink of an eye was vividly illustrated in the dense isobars that rolled in on the weather charts, mountains of wind on the move, immense and morose. By now it was well into autumn, and the sea was going through an identity crisis, sloughing off the genteel mantle of summer and undergoing a personality change. The waters had become grey and heaving, flecked with dead seaweed, looking dark, menacing and entirely forbidding. I needed one more high-pressure system, a window of opportunity to tow the boat to the islands one day and then row it back the next. I combed through websites and television reports, becoming something of a dab hand at identifying my occluded fronts from my anticyclones. After two postponed attempts in the space of a week, I was beginning to despair when, meandering in from the open sea with a faint whiff of the Caribbean, came a lovely, plump, rosy cheeked high-pressure system.

I had three days to prepare, ample time to buy food, energy drinks, and various lotions and unguents for the seriously chafed posterior. By the end of the third day, I had so many energy bars that if I hired a specialist to ram them into my mouth continuously for the entire row, I still would have been left with enough for the entire village. It became a compulsion. Have a brief moment of calm – buy an energy bar. Stop at a petrol station – buy an energy bar.

Paddy was, if anything, even worse than me. He phoned me regularly to check on my preparations and continually modified the currach until it bristled with spare pins for the oars, spare tools, string, rope and safety gear.

'Now you will have a life jacket, won't you?' he asked for the twenty-fifth time when we met for our final training session.

'I will, Paddy,' I mumbled through a mouthful of fruit energy bar.

'Good man, good man. And how about tools? Show me your hammer and screwdriver.' These were duly produced and inspected thoroughly. We both circled the boat several times, studying it from all angles – Paddy wondering where he could stick some extra pins for the oars, and me surreptitiously eyeing deck space for storage.

The great day finally dawned when we would tow the boat out to the Arans for a dawn start the next morning. Paddy shook my hand as I left Roundstone, the currach sitting proudly on a trailer looking resplendent in a new coat of paint.

'Have you got a life jacket?' said Paddy sternly.

'I have, Paddy.'

'Good man, good man. Now, I've got every faith in you – it's a good pull all right, but you're the man for the job.' He shook my hand warmly, and I positively beamed, sent on my way with a ringing endorsement from a man with brine in his bones.

Martin O'Malley met me at the pier in the harbour of Rossaveal an hour later. This was to be our launch point for the tow out, and I could see the Aran Islands as a dark shadow on the horizon. He was to drive the RIB for the tow out and then follow me home as a safety boat. We heaved the currach off the trailer, and lowered her gingerly into the water by the slip, standing back to watch her settle her ample behind into the shallow sea.

She leaked like a sieve.

We had taken her out of the water to do some repairs the week before and, during her time on the trailer, the planks had dried slightly, opening up a series of minuscule cracks and one rather large gap that sluiced water enthusiastically down the insides of the boat, dribbling down the interior to settle in clear pools in the footwell. Martin and I studied the scene in silence for a moment, until he finally broke the silence.

'Not to worry, Monty,' he said firmly. 'I'll have something in the van, you wait and see.'

He stomped off and opened the doors of his van, returning in moments with armfuls of tape, cord, tools and exciting-looking tubs. In the interim, I had phoned Paddy to tell him the news and been treated to a stream of invective that made my ears ring. It was now pushing towards evening, with the sun slipping over the horizon. He had promised to come down should the situation not be resolved; however, even this meant that more time would slip away and the night would close in.

This was a genuine problem, one that could derail the entire venture. The rowing itself would be bad enough, but to have to bail continuously throughout would be nigh-on impossible. Martin set about applying tape and glue, muttering darkly to himself all the while. Eventually he stood, brushing his hands on his thighs.

'Monty, it's no good. Do you have access to any other currachs? She's leaking really badly, and I can't see a way out of this unless we get exactly the right kit.'

At that precise moment, that exact second, even as the words hung between us in the air, a car drew up at the head of the slip. Out of the car stepped Padraig – the skipper of the hooker in which I had raced several weeks before. He stretched lavishly, peering round him at the soft light of another Connemara dusk, then gave a comic little jump when he saw us at the foot of the slip.

'Padraig,' I said, 'what the hell are you doing here?'

He took off his flat cap and scratched his head in bewilderment.

'I was going to ask you the same question. I come down here most nights just to take in the air and get a whiff of the sea.' His eyes lit up at the sight of our upturned boat. 'Is there a problem?'

Within moments, Padraig was studying the gap between the planks, peering over the top of half-moon specs. Within minutes he had produced caulking, tar and a number of specialised tools that created an expert seal, saving the boat, and therefore saving the day. My role in all this was to stand to one side, shaking my head slowly and reflecting on the vagaries of fate.

I thanked him profusely.

'Ah, it's my pleasure,' he said modestly. 'Now get out there, and good luck to you.' He smiled, 'Oh, and one more thing. We definitely had the bloody right of way.'

Twenty minutes later, I was sitting in the currach being towed briskly towards the islands, feeling like some bizarre carnival princess as the boat bobbed and weaved behind the RIB. It was an absolutely beautiful evening, the sea oily calm, and the lights of the islands glinting like jewels on the horizon. The wind of our passage murmured past, the hull of the currach shivered and trembled in the seething rapids of the wake, and I felt completely alone in the darkness. I also felt very, very happy indeed, racing towards three legendary islands and the great challenge that awaited me.

Having arrived at Kilronan – the harbour on the largest island of Inishmore – we pulled the currach high up onto the beach in the darkness and caught a taxi to our bed and breakfast. The cab was driven by a substantial figure who introduced himself as Joe. Joe turned out to be the rudest man I had met in my entire life. Martin knew him of old, and suggested that I sit in the front for the short drive.

'And how's the fishing going, Joe?' Martin asked innocently from the back seat as we drove.

'Ah, load of arse, mackerel' was pretty much all I understood from the response.

'Aha, mackerel,' I trilled nervously. 'Do you see many orcas following your boat? I hear they do that with the mackerel boats.'

Joe glanced across at me with withering scorn.

'I don't see too many orcas, but I see fekkin' loads of killer whales.'

I glanced up to see Martin grinning delightedly in the rear-view mirror, and the rest of the mercifully brief journey continued in silence.

As we unloaded the gear at the B&B, Joe glanced up at me for one last time.

'Are you the guy who's rowing back to Roundstone?'

'I am, Joe,' I said proudly.

'Well, you're a bloody eejit.'

I would have said something in response, but secretly suspected that he might be right.

After a truly terrible night's sleep, writhing in the grip of horrible dreams about having to have my buttocks removed, I was up at 5 a.m. to commence the final preparations. To go to sleep beyond dusk and wake before dawn is always a peculiar sensation, but one that invariably means that mischief is afoot. The adrenalin had kicked in, and I wanted nothing more than to make that first mighty heave on the oars and be on my way.

The currach sat on the beach precisely where we had left it, leaning on one side, an inelegant position for a lady of her class, causing her plump belly to be exposed. She looked vulnerable and lost, a tiny scrap of timber staring out into a grey sea. I jumped down onto the sand, icy cold in the stillness of dawn, and walked towards her. A few final preparations saw her ready to go to sea, and a few final stretches did the same for me, both of us creaking and groaning as we approached the water. I sat on the wooden seat, gripped the oars, and away the two of us went.

It was perhaps the first two or three miles that were the hardest of the entire passage. The real snag with rowing is that you are facing the place you came from, and that place is receding into the distance unbelievably slowly; it's a stark and perpetual reminder of how appalling your rowing technique is. As I pulled on the oars, I noted that the wooden grip under my left hand was slightly rougher than the right, a seemingly insignificant factor that would loom ever larger as the row progressed.

Eventually, the harbour lights receded, giving the island context and scale as they sparkled in the lee of the hills. Inishmore looked immense and ominous in the darkness, great buttresses of granite rising from the sea floor to shoulder aside the ocean. The only sound was the rhythmic clop of the oars, the creak of the pins, and the rustle of the water against the hull.

As the light increased, so my distance from Inishmore grew and I began to see the full length of the island. This was absolutely the best way to view the Arans, from a position virtually level with the surface of the sea and with the only sound the passage of a boat over the water. I watched the morning sun enfold them with low light, claiming the land back from the dark seas around it.

Martin had hovered a discreet distance away from me for the first hour or so, the RIB's engine muttering in the gloom and the navigation light shining reassuringly. As the sun rose over the horizon, he motored over to me for a quick check to see how I was faring.

'You're doing grand,' he said. 'The waves and tide are pushing you along very nicely. You're up to four knots at times – good man, good man. Give me a shout if you need anything, won't you?' With that, he motored off to hang in the middle distance once again, a piratical O'Malley entirely happy to be bobbing in an open stretch of sea.

In the currach, things were actually progressing very nicely, and my first objective of Golam Head rapidly hove into view. I was being borne in precisely the right direction on wind and wave, and occasionally the currach would hitch up her petticoats and surf down the face of a small breaker, like a little old lady who forgets herself at the beach. I would touch the oars and drag her nose back to the job in hand.

Golam Head was a steep promontory of rock that jutted like a crooked finger pointing at the islands from the mainland. The sea surged and crackled round the edge of the cliff faces, a suitably dramatic waypoint for my progress towards Roundstone. This was the last place that basking sharks had been sighted during the summer only a few weeks previously. By the time I had launched the RIB and motored to the position of the sighting, they had moved away, and I felt a moment's regret that I had missed the spectacle of those jet-black fins criss-crossing the surface with the headland behind and the Aran Islands crouched on the horizon.

I was now nine miles into the row and feeling fairly perky. The only problem was my backside, which was starting to feel somewhat anaesthetised by the hard seat beneath. Nature has not seen to equip me with a bum that is ideal for long-distance events, it being a somewhat skinny affair, and even though I had padded out the bench on the currach I had received some fairly strong signals in the early stages of the row that not all was well. I would periodically lift my rear from the seat and give it a brief massage, causing

Martin to edge slightly further away in the RIB and stare fixedly into the middle distance.

I was delighted to see Paddy appear around the headland at the helm of his own RIB. He gave me a delighted thumbs up and bellowed, 'Fair play to you, Monty,' spurring me on to a spectacular three or four heaves on the oars. He would stay with us for the rest of the day, ever watchful, occasionally motoring alongside to offer advice or mutter a few words of encouragement – living every stroke that took the currach closer to Roundstone.

From Golam Head to my next checkpoint was seven miles of small islands and sandy shallows. These bottlenecks funnelled the tide splendidly, and soon I was racing along at a brisk four and occasionally even five knots. The low islands were absolutely beautiful, and I passed several grey seals that humped and flopped their way towards the sea, startled at my passing. They would appear in my wake, heads shining and eyes wide, to peer at my passing with genuine curiosity. On one long reef that broke the surface like the spine of a dark crocodile sat lines of shags. There is something faintly prehistoric about the shag, looking more like pterodactyls than birds, and I got very close to them before they were startled into clumsy flight. They were sitting with their wings outstretched, harvesting the rays of the morning sun, their feathers as dark as the night and their eyes glinting quartzite. They leaped from the reef, serried ranks of flapping, thrashing forms seeking the sanctuary of the sea, all gone in an instant beneath the surface to appear as a row of reptilian heads that twitched and dipped in alarm.

By now – four hours into the row – my left hand was starting to smear and blister on the rough wood of the oar handle. This was becoming fairly uncomfortable, but I was pleasantly surprised by how my body in general was bearing up. Paddy's training was paying dividends in the rhythm I had been able to establish, in the long low sweep of the oars, and the rocking of my entire upper body to ease the blades through the water. I had often watched the men of Connemara row, and had been mystified at the exaggerated motion they employed. Now I understood completely – it was a movement in time to the sea itself, easing along with the momentum of the waves and the rush of a currach sliding down the face of the sea. It was an almost hypnotic sensation, which when combined with the wind in my face and the gentle rustle of the sea around gave the row a timeless feel. It was a throwback to another age when the passage of minutes and hours did not hold sway over everything a man did, when we were borne from place to place by the sea and arrived when the wind and tide allowed us.

The occasional glance over my shoulder now showed Saint MacDara's Island coming into view. This was a significant waypoint for two reasons. The first was that as I turned away from the island I would be able to see Roundstone for the first time, and the second was that the island had always been considered a special place for seafarers along this coast, a harbinger of good fortune and fair winds. The island is named after the patron saint of fishermen and sailors in Connemara. As the island rose steadily from the sea behind me, I could make out the roof of the small monastery he had built there in the sixth century, the memory of over a thousand years of Atlantic storms in its walls. Tradition demands that passing boats dip their sails as a mark of respect. Failing to do so was said to result in terrible misfortune, something of a dilemma for me as a man in a rowing boat. I settled for tipping my cap as the island slipped past, a sheepish salute that reflected a respect for folklore and superstition that remains in seafaring folk to this day.

I remembered a dive trip a few years before on a vessel which had every piece of communication, navigation and satellite navigation kit available. This boat was a bleeping, glowing collection of cutting-edge equipment that made the bridge look like the cockpit of a jumbo jet, lighting up the skipper's face in an eerie green glow. Bored during the long passage to the dive site, I stepped out onto the main deck and started to eat a banana, only to have the skipper charge out from the wheelhouse, snatch it from my hand and hurl it overboard.

'A banana!' he shouted, eyes wild. 'On a boat! What the hell were you thinking, man?' He duly stalked off, shaking his head in disgust and muttering darkly at the foolish ways of landlubbers.

There is no environment in the modern world that is more hog-tied in tradition and impenetrable myths than the sea, so it made perfect sense to this modern, well-educated skipper that bananas are very bad news indeed. As was whistling. And Fridays. And anything with thirteen in it. And women. With all the complex rules to negotiate and the dazzling array of things you're not allowed to take on a boat, I'm amazed anyone ever manages to get to sea at all.

Perhaps I had tipped my hat incorrectly as the row was about to get very emotional indeed.

*

As I rounded the tip of the island, I stopped the currach and leaned on the oars, allowing the stern to swing round in the wind so the boat faced the mainland. Before me was the reassuring bulk of Errisbeg Mountain, the unmistakable silhouette that greeted me every morning when I stepped out of the cottage. It looked familiar and reassuring, close enough that if I reached out with one of my slender oars I could tap it on its ragged summit. Nestling at the base of the mountain was the village, shining in the early afternoon sun, an oasis of beer, coffee, bottom rubs and soft places to lie down. At my present rate of progress, I would be there in just over an hour, so I gave a swift pull on my right-hand oar, spun the boat around and set off in an appropriately determined fashion.

Only now I had turned sideways on to the wind that had, up to this point of the row, been ushering me along by shoving the currach's plump rump. The boat immediately tried to turn sharp right, swinging her backside around so the wind could once again ruffle her petticoats. Sharp right was very much at odds to where Roundstone lay, so I gave a vigorous heave on my left-hand oar, the skin of my hand smearing like old papier mâché as I did so. This worked perfectly well for all of five yards, after which the currach once again petulantly kicked her stern around, causing me to pull mightily on the left-hand oar once again. And so we went on, crabbing, slewing and arguing like an old married couple for the remaining six miles to Roundstone. The swirling grains of the wood on the handle of the oar, which I had idly noticed as I pulled out of Kilronan Harbour, snagged and twisted the soft skin of my palm. I could feel the blisters rise and skin break, with small flaps of flesh tugging and weeping at each stroke. My progress – up to this stage triumphal and serene – slowed to a snail's pace, each pull accompanied by a considerable amount of grimacing, snorting and lavish expletives.

Two hours later, Inishlacken Island finally appeared at my shoulder, a period of time that had seen my relationship with the currach descend into smouldering silence. Once in the lee of the island, however, with only two miles to go, we both dramatically perked up. She seemed to spot the haven of her home harbour, and for the first time in four miles compliantly turned her nose and surfed gleefully down the small waves. I imagined I caught a distinct whiff of Guinness and increased my stroke, keenly aware that the eyes of the village would be upon me as I swept up the channel. As I finally left the northern tip of Inishlacken behind me – the white sand of the beach crowning the shore like snow on a craggy summit – at last I could make out the harbour. Behind me were almost twenty-four miles, seven and half hours and the lingering memory of the great, granite bulk of the Aran Islands fading into the Atlantic. With me was an extraordinarily numb backside, so bad it really didn't feel like mine at all any more. Ahead of me lay Roundstone Harbour, Nimmo's magical piece of civil engineering and my journey's end. My left hand was a real mess, a painful collection of blisters and open skin that sent jagged bolts of pain up my arm at every pull of the oar. The rest of me, though, had stood up to the trip surprisingly well. All I wanted to do now was pull the currach ashore, stumble up to O'Dowd's, order a bucket of coffee, and wait for my bum to return from wherever the row had taken it.

I was rather hoping there might be one or two people

passing the time of day on the harbour wall when I appeared. If nothing else this would give me the opportunity to idly respond, 'Oh, the Aran Islands,' when they asked me where I'd rowed from. Word had, however, plainly got around.

Rowing a currach strikes at the very heart of small communities on the west coast of Ireland, and even in this age of mechanisation it still elicits a deep response from anyone who has grown up on this crackling Atlantic frontier. As I came within a few hundred yards of the harbour, I heard a babble behind me, a collection of voices brought to me on the wind. Mixed in amongst them was a young voice that piped up a shrill 'Come on, Monty!'

This was the signal for a bellowing wave of support and encouragement from my friends in Roundstone that swept me the last few yards. I glanced up at the quay wall and there, surrounded by his family, stood Michael King holding out a pint of Guinness, Simon Ashe and his wife Anne, Padraig, Mary McDonagh, the good Duke Richard de Stacpoole, as well as Lynn and Lorna bouncing up and down on the spot and clapping furiously. They had brought Reuben down to greet me, and as I glanced round I saw his dark form hurtle into mid air from the harbour steps, hitting the water with a percussive thump that drew an even bigger cheer from the crowd. Paddy clapped his hands above his head from his own RIB and shouted his approval, Martin gave me a lavish thumbs up, and so the last few strokes of the Aran Sweater saw me circled by a joyously barking dog, pulled into the still waters of the quay by the warmth and encouragement of the village that I now thought of as my home.

As I tottered round the village for the next few days, creaking and grimacing as I climbed out of the car before lowering myself gingerly onto a stool in the Shamrock, I noticed that I had even made several new friends. Some of the older, more grizzled fishermen who had studiously ignored me for the last six months would glance up and nod as I passed. There was even the occasional pint raised in my general direction. The elder generation of Roundstone, their blood made up of the briny of many a spring tide, quietly acknowledged the row in their own way. Tinkering with the Land Rover on the main street several days afterwards, I was startled by a tap on the shoulder, and turned to see an old lady who smiled sweetly, pressed my hand in hers, and said, 'Well, you're a mighty man. A mighty man,' before shuffling off. I had absolutely no idea who she was, and strangely enough would not see her again during my time in Roundstone, but wanted very much to run after her, sweep her off her feet, and waltz her down to O'Dowd's. Even in Galway – a place I had begun to think of as a teeming metropolis – a swarthy lad wound down his car window beside me to raise a grimy thumb in my direction, before assuring me he would be smashing the record imminently.

It seemed to me that the Connemara folk – that great oceanic tribe – particularly embraced any event that represented a small victory over the sea. The support of my friends in the village meant a great deal to me, but the subtle recognition that the row engendered in the wider community was extremely gratifying. We all aspire to belong, and for the first time I really did feel like I was part of the village and its intimate relationship with the ocean on its doorstep.

22

A Few Answers (and rather a lot of questions . . .)

A s though to emphasise that summer was truly over, the day I spent preparing the boat to recover the acoustic pod, which had lain in the bay for nearly four months, silently monitoring the movements of the dolphins and porpoises, was also the day that the calves on the island were taken to market. My landlady Bridie had mentioned this to me a week or so before, asking me to leave enough space in my drive so the truck could reverse and turn as it left with the calves onboard. I had given it very little thought, but it precipitated a deeply touching saga that created a heartbreaking soundtrack to my preparations to go to sea.

To collect the calves, they first had to be separated from their mothers, the heifers who had suckled, guarded and nurtured them. This was done by herding the heifers into a large shed, and then rounding up the bewildered calves and moving them onto the waiting truck that in turn drove off the island. The heifers were then released from the shed, lowing and bellowing as they ran on heavy legs through the fields that had been their home for the last few months. They explored every dip and hollow, every boggy ditch and bent bush, all the while wide-eyed and clumsy in their haste. They seemed to me almost mad with grief, their calls becoming ragged, utterly bereft at the sudden disappearance of their young. This scene would go on throughout the afternoon and, even as night settled, I could still hear them calling on the hill, their resonant bellows drifting out over the channel and echoing in the wind.

It was therefore a considerable relief to reverse the RIB down the slip one last time and head away from the island. This trip had particular resonance – it was not only the final patrol, a last chance to encounter the animals that were now so familiar to me, it was also an opportunity to recover the piece of equipment that might just answer so many questions about them. My encounters over the course of the summer had been many and varied, with some mere fleeting glimpses of a hurtling grey form, and others languid afternoons when the dolphins had circled the boat for over an hour. During these more sustained meetings, the adults and young seemed to peer up at me in genuine curiosity and I would stare straight back, two species perplexed and intrigued at each other's presence in the cobalt waters of Gurteen Bay. I knew these latter encounters would remain with me as treasured moments for the rest of my days, to be idly thumbed and cross-referenced in the back catalogue of my life, wherever that life may ultimately take me.

However powerful the emotions, though, the data remained

relatively scant. The acoustic pod that had swung silently on its mooring for the last four months held a great deal of what might be key information. The pod had the ability to record every click and whistle of dolphins and porpoises as they passed within a 400-metre radius in the bay, and its electronic innards held the real story of the dolphins of Roundstone.

I had decided to take Reuben out on this final trip as a special treat. He behaved with his normal unflappable decorum on the RIB, alternating between standing at the bow bouncing on the tubes with stiff legs, and charging back to where I sat to drape his paws over the side of the boat and bark furiously at the passing waves. Occasionally, one would leap up in a threatening manner to hiss against the bright orange hull, and he would snap at it with flashing teeth and folded ears, causing it to fall back towards its heaving companions. Reuben would glance round at me in triumph, before turning his gaze once more towards the thrashing surface, ever watchful for a rogue peak that might snatch his master away.

Inishnee Island slipped slowly alongside as we motored out of the channel. In the ragged shallows stood a heron, a frozen monument to patience and fortitude. It was startled into flight at our passing, launching itself into the morning sky under an immense cloak of dark wings. I glanced up at the cottage sitting on the shoulders of the hill, the slopes now a rich tawny brown as the bracken died off at the approach of winter. It looked to me at that moment just as it had the first time I had seen it six months before – friendly, compact, a haven staring out over the great expanse of the sea. I had been very happy indeed living on the island, immersed in the wind and touching the face of the sea.

As we moved towards where the lighthouse stood squat and reassuring on the headland, a raucous group of oystercatchers exploded into the air, shrieking furiously at man and the thunder of engines that accompanied him. A black-backed gull stood impervious to it all, sinister and powerful, staring at me with eyes as lustrous and dark as gems.

Soon the RIB was lifting its nose towards the wide open spaces of the bay, driving towards Deer Island. The dark hump of the island curved up and out of the water like the glossy back of a diving whale, and I pushed the throttles forward to lift the boat onto the plane and allow her to approach the island at a good old gallop. Reubs finally gave up the uneven battle with the maelstrom of the bow wave, and came to sit with his back pressed against my leg, head up and ears flapping in the breeze. I was rather hoping that I would see the dolphins one last time, but the waves were of a good size and in my heart I knew it would be a very lucky encounter indeed should I stumble upon them. This was their realm, the sounding main and the tumbling crest, and they would have no need for men and boats on a day such as today.

I finally arrived at where the buoy marking the acoustic pod bobbed and weaved on the water. Slowing the boat, I allowed the wind to push us towards where the lurid buoy sat, the line snaking mysteriously into the depths beneath it. I leaned over and snagged it with the boat hook as we drifted past, and after a truly eye-popping effort to raise the weights anchoring it to the seabed, fell back into the well of the boat cradling the nondescript cylinder which housed the batteries and memory chip. This rather dull-looking grey tube had harvested the mysterious echoes that had resonated around the bay over the last four months. This was the record of the dolphins' movements, and I could hardly wait to get it home.

Despite my enthusiasm, I keenly felt the weight of the journey back, knowing as I did that this would be the last time for many months – possibly years – that I would surf the waves towards Inishnee Island and home. I was due to leave Connemara by the end of that week, leaving behind the wide sweep of the bay and all its mysteries.

The RIB surfed gleefully down the rollers as they rose in the mouth of the channel, driven upwards by the shallows beneath and the narrowing rock walls alongside. I lifted my head to look at Errisbeg to my left, craggy and wild, riven by fissures cut deep by tumbling streams. Beneath me, stark on the echo sounder, were undersea ridges and gullies patrolled by flickering shoals of pollack and mackerel, each overhang the home to an armoured crab or a slate-grey eel. Inishnee Island hove into view beside me, all tumbling walls and compact cottages. On this day it looked neat and genteel, but the trees on the skyline told another story, of dark nights and whistling tempests, of being an outpost on a seething frontier between two very different kingdoms.

Joanne O'Brien had agreed to meet me at the cottage a few days later, and was treated to the novel sight of both myself and Reuben charging out of the door to greet her when she turned up. I had met Joanne on a number of previous occasions throughout the summer, either on survey boats or at the headquarters of the Irish Whale and Dolphin Group. She was a formidable presence in terms of her accumulated knowledge, but happily she was also great fun, with a ready smile and a nice line in self-deprecating banter. She was very much the expert from the IWDG when it came to deciphering the information on the cards within the pods, and had driven up from Galway specially. The poor girl was duly dragged out of her car and bundled indoors, laptop tucked under one arm, with me talking in one ear and Reuben barking in the other – although occasionally that switched round depending on the mood. Although I had recovered the pod itself, I lacked both the knowledge and the technology to read the memory card within, and had spent the last two days staring at it on the kitchen table. Occasionally I had picked it up and turned it slowly in my hands, before placing it reverently back down like some delicate ancient parchment. It was always a pleasure to see Joanne, but this time I was like a child on Christmas morning. As for Reuben, he had plainly detected that something was up and had decided that barking a great deal would move things along nicely.

A few minutes later, Joanne was sitting at the table with a cup of tea, peering intently at the pod.

'Well, it looks fairly good,' she said finally, to an audible exhalation of relief from myself. 'We had a devil of a time with these things initially, but gradually the technology has improved and of course we've learned a lot too. It's always a risk to put any piece of electronics in the sea, but to leave it there for four months being battered by storms . . . Well, let's just say we've had our little dramas in the past. Now, could you hold the pod firmly, please?'

I did so, whilst Joanne inserted a screwdriver into the top section, both of us grimacing as she twisted one way and I the other. With a creak that may or may not have come from my wrists, the top of the grey tube twisted off revealing an exciting collection of wires and plates, in the midst of which sat the chip.

'Well, there it is,' said Joanne.

And indeed there it sat, a scrap of bright plastic full of mysterious clicks, cheeps and whistles. Joanne carefully extracted it from the tube and placed into a slot at the side of her laptop. There was a great deal of whirring, some very impressive ragged lines appeared on a series of furiously scrolling graphs and, after a tense five minutes or so, the computer finally calmed itself.

Joanne patiently talked me through the data for over an hour. The presence of the dolphins on a regular basis was unequivocal, with an average of one day in five registering the unmistakable sounds of them going about their business in the bay. The rest of the data was made up of the lesser clicks of harbour porpoises, smaller cetaceans that lacked the flamboyance of their larger cousins. Despite them being in the area of the pod almost as frequently as the dolphins, I had never seen them on my patrols. The most one ever glimpses of a harbour porpoise is a gently rolling back that just breaks the surface, and in the maelstrom of the bay I had simply overlooked them. Interestingly, on the days when the dolphins were recorded by the acoustic pod, the porpoises were never present. They have none of our preconceived ideas about dolphins, and know that to stay in the vicinity of a group of bottlenose dolphins would mean injury and even death. They would skulk away into the open ocean at the first hint of those great, gunmetal-grey bodies appearing. The pretty traces on the graph were a tiny illustration of the drama that takes place in the echoing spaces of the sea.

I thanked Joanne, the two of us chatting for a little longer as the sun tracked across the sky and the tide slipped away from the shore. The acoustic pod had indeed revealed the beginnings of an intriguing story, which could be combined with the photographs of the dolphins' fins to reveal a little more about their whereabouts throughout the year.

'My theory is that they use this area as part of a wider range,' said Joanne, tracing a finger along the data displayed on the screen. 'You can see that they appear periodically, but then seem to hang around for a wee while. Your photos have shown they can appear here from as far afield as Donegal, so perhaps you have a transient group who come to Roundstone for the summer? Heaven knows, everyone else in Ireland does.'

She smiled, and began to pack away her equipment.

'You'll just have to come back,' she said as she loaded her car, smiling over one shoulder. 'There are so many questions that remain unanswered about these animals, you could quite happily spend the rest of your life studying them and still only begin to understand their biology and social structure.'

She had a point. The results from the pod had shown that there was a significant presence of bottlenose dolphins in the bay, but suppose I had placed it a few hundred metres further inshore? Suppose I had used two pods, one each side of Inishlacken Island? Suppose next summer was a balmy, windless affair, ideal for photographing shining dorsal fins as they swept past a boat? The pod had revealed only a tantalising glimpse of what lay beyond the island.

23

The Rescue Pontoon

Despite the heroics of the Diving Festival and the emotion of the Aran Sweater, we were still a few hundred euros short of the five thousand required to pay for the rescue pontoon. Time was short, so I decided to run one final fundraiser. Lorna made a gigantic map of the Aran Islands and the coast leading to Roundstone on a bed sheet. Then I set up the rowing machine one crisp October morning near the sea wall. The goal: to count down the miles on the computer readout of the rower, and draw a line on the map as we drew ever closer to the village. We had a total of 38,000 metres to row, which is four times the height of Mount Everest, and a day to do it.

I took my seat, hoping that the sight of me huffing and puffing would inspire the locals to have a bash, and we would oh-so-slowly creep towards Roundstone on our splendid map that flapped and twitched on the flagpole behind me. I rather self-consciously completed three minutes – the period I had decided would be best for all and sundry should they want to have a go – and climbed stiffly off the rower wheezing and red-faced. Lorna was next, all flying hair and a beaming grin. There was steel behind the smile though, a Connemara lass with a challenge before her and an Englishman beside her. She posted a very respectable time indeed, throwing the gauntlet down to Tam, who hopped aboard with a glint in her eye.

'Now, ladies, please,' I murmured under my breath. I was roundly ignored.

Three minutes later, Tam had finished her stint, and curtains were beginning to twitch along the length of the main street. Lynn appeared, beaming at the prospect of putting the younger generation in its place.

She gave me a hug of welcome, then turned to eye the machine.

'I used to row, you know,' she said, rolling up her sleeves. 'Now, watch this!'

She leaped aboard, brow furrowed in concentration, and covered over 500 metres in her three minutes, legs pumping and brow furrowed. She was delighted when she climbed off the rower, glowing and beaming in the post-exercise rush.

A combination of healthy female rivalry and my own brief efforts had already shoved our cartoon boat a respectable distance along our map. By now several kids had gathered, and were immediately press-ganged into service, a scene akin to a Victorian sweathouse developing as bewildered children were secured into the foot straps and told to heave away. By now it was mid-morning, and strolling tourists would stop to idly glance at the scene and then find themselves gasping for breath on the sea wall moments later, all to move a small drawing of a boat along a wildly inaccurate map. A kind of collective madness descended on the village, with more and more people emerging from their houses to take part, with every three-minute stint completed to thunderous applause.

It was yet another beautiful day – 'You plainly have some very impressive contacts indeed,' Lynn said to me halfway through the morning as she glanced up at the sky. The village shone in the clear October sun, with the channel sparkling below the village, and the mountain behind a riot of green shot through with the sepia tints of autumn.

'Oh, I can't believe you're going,' said Lynn. 'I'll warn you right now, you know – you can leave Connemara, but Connemara will never leave you.' She smiled brightly and charged off to encourage one of the kids who was already strapping his feet into the footrests of the still-spinning rower.

I had set up a bucket next to the machine and watched it fill steadily with donations, a glistening pile of silver and notes that grew to respectable proportions very quickly. All was progressing splendidly and then, around the corner, came a nightmare.

Appearing abruptly with a collective hiss of wafer-thin tyres and the expensive rattle of carbon-fibre frames came a cycling club. Gaudy and ornate in skintight Lycra, like a flock of exotic birds blown in from the sea, they stilled beside the rowing machine. Energy drinks were sipped, quiet words exchanged, and from their midst emerged a colossus, a legionnaire in spandex, a vacuum-packed physiology lecture.

'C'mon, Andrew,' one of them shouted, a call taken up by the rest of the group.

He smiled sheepishly, took a seat, bunched thighs that looked like a sack of rabid pythons, and began to row. The machine howled and hissed, sliding along the pavement with the power being generated, the milometer whirred like the meter of a late-night minicab, and three minutes later the big fella rolled off the rower heaving and perspiring, an entire kilometre nailed. The rowing machine took several minutes to stop revolving, and I'm sure I saw a wisp of smoke emerge from one of the cogs. The applause was rapturous, and big Andrew was led away on wobbly legs for a sustaining pint across the road.

The snag with all this was that I was still basking in the warm glow of my newfound reputation as Aran Sweater man – I really couldn't have strangers in Lycra smashing my record. 'Come on, Monty,' a small voice piped up from the watching group of children. 'You can do it. You rowed from the Aran Islands to Roundstone.'

The crowd took up the chant and, mainly because I'm an idiot, I walked forward, raised a hand to hush the mob, and re-took my seat on the rower.

The three minutes that followed were, I felt, impressive enough. The combination of months of training, Paddy's careful tutelage, and absurd middle-aged pride meant that I managed to beat Andrew's distance. It was the ten minutes that followed, after I was lifted off the rower like some medieval knight being removed from the field of battle, that created the real issues. These were spent in a similar position to that adopted by a cat with a persistent hairball – on all fours behind the Land Rover with my back arched and my breakfast hosing out of what appeared to be every aperture in my head. Tam rubbed between my shoulders and told me that I was still impressive, and of course it was important nearly to kill myself in order to beat a chap I'd never met before, on a static rowing machine to move a cartoon boat along a bed sheet. I wasn't a shallow, foolish, tragically competitive buffoon in the slightest.

I emerged from behind the Land Rover after a period of meditation, my breakfast, my dignity and my reputation on the pavement behind me. The crowd – thankfully – were enjoying the spectacle of the row too much to have noticed their vomiting compère, so operations had continued unabated.

It was the kids who brought us home. I had always enjoyed their presence in Roundstone, a colourful collection of all ages who would invariably shout a greeting as the Land Rover passed, with some pedalling their bikes furiously alongside as I sped up the lanes. When I had been working in the harbour, there would invariably be a group of them asking questions about the dolphins and the sharks – these were after all the offspring of fishermen and farmers, attuned to the wild waters around them and full of curiosity about its hidden treasures.

It was therefore particularly fitting that the last few kilometres were completed by the next generation from the village. We pulled into our theoretical harbour late in the afternoon, having rowed our little machine a distance equivalent to reaching the summit of the world's highest mountain four times, having sweated and gasped together, having clapped and cheered every man, woman and child home. The last few pennies of the rescue pontoon were, fittingly, raised by the people who would probably be the first to use it.

The rescue pontoon was presented to Simon and the members of the Irish Whale and Dolphin Group at the gleaming edifice of the Galway and Mayo Institute of Technology. The GMIT had been instrumental in funding several of the projects we had undertaken during the summer, including paying for the acoustic pod that had revealed so much about the bay and its chattering inhabitants. Simon had invited marine biology students from the Institute, as well as patrons and members of the IWDG to the ceremony, so a goodly crowd were present as I hefted the gigantic yellow bag containing the pontoon out of a side room. They were an excellent group of people to be present at this ceremony, knowing better than most the value of that yellow container, and the applause was warm and genuine.

I had another insight into the contents of the bag, though. Inside was the expertise and generosity of Paddy 'Shoulders' McDonagh, the watchful eye and acquired knowledge of John Brittain and Martin O'Malley, the sweat of the kids on a long hot day on the rower, the paintings donated by local artists for the auction at the Diving Festival, the energy and support of Duke Richard de Stacpoole, the unstoppable drive of Lynn and Lorna, and the unflagging support of the people of Roundstone. It was the culmination of six months' work, and a perfect illustration of the intense relationship between the little village at the base of Errisbeg Mountain and the great oceanic plains that stretch away before it.

Over a cup of tea afterwards, I chatted to Simon about the work over the summer, and his thoughts on the dolphins of Roundstone. He paused for a moment, searching for the right words.

'You know,' he said finally, 'it is so complicated trying to establish exactly where these animals go, how they live their lives, and extracting the hard science from all the hysteria that seems to surround them. What you have done, unequivocally, is show that there is a very significant population of dolphins along that stretch of coastline, and that further studies should be conducted into their movements.' He paused again, a most uncharacteristic state of affairs for Simon, and I briefly considered calling an ambulance. He finally took a breath and continued, picking his words and speaking more quietly.

'There's so much work to be done here. The place where the Atlantic meets the land, I think it's one of the most exciting ecosystems on our planet. We need to use places like Connemara as launch pads into the open sea, as viewing points, as base camps to make forays into the wide open spaces. You've touched on some very intriguing things here, Monty, but there's a lifetime of work off that coast, should you or others wish to follow it up.'

He paused again, then continued in an altogether brighter vein.

'Anyway, I think you'll be back. You've got the fever. You simply can't tag a couple of basking sharks then just bugger off; it's actually not physically possible.' He glanced down at his cup, swilling with weak tea. 'Come on, let's go for a pint.'

24

The Magic
of Connemara

Study a map of Europe, allowing your eyes to trail to the ragged western edge of the continent, and sooner or later you will find yourself looking at Connemara. This is the place where the mountains reach the sea and where the ocean itself encroaches on the land, threading through steep valleys with icy tendrils that form dark loughs and still fjords.

Every day the tide creeps into endless coves and inlets, sliding and chuckling over stone and bog, the sea making the shore its own for a few brief hours until called away by the moon. It is a timeless change, unhurried and relentless, completely oblivious to what takes place in the bustling world of mankind. For half a day, every day, the bladderwrack becomes a waving forest of leathery fronds, the slimy rocks of sea wall and harbour steps are immersed, and every cove becomes a uniform metallic grey, seething with the nomadic life of a temperate ocean.

Tucked away at the head of one of the loughs is a typically sleepy inlet. It is surrounded by trees that are rheumatic with age, their limbs twisted by the power of five generations of storms. It has become one of Tam and my favourite places during our time here, and there is even a natural seat for the weary traveller – a large flat rock buried in the hillside, emerging from the heart of Connemara itself to peer out over the water at the setting sun. Along the fringes of the cove, otters forage and hunt, their squeaks and splashes punctuating the cathedral hush of an autumnal evening. Seals raise their shining heads to peer at the land, at once curious and fearful at the strange goings on of man. They wait patiently for the tidal waters around them to swirl and bulge in the early summer, as salmon pick up the first scent of their home river, silver bullets crammed into a dark bottleneck preparing for their final, great physiological effort after a lifetime of defying impossible odds. Close to the rock on which we sit, a waterfall thunders down steps of slick granite, pounding at the earth beneath with relentless energy and purpose before meandering down to the shore to be lost in the sea. Legend has it that the cliffs and hollows that line the cove are a fairy fort, and even to the most rational mind there is something faintly mystical about the place.

We sit with our backs to the hill, wrapped in a blanket against the chill, watching the sun settle into the inlet at the end of another day. It seems the most logical thing in the world to spend our summers for the next few years (and a few after that, I suspect) attempting to unravel some more of the mysteries that lurk in the sea on our doorstep, and so we have resolved to return. It's a brisk evening, a reminder for us that the cove will transform over the next few months to become a brutal place of freezing spume and icy winds. Then will come the first hint of spring: the sea will still, the shallow seas around Gurteen and Deer Island will once again echo to the calls of hunting bottlenose dolphins, and a new cycle of life and death will begin.

We shiver with the cold, the heat having long seeped out of the day and fled over the horizon. Rising stiffly to our feet, we gather up the blanket and hurry back to the warmth of the car. Before closing the door, I glance back and see the channel sweeping round the back of Inishnee, the island's dark spine rising in a series of ridges that plunge into the ever-changing, mysterious waters of the shallow bay in the shadow of Errisbeg Mountain.

Acknowledgements

I was so very fortunate to be surrounded by such knowledge, enthusiasm, and unselfishness during my six months in Connemara. Living in the cottage would have been a great experience if it had just been Reuben and me entirely alone, but it was enriched beyond measure by numerous friends. They helped me out at every turn.

As ever, the team at Tigress Productions played a blinder – Dick Colthurst, the unflappable skipper, with Louisa, Nikki (congratulations!) and Gina his imperturbable crew. On site Martin Pailthorpe somehow managed to keep it all on track – he is a relentless source of creativity and soup. James Hemming performed way beyond his remit, James Lovick was absurdly talented, and Rob the sound chap was a very sound chap. Adam Keltie even flew down from the Hebrides to recreate the dream team. Lorna Hill was inspirational of course – she really is an unstoppable force of nature, that girl; every film crew should have one.

A huge thanks to Simon Berrow – it is amazing what he has achieved with the IWDG, and when you meet him you realise that it is his unique energy and drive that makes the organisation prosper. Thanks also to Emmett, Conor and Joanne – I learned so much working with you.

Thanks to the divers who came out to help, and to Plymouth University for making it all possible. Dan Stevenson worked wonders, particularly with the baskers. Thanks to Andy, Becks, Finn, Jo, Ali and Martin for giving up their time for nothing. I owe you all lots of beer – which I assure you will appear at some future indeterminate date.

Within Roundstone, there are so many who helped me I might as well list the entire village – they are, en masse, a credit to Connemara and to Ireland. In particular there was Lynn Hill – Reubs still looks for you every time we take him for a walk, Lynn – Richard, Duke de Stacpoole, Martin O'Malley, Bridie Davis, Paddy 'Shoulders' McDonagh, Christina Lowry, Michael Reynolds, Michael King, Mary and Patrick McDonagh, Pat Mullen, Ronan Creane, and Nicky from O'Dowd's. And thanks to every kid in the village – the next generation of Roundstone will be of a particularly fine vintage.

Beyond the village, thanks to John Brittain – a more knowledgeable guide to the dark art of finding sharks you couldn't hope to meet. A big thank you to Donal, Padraig, Joe and Ronan – we definitely had the bloody right of way!

At Ballynahinch – what a place – there was Simon Ashe and his lovely wife Anne, Patrick O'Flaherty, Des Lally – your notes were invaluable, Des – and the entire staff.

The Dive Fest wouldn't have happened without Nigel

Motyer, Michael Gibbons, good old Martin P, Bernie Mullen, Paddy McDonald and his gigantic pig, Rosie McGurran, Brendan and Proinsias Hernon, Marty and Catherine Nee, Graham Roberts and Connemara Smokehouse, Brenda Mullen, Jim and Leo from Fourth Element, and Paul from Dive Magazine.

Thanks to John Wright for writing *The Edible Seashore* – a truly wonderful guide to inter-tidal foraging. Thanks also to Tim Robinson – *Listening to the Wind* really is the definitive work on Connemara, and an invaluable means of discovering the real story behind an extraordinary place. He is a master of his art.

To Julian Alexander my gratitude for – as ever – providing a steadying hand in the writing process. Thanks to Albert DePetrillo at Ebury – we didn't even shout at each other this time, Albert, which I find strangely worrying.

To Suze, you are a legend. Whatever you're being paid, it's not enough.

To Reuben – you are my number one mucker. Please stop eating my seatbelts, though.

And to my Tam – these are moments I'll never forget. Thank you.

Index